P9-BVH-591

Ethnographic Writing Research

Ethnographic Writing Research

----

writing it down, writing it up, and reading it

WENDY BISHOP
FLORIDA STATE UNIVERSITY

Boynton/Cook Publishers
HEINEMANN
Portsmouth, NH

Boynton/Cook Publishers, Inc.
361 Hanover Street
Portsmouth, NH 03801-3912
http://www.boyntoncook.com

Offices and agents throughout the world

© 1999 by Wendy Bishop

All rights reserved. No part of this book may be reproduced in any form or by any electronic or mechanical means, including information storage and retrieval systems, without permission in writing from the publisher, except by a reviewer, who may quote brief passages in a review.

The author and publisher thank those who generously gave permission to reprint borrowed material:

Excerpts from Norman K. Denzin and Yvonna S. Lincoln, *Handbook of Qualitative Research,* copyright © 1994. Reprinted by Permission of Sage Publications, Inc.

Excerpts reprinted by permission of Elizabeth Chiseri-Strater: *Academic Literacies: The Public and Private Discourse of University Students* (Boynton/Cook Publishers, A subsidiary of Reed Elsevier, Inc., Portsmouth, NH, 1991).

Excerpts from *Writing the Qualitative Dissertation: Understanding by Doing* by Judith M. Meloy. Copyright © 1994. Reprinted by permission of Lawrence Erlbaum Associates, Inc.

"Ethnography or Psychology? The Evolution and Ethics of a New Genre in Composition" by Keith Rhodes, and excerpts reprinted by permission of the Authors. In *Voices and Visions: Refiguring Ethnography in Composition,* edited by Cristina Kirklighter, Cloe Vincent, and Joseph M. Moxley (Boynton/Cook Publishers, Inc., A subsidiary of Reed Elsevier, Inc., Portsmouth, NH, 1997).

Excerpts from Paul Atkinson, *Understanding Ethnographic Texts,* copyright © 1992. Reprinted by Permission of Sage Publications, Inc.

Excerpts reprinted by permission of the State University of New York Press, from *Representation and the Text* by William G. Tierney and Yvonna S. Lincoln (eds.), © 1997, State University of New York. All rights reserved.

Library of Congress Cataloging-in-Publication Data
Bishop, Wendy.
    Ethnographic writing research : writing it down, writing it up,
  and reading it / Wendy Bishop.
      p.   cm.
    Includes bibliographical references and index.
    ISBN 0-86709-486-9 (alk. paper)
    1. Ethnology—Authorship.   2. Ethnology—Research. I. Title.
  GN307.7.B57   1999
  305.8'0072—dc21   98-55915
                                      CIP

Editor: *Lisa Luedeke*
Cover design: *Tom Allen/Pear Graphic Design*
Manufacturing: *Louise Richardson*

Printed in the United States of America on acid-free paper
Docutech RRD 2008

Contents

Acknowledgments and Introduction

Ethnographic Writing Research

Ethnography, like composition, is a relatively new field of inquiry, and it has an analogous modern history: for the past century or so, it has been practiced by many people who called it different generic names—history, autobiography, journal writing, diary, travel account—while also affiliating it with the narrower and more academically prestigious discipline of anthropology. At about the same time that composition research began its current period of growth, ethnography developed a more autonomous identity. . . . The field of ethnography as we understand it today may also be expressed as "writing culture," the term James Clifford and George Marcus use in the title of their 1986 ethnographic essay collection.
—David Bleich 1993, 176

In a sense, we have all engaged in classroom inquiry since our earliest experiences as teachers, for we have listened, observed, questioned, and hypothesized, all to the hoped-for end of improving the quality of learning in our classrooms.
—Dixie Goswami & Peter Stillman 1987, "Preface"

After all the interviews were transcribed, all the drafts examined, all the revisions noted, after the methodological machine had come to a halt, I still had to find the narrative thread that led me through the material. I had to "intensely consult and intensely ignore," keeping the data I needed, putting aside the rest, grieving for a bit for all I had to leave out.

It is a lonely feeling, and for a while an empty feeling. But I was not totally alone because I had patterns of other narratives to draw on. I could make new stories out of old ones.
—Thomas Newkirk 1992, 150

Although ethnographic writing research is a rapidly growing area of composition studies, the words themselves—*ethnographic writing research*—quickly become problematic. Am I talking about naturalistic research or teacher research or case-study research? What makes some research ethnographic and other research not? Where would this writing research take place? In classrooms, outside classrooms, in the university, in writers' homes and workplaces? Definitions are definitely in order, and much of this book will grapple with them. Yet by limiting my discussion to ethnographic writing research, I hope, at the same time, to open this methodology to scrutiny, discussion, and practice.

> Ethnography is a human model. Born out of anthropology as a way for the lone anthropologist to immerse herself in and come to understand a foreign culture, it now enables us to approach classrooms (something we are very familiar with) with freshness and clarity. In ethnography, researchers do not reduce classrooms to lesson plans or test scores, but rather we seek to bring to the surface what is intangible, hidden or overlooked in the unfolding of classroom dynamics. . . . When we take this kind of approach to such complex phenomena we don't end up with neat research designs, clear-cut boundaries and controlled variables. But we do find ourselves involved in an enormously rich task that often requires us to respond on a human level.
> —Sondra Perl 1983, 11

As a research methodology, ethnography has firmly arrived—along with other, related, naturalistic inquiry approaches. In 1987 Stephen North claimed that the community of ethnographic research was one with edges but no center; in the same year, I began my own ethnographic research project. Since I completed that dissertation in late 1988 and published a revised version of my work in 1990, I have watched the surge, development, and now—perhaps—the cresting of a wave of similar projects. Studies labeled *ethnographic, naturalistic,* and *case study* are well represented in *Research in the Teaching of English* bibliographies of the past several years; through the 1990s, conference programs at the Conference on College Composition and Communication have listed more reports, and, in general, much talk about ethnography has been taking place. Our conferences now regularly include panels on the subject as well as workshops. In 1987, when I commenced my research project, however, I felt I was inventing ethnographic writing research on my own. Aside from Shirley Brice Heath's *Ways with Words* (1983), Glenda Bissex's *GNYS at WRK* (1980), Sondra Perl and Nancy Wilson's *Through Teachers' Eyes* (1986; 1998), and a few teacher–researcher articles, my "bibles" were written for social scientists and anthropologists, and I had few studies to study. The methods texts I did have—

Ethnography and Qualitative Design in Educational Research (1984), by Judith Goetz and Margaret LeCompte, and *Qualitative Data Analysis* (1984), by Matthew Miles and Michael Huberman—were valuable. They told me how to design research and collect data (how to "write it down"), and I scoured them for hints on ways to adapt my borrowed methodology to my own new field—writing research.

I learned to design research, and I designed in, I thought, reliability. I would "write it down" through field notes, personal memos, and copious participant–observer data collection (i.e., video, audio, interview transcripts, etc.). I knew I would increase validity through rigorous data analysis (charting, cross-checking [triangulating], coding, etc.).

Along the way, over a thirty-month period, as you can imagine, I became less sure, less able to translate methods-book injunctions into research realities. Questions arose. Not just what is *ethnography*, but why did "doing ethnography" seem to have elements of "doing literature" and "doing creative writing" that no one and no methods book was mentioning? Or, how could research that seemed more and more to rely on my subjectivity, interpretations, and, finally, storytelling skills be a vehicle for reliable and valid results?

This book takes you through such questioning to questions of your own. This is not a book about certainty. It's a place where my thinking will resonate with and (hopefully) prompt your thinking but not duplicate your thinking, which is impossible, by definition, in this phenomenologically situated method. I hope to anticipate and prompt questions that are bound to arise as you undertake your own ethnographic enterprise. Thinking along with me, you'll encounter methodological questions, some that only your best judgment and evolving experience can help answer.

Research methods in general are receiving more attention as many colleges and universities begin or expand degree programs in rhetoric and composition and include required methods courses to prepare students for completing research theses and dissertations. In fact, you may be reading this book in conjunction with such a course. While methods books have been published that survey the spectrum of available research methods or offer essayist voices on a theme or topic of concern, most ethnographic writing researchers have to reinvent the methodology, going to classic texts in anthropology, and sometimes sociology, and to cognate but not perfect (for our purposes) works in educational ethnography. In books and journals we find discussions of ethical issues in research, service learning, and representations of students. A lot of translating and interpreting must be done, but that's not completely problematic because we all benefit from being broadly read in our area. This book, in a way, may be seen as one translation, or an introduction to translations.

For those initiating smaller classroom-based ethnographies, this text may provide a fieldguide or a blueprint, an initial talking-through of issues and decision points. For those already involved in a deeper, long-term engagement with the methodology, this book will serve as part of the conversation, pointing you toward issues (that no one can resolve, however much we enjoy and need to talk about them) and sources as you make your own contributions to field discussions in the form of finished ethnographies and meta-analyses of your methodology.

Because of this dual vision—we need to do ethnography to learn ethnography, and the more we learn about ethnography, the more there is to learn—this text has two voices. Clearly it is personal and anecdotal. I have intentionally not chosen the high academic road. Rather, I will talk you through issues, pose real and imaginary research problems, share research anecdotes, and offer guidelines and checklists that I know you will modify. At the same time, I will share my scholarly reading in the form of discussions of the writings of others, suggestions for further readings, mini-bibliographies and pointings toward other resources, and, as you have already seen, block quotes from other researchers, which I hope will continue, aphoristically, to prompt thinking about our subject at hand.

Using my personal and anecdotal voice, I need to mention that this book owes much to my own professors—Patrick Hartwell, Donald A. McAndrew, and Michael Williamson—who allowed me to go where no Indiana University of Pennsylvania graduate student had gone before. It owes as much, or more, to the many fine graduate student researchers in several research methods courses at Florida State University: I can't list all of your names, but you all more than earned your ethnographer's badge as well as my continuing thanks.

Peter Stillman, way back when, asked me to write this book. His faith in my ability to do so has been fundamentally important. Lisa Leudeke gracefully inherited the project and guided it to completion. Elizabeth Chiseri-Strater offered timely and strategic revision suggestions. She and Bonnie Sunstein at other times shared conversations about research that helped me to think better (and they included, most recently, some needed clambake etiquette lessons). Any infelicities here are mine, never the result of all this help, and any felicities I am sure flow from my life's main resources: Morgan and Tait. Once again, this book is for you two.

Reverting to my scholarly voice, I would remind you that many other authors and researchers inspired this work with their excellent prose and trenchant observations. I cite and salute their projects, hoping you'll add all of their books to your ethnographer's bookshelf. My primary goal in this book is to help readers conduct their day-to-day research—whether in developing an informal classroom report, writing a dissertation prospectus and study, or participating in local, civic literacy research. I also provide discussions that should help you to read ethnographic work—your own and that of others—with more critical sensitivity and insight.

This text, then, could be considered a set of mini-lectures, the ones I never manage to offer to my classes because we're usually trying to learn by doing, by pooling our resources and examining our practices. However, when we return home from classes, lectures, presentations, and/or discussions, questions arise, and we all find it useful to pull a methods book off the shelf, using it to complicate our thinking. And we read them—as you should this one—for what we need: perhaps Chapter One to the end of the book; perhaps for a spot check on a particular issue (e.g., keeping field notes) that points to other considerations (turning notes into narrative) and yet another issue (problems of postmodernism and verisimilitude!). However, after my final introductory quote, this book opens in Chapter One with definitions and initial research decisions.

> How we do research, like how we teach, reflects our underlying assumptions about human nature and learning.
> —Lucy Calkins 1985, 126

Chapter One

Defining *It*

> Ethnographers are rightly accused of making the obvious obvious (or, more kindly, of making the familiar strange . . .) because, quite literally, their task is to describe what everybody already knows.
> —Harry Wolcott 1987, 41–42

Writing teachers know better than to begin a chapter with the word *it*. But the fact that I have done so in my chapter title speaks to the difficulty researchers experience when talking about this specialized but complex *it*—ethnography in general and ethnographic writing research in particular. Ethnography is a research approach that is best learned by doing, but before doing, the doer needs to get a handle on what should be done. Ethnographic writing research borrows from three distinct genealogies. For me, this research takes place in a sociological space—often (but not always) writing classrooms or other sites of literacy learning: libraries, workplaces, preschools, alternate schools, prisons, community centers, homes. Instead of studying a group of people who inhabit a certain urban location (say, a Chicago streetcorner) or a certain town (say, a small, seemingly typical one in Indiana), ethnographic writing researchers look to study how individuals write (or don't write, or resist writing, or combine reading and writing, or are asked to write and perceive those jobs or academic assignments and carry them out).

> Schools are communities (within larger communities) and classrooms are subsets of schools. Within the culture as a whole (for example, the USA), schools have their distinctive patterns of behavior, attitudes towards literacy, for example, beliefs about education and about the roles of teachers and students.
>
> —Nancy Martin 1987, 20

At this point, ethnographic writing research intersects with a history of modern composition research that most of us in the field date from the early 1960s, when regularized study into composing processes began and study into how writers write was carried out within the dominant scientific tradition, which was positivist and experimental, often using artificially controlled clinical and case-study settings. When classrooms were studied, they were often paired and studied in terms of treatment and control groups. "Composition scholars began to refer not to the 'writing' process but to the 'composing' process, as in the pioneering work of Janet Emig. . . . The significance of this shift in terminology was its emphasis on the cognitive activities involved in writing. 'Composing,' in other words, is what goes on in the writer's head and is then recorded in writing" (Bizzell & Herzberg 1996, 8).

Early case-study research—a single writer writing on a set, assigned task—led to more complicated cognitive research, adapted from the traditions of clinical psychology. Through testing, refining hypotheses, retesting, replicating, and extending their hypotheses, cognitive writing researchers developed a generalizable model of the steps writers go through to produce a text. Although cognitive models illuminated the processes of writers in general, such models did not suggest treatments for classes or for writers who were writing under uncontrolled and uncontrollable real-world conditions. Researchers who were less sure that the dominant tradition could address their research needs came to qualitative approaches in general and the ethnographic approach in particular because it represents a different philosophical attitude toward studying the world. W. James Potter (1996), a quantitative researcher exploring qualitative approaches, emphasizes the breadth of such work:

> For example, the following is a partial list of synonyms . . . phenomenology, interpretation, humanism or humanistic studies, naturalism, hermeneutics, ethnography, critical theory, cultural science, postpositivism, interaction, and ethnomethodology. Although these terms overlap somewhat, their individually subtle and sometimes nuanced elements distinguish them from one another. (7)

Ethnographers admit—sometimes even celebrate—the subjective nature of their inquiry, and *ethnography* as a research label has come to represent a phenomenological attitude toward writing research as writing researchers have adopted these methods in an attempt to contextualize their study.

A third response is to deny the opposition of subjectivity and objectivity and overcome it by fully accepting the hermeneutical character of existence. Paul Rabinow and William Sullivan (1987) endorse this view, following a line of argument advanced by Martin Heidegger, Hans-George Gadamer, and Charles Taylor. They claim that the activity of interpretation is not simply a methodological option open to the social scientist, but rather the very condition of human inquiry itself: The interpretive turn is not simply a new methodology, but rather a challenge to the very idea that inquiry into the social world and the value of the understanding that results is to be determined by methodology. (20)

—Thomas Schwandt 1994, 119–20

An ethnography becomes a representation of the lived experience of a convened culture. Ethnographers "seek to document the cosmology, that is, the knowledge and belief systems that contribute to the coherence of the group" (Potter 1996, 51). The culture cannot be replicated or tested because it is experienced for a finite time through the researcher's participation and attention. The culture can be entered and participated in—to the degree that the researcher is canny enough to gain entry and the members are willing to afford entry—and then that research experience is textualized through the analysis of field notes, transcribed interviews, and physical (in this case, usually textual) artifacts. By the time the researcher is writing up a report, the culture has gone elsewhere, continued on without the researcher, or, in the case of classrooms (which for the purposes of this discussion will be viewed as temporarily convened cultures), disbanded entirely and dissolved in the larger matrices of school, work, or civic life.

Culture is not lying about, waiting patiently to be discovered; rather, it must be *inferred* from the words and actions of members of the group under study and then literally *assigned* to that group by the anthropologist. "Culture" as such, as an *explicit* statement of how the members of a particular social group act and believe they should act, does not exist until someone acting in the role of ethnographer puts it there.

—Harry Wolcott 1987, 41

Sites of ethnographic writing research, by the very nature of the academic calendar, have a much shorter span (longitude) than do the studies undertaken by classic ethnographers who entered a culture in Samoa or Borneo or Morocco or Mexico and lived some years there, attempting to describe the beliefs, practices, rituals, and ways of thinking of those they encountered from those peoples' own points of view. While ethnographic writing researchers do not usually reside long-term in unknown cultures, they do attempt to understand the learning-to-write situation from the learners' points of view; researchers may study the dynamics of the entire classroom or corporation, of teacher-education classes, of curricular "projects" such as writing across the disciplines programs, and so on. Note, for instance, the relatively short duration of the projects cited in the ERIC Document abstracts at the end of this chapter: a four-day study (Campbell), a three-week study (Tinberg), and a term-long project (Bullion-Mears).

It, then, represents a complicated hybridization of research traditions—sociological, cognitive, and anthropological—and, like any hybrid, is easier to describe by negation or by comparison and contrast. For instance, definitions often draw on the oppositions between quantitative (experimental) methods and qualitative (ethnographic) methods. Michael Kamil, Judith Langer, and Timothy Shanahan (1985) define the following characteristics of the former—the dominant, objective, experimental research tradition—as

1. positivist, seeks facts and causes
2. sets variables and tests relationships
3. preformulates research questions or hypotheses
4. uses laboratory or field settings

They list the following characteristics for the latter—the emergent, ethnographic tradition—which may be viewed as occurring at the other end of the objective–subjective spectrum:

1. phenomenological and seeks to understand human behavior from participants' frame of reference
2. systematically observes recurring patterns of behavior as people engage in regularly occurring activities
3. uses field settings and develops hypotheses grounded in events and driven by the conceptual framework of the study
4. confirms across a variety of information sources, contexts, times (summarized and adapted from page 72)

Like any genre or classification, *it* is clear in a clear case and fuzzy when researchers push the borders of what is generally agreed upon.

This book, though, is for those who want to start by constructing praiseworthy, ethnographically oriented research designs. When we enter a discipline and undertake a new methodology, we seek to gain acceptance into our research community and at least temporarily claim certainty about our project. We look at methods that conform and methods that don't, usually deciding to master the former as we begin to understand how we might, (soon) in the future, need to try more of the latter. A major goal of this book is to examine what constitutes a strong ethnographic writing research project, knowing that immediately local circumstances will suggest needed modifications from that design. And that's as it should be, because research of this sort is more a matter of worldview and attitude, orientation and approach, than it is of standardized methodological practices.

I should point out that there are currently conflicting understandings about how this approach can be incorporated into composition studies. There are researchers who argue for a pluralism of methods, who see naturalistic methods as augmenting and supplementing cognitive research (recent work by Linda Flower is moving in this direction), or those who see ethnography and all methods of descriptive research—case study, survey, and ethnographic—as *merely* hypothesis-generating, as in the research taxonomy presented by Lauer and Ascher in *Composition Research: Empirical Designs* (1988). In this view, ethnographers identify and develop hypotheses that may then be tested under more controlled conditions and contribute to comprehensive models of composing. I am of the school that argues, instead, that ethnographic approaches and methods are not *in service of* but are *equal to.*

Ethnographic inquiry represents a researcher's grounding in a different set of beliefs—naturalistic, holistic, subjective beliefs—about empirical research. Researchers like myself believe that all research is rhetorically situated and all research reports rhetorically structured and that researchers within both the positivist and the ethnographic traditions make arguments from their structured observations as well as from their philosophical beliefs. Books concerning methodology consider these issues and more; some researchers are concerned with ethics (see Mortensen & Kirsch 1996) and the varied ways ethnographic methodologies are being deployed in composition studies today (see Kirklighter, Vincent & Moxley 1997), with reading and interpreting such research (see Potter 1996) and with carrying out dissertation projects in this vein (see Meloy 1994).

> To the charges that the researcher brings her own biases, qualitative feminist researchers would reply that bias is a misplaced term. To the contrary, these are resources and, if the researcher is sufficiently reflexive about her project, she can evoke these as resources to guide data gathering or creating and for understanding her own interpretations and behavior in the research. . . .
>
> —Virginia Olesen 1994, 165

Because researchers in writing have been calling their work ethnographic for a scant twenty or so years, it is not easy to call on tradition when invoking parameters for what might make good, useful, or effective ethnographic approaches to writing research. My purpose in defining, then, is to help researchers clarify and articulate where they stand, to ask them to qualify what particular hybrid they are proposing. Still, change happens. Variations occur. When we cross-breed roses, we can get new, namable colors; we can do this again in the largest sense, that we know each parent variant and what each will contribute to our new offspring. When we cross-breed ethnographic research traditions and graft those onto our site of interest, we can mainly indicate what practices would make our work more or less ethnographic, more or less namable in this way. But, of course, these are reasoned and reasonable predictions, nonetheless.

> Ethnography has four core features, according to Atkinson and Hammersley (1994). First, it is inductive rather than deductive. Second, the data are open to many interpretations and are not collected in a closed set of analytical categories. Third, investigation is intensive on a small number, even as small as one, of cases. And fourth, the analysis is an explicit interpretation of the meanings of language and human actions. When statistical analyses are used, they play a subordinate role.
>
> —W. James Potter 1996, 27

This said, I also have to remind readers that ethnographic writing researchers must have a capacity for ambiguity, for withheld and delayed certainties. Along with that capacity, they have to have personal integrity and rigor so that when the product, an ethnographic writing research report, is completed, they know they started with the best design possible, made reasonable adjustments, and can articulate where they are (even who they now are) when they stop.

> We imagine, therefore, that in the construction of narratives of expe-
> rience, there is a reflexive relationship between living a life story,
> telling a life story, retelling a life story, and reliving a life story. As re-
> searchers, we are always engaged in living, telling, reliving, and retell-
> ing our own stories.
> —Jean Clandinin & Michael Connelly 1994, 418

The remainder of this chapter looks more closely at historical and methodological genealogies: We'll take a whirlwind tour of twenty-plus years of writing research (those already familiar with this review will want to move to later sections) and then explore the rise of and reason for interest in ethnographic approaches.

Writing Research: The 1960s to the 1980s

In his 1986 *College English* article, "Competing Theories of Process," Lester Faigley discusses writing research of the previous fifteen years and divides process theories that result from writing research into three broad categories: expressive, cognitive, and social. Of these categories, cognitive theories dominated because they provided a starting point for building a model of the composing process, something that had not formerly existed. Before this time, we relied on writers' self-reports. Often these were the reports of literary authors who composed under circumstances very different than those of student or professional and/or technical writers. It is interesting, for instance, to learn that "Dame Edith Sitwell sought inspiration by lying in a coffin. George Sand wrote after making love. Friedrich Schiller sniffed rotten apples stashed under the lid of his desk" before composing (Wyche-Smith 1993, 111). But such reports are unreliable, possibly a result of cultural myths we hold about writers and writing that writers echo back to interviewers. Self-report also breeds misconceptions (for instance, that *great* writers apprentice to a single genre and master it) and misrepresentations (for instance, that writers must wait to be inspired by the muse or that *real* writers are always so inspired). It is clear, for example, that authors often edit their composing memories to present a more interesting self.

Writing teachers could not draw solely on authors' reports to help their students learn to write better. Cognitive researchers, therefore, worked to make observable the invisible, the composing activities that take place inside a writer's head. Because of writing teachers' interest in and need for more reliable teaching methods for required first-year writing courses, research in the cognitive domain of writing developed

dramatically in the late 1970s and early 1980s. Cognitive models became more sophisticated, and techniques for studying writers' writing
improved.

A generally accepted starting place for cognitive research is Gordon
Rohman and Albert Wlecke's 1964 model of writing, which included
three stages: prewriting, writing, and rewriting. These researchers were
studying invention and not intending a complete description of the composing process, yet their model prompted further research. The main
drawbacks to the model was its linearity and the fact that it was derived
from the analysis of products, written texts, and not the observed process of writing, writers at work.

By 1977, Janet Emig had studied the composing process of twelfth-
grade student writers and expanded both the research model and research methodology. Emig used case studies and composing-aloud protocols. She observed eight American high school seniors while they
composed and used her interviews with them to verify her observations.
In a single, detailed case study of one of these writers, she found data
that led her to expand Rohman and Wlecke's categories of prewriting,
writing, and rewriting. For instance, in the writing stage, she observed
that writers exhibited silences and hesitations (areas studied by later researchers). She broke down the rewriting stage into correcting, revising,
and rewriting (which meant stopping and starting over). One of her
most important discoveries involved the recursive nature of the composing activity. She found writers planning in the prewriting *and* in the
writing stages, and so on.

In 1977, Mina Shaughnessey defined and explored the problems
of basic writers. "In her analysis of successive drafts of papers by extremely unskilled college writers, Shaughnessy has found attempts at
meaning making where there appears to be no order at all" (Bizzell
1986, 61). Basic writers, Shaughnessey found—contrary to the expectations of teachers—were working by a rule-governed system. Their
mistakes were often the result of mis- or overapplying rules in their
writing. Through careful error analysis, conducted on large numbers of
students' papers and giving attention to their writing process and classroom development, Shaughnessey found ways to enable basic writers
to become more fluent, successful writers.

Interest in the problems of basic writers (who flooded schools in
the 1970s due to open admissions policies) led researchers to study the
differences between basic writers' composing strategies and the strategies of traditional college students or experienced professional writers.
In 1979, Sondra Perl found that the basic writers she observed were doing exactly what Shaughnessey had said they were doing: applying in-
effective rules throughout the composing process. These writers would
often stop and scan and correct their papers at the sentence or word

level. This self-imposed interruption would keep the students from achieving any type of global development in a piece of writing.

Perl found more efficient writers participating in projective structuring (worrying about audience) and retrospective structuring (checking the text written so far in order to guide future development). She found successful writers listening to what she termed a "felt sense," which helped them negotiate the demands of their text in process.

Sharon Pianko (1979) also found basic writers to be overly rule-governed and concerned with correction. For her project, Pianko scheduled five writing episodes—one per week—for ten remedial and seven traditional writers. Assignments for episodes were set, and each student was observed and videotaped during one of the writing episodes. Writers were interviewed as well as observed. Basic writers in Pianko's study spent little time prewriting or writing and did not appear to value writing. The traditional students that she observed did have more successful writing strategies than did the basic students.

By 1980, as a result of this research, the composing process appeared much more complex than formerly thought. By observing writers as they wrote in controlled, clinical settings, a great deal could be inferred about their cognitive activities, and new issues seemed worth studying. Specifically, what were the differences between basic and expert or professional writers, what were the steps in the revision process, and what kept certain writers from becoming more successful in their composing process?

In 1980, Nancy Sommers and Lillian Bridwell each reported their studies on revision. Sommers found that basic writers relied on two main types of revision—addition and deletion—neglecting substitution and reordering. However, experienced writers used all four types of revision techniques. Experienced writers also had a metacognitive awareness of their revision process, while student writers, on the other hand, spoke of "cleaning up" their writing and showed underdeveloped revision strategies.

Bridwell's study—"an analysis of 6,129 revisions in 100 randomly selected sets of twelfth grade students' drafts of an informative/argumentative essay" (Bridwell 1980, 197)—supports this difference between successful and unsuccessful writers. In her study, the most effective writer revisions occurred *between first and second drafts* while writers were rereading their work. However, less successful writers, as in earlier studies, interrupted their work to make meaning-destroying, sentence-level corrections.

By 1981, Linda Flower and John R. Hayes had developed an initial version of a full-scale cognitive model of the composing process. "Flower and Hayes ask writers to describe their thought processes aloud while they are composing. The transcript of what they say is the protocol, which the researchers then analyze for regular features of a composing process" (Bizzell 1986, 56). Using this method, Flower and Hayes divided composing into generating, translating, and reviewing. Further, they discussed several important aspects of composing that connect to the results of the research I have reported so far. First, the composing process is also dependent on the text written so far (as in Perl) and on the rhetorical situation (audience demands, and so on) and is limited by the capacity of long-term memory. In this case, memory is linked to meta-cognitive and metalinguistic ability developed through previous writing experiences. Finally, and most important to Flower and Hayes' model, writers are influenced by self-developed goals. Flower and Hayes found successful writers relying on a hierarchy of sub-, mid-, and higher level goals, which took them from sentence-level to global concerns. Less successful writers seemed to lack mid-level goals and became stuck at the sentence level (as in the revision studies by Bridwell and Sommers) or on more global concerns.

Three other studies need to be mentioned to round out the composing picture, for "research into the cognitive processes of writers continued, but it was informed by new interest in how these processes are conditioned by social circumstances" (Bizzell & Herzberg 1996, 10). In 1980, Mike Rose published case-study cognitive research on blocked and unblocked writers. He found that blocked writers were often applying inappropriate, algorithmic rules to their writing, a characteristic of basic writers. On the other hand, unblocked writers had flexible planning and composing strategies, which allowed them to write in a variety of situations for a variety of audiences (like Sommer's expert writers).

In 1979, Linda Flower discussed writer-based prose. Writer-based prose, she posited, is generally narrative and associational in structure, internal, expressive, and intended by the writer to explore a situation. Nonetheless, many writers have trouble moving from the useful medium of writer-based prose to the more public medium, which Flower termed "reader-based prose." Reader-based prose is expository in nature and organized with the reader in mind. Work by James Collins and Mike Williamson (1981) provided some insight into the problems experienced by composers of writer-based prose. Often these writers seem to be writing down speech, relying on unavailable references, which are external to the text.

Cognitive research, then, through composing-aloud protocols, textual analysis, and case-study reporting, develops a picture of the basic writer as someone who is rule-governed (generally inappropriately so), who has trouble imagining audiences other than himself, who doesn't value "school" writing, and who has inflexible revising and writing strategies and an underdeveloped sense of the composing process. Successful writers are much more closely aligned to the Flower and Hayes model, able to decide upon audience and able to tailor the developing text to audience demands and rhetorical demands. The successful writer not only has flexible composing and revising strategies, but also has a wealth of successful previous writing experience to draw upon, enabling her to make and adjust writing goals to suit a particular writing situation.

Authors' self-reports, as elicited in interview, were not a strong enough foundation for teaching all writers how to write. Neither was the developing cognitive model wholly satisfactory, in that it represented thinking at the other pole. For instance, those who believe in expressive theories of composing see the writer as an individual who is learning through writing. Other theorists at this time, such as Ken Macrorie, James Moffet, Frank Smith, John Mayher, and others, viewed writing as a natural process, and many of their theories are derived from observing writers in the classroom, arguing that cognitive researchers, in order to study writing, had to break down writing activities into unnatural and unrealistic stages, procedures, and so on. Additionally, they pointed out the problems that arose when such studies take place in unrealistic testing contexts and settings.

Cy Knoblauch and Lil Brannon (1984) argued that breaking down the writing process into stages greatly misrepresents the composing process and encourages teachers to take a smorgasbord approach to writing instruction—picking and choosing those stages or those models they wish to emphasize—and that such an approach will lead to misinformed instruction. They preferred to emphasize a holistic approach to the teaching of writing.

Expressive theorists have made valuable contributions to composition instruction. They suggest that we start where the student is, use student-centered classrooms, and help students develop as individuals as they develop as writers. Unfortunately, these theorists do not always take into account the very real constraints under which composition teachers work, such as large classes, department or district control of curriculum, diverse student literacy backgrounds, and so on. However, expressive theorists did offer an important corrective voice when considering cognitive theory, which still offered an incomplete model for the complex activity we call composing.

A different outlook for composing theory developed from the work of social theorists. Structural social theorists such as Patricia Bizzell (1986), Marilyn Cooper (1986), and Kenneth Bruffee (1984) insisted that neither the cognitive model nor the expressive models are complete, for composing does not occur only for an individual (expressive) or in the head (cognitive), but also in complex social settings, which affect the ways in which both basic and professional writers write. To define a new, contextual base for composing, Bizzell explored the idea of discourse communities; Bruffee, interpretive communities; and Cooper, an ecological system that supports writing.

The Move to Ethnographic Approaches: The 1980s and 1990s

It was not long before social theorists were learning about composing through the results of ethnographic research like that undertaken by ethnographers such as Shirley Brice Heath (1983) and Jerome Harste, Virginia Woodward, and Carolyn Burke (1984). These researchers pointed out that composing is negotiated by writers within households, schools, and communities, and that these social and/or biographical factors also affect the writing of any individual. It is at about this time, 1985, that the dominant model of cognitive, positivist research into composing began to undergo a sea change, with more and more researchers looking at naturalistic methodologies and gravitating toward ethnographic methods and the more naturalistic methods of teacher research.

Ethnographic writing researchers borrow from the anthropological model of naturalistic, participant-observation inquiry. Traditionally, the anthropologist would "enter the field" of another (almost always distant) culture, identify a "key informant," and begin to try to "learn" that culture, in hopes of making manifest that which normally isn't manifest—cultural definitions, practices, and community understandings. While sociologists also practiced naturalistic research, conducting community studies in the more familiar cultures of American cities and local communities, their work was often undertaken to support the work of social theorists "who build broad conceptual models for others to test and modify in humble social settings. These models are supposed to predict and explain patterns of thought and action across cultural domains" (Van Maanen 1988, 20). In anthropology, on the other hand, ethnographic research was—and remains—the primary research methodology.

In *The Making of Knowledge in Composition*, published in 1987, Stephen North offered an initial definition of ethnographic research in composition along with a fairly pessimistic discussion concerning the function, usefulness, and reliability of field practices in this area, pointing to the variability of research designs and lack of projects in general. Although there are still fewer published projects than might be expected or hoped for, there has been greatly increased interest since that time, in what William Irmscher (1987) calls "a model of inquiry appropriate to our own discipline—composition as part of English studies—consistent with its values, supporting and enlightening it" (82).

Since North published his influential book, many in composition have argued that naturalistic research methods, particularly ethnography and teacher research (ethnographic researchers *study other teachers' classes,* while teacher–researchers *study their own classes*), may be primary methods for understanding the complex literacy cultures and communities that occur in schools and communities. Many in composition claim that context-based study illuminates previously neglected areas (for example, classroom cultures) and produces holistic understandings of complex processes (composing, becoming a writer or a writing teacher, undertaking or resisting university literacy). "To Study this rich network, we need to look not only at the individual writer but at the collaborative situation of his or her classroom, personal and institutional histories, and writers' and teachers' political hopes" (Bizzell & Herzberg 1996, 13).

For instance, here's how I justified this methodology in my own initial (dissertation turned book-length) study:

> Ethnographic studies involve a major paradigmatic shift from the prevailing experimental tradition. The ethnographic mode, based in a cultural context, presents a phenomenological and empirical approach to research. It is holistic and naturalistic. Macroethnographies report research on multiple sites and involve larger or longer projects than do microethnographies. Microethnographies can report on the culture of the single classroom, the single learner, and even the single learning event.
>
> Ethnographic inquiry can be misapplied or misconceived. Too often, research using a single ethnographic technique (case study, life history interviewing, participant observation, and so on) is claimed as ethnography, resulting in what Ray Rist calls "blitzkreig ethnography." To avoid misapplication, ethnographic data analysis must derive its reliability and validity from a fully developed scheme of data collection, data reduction, data display, and conclusion drawing/verification which takes place recursively, with steps being repeated and refined until conclusions may safely be presented. Additionally, data is collected by more than one method (interviews, direct observation, artifacts) in order to assure triangulation, verification from multiple sources, while research reports rely on the "thick description" described and utilized by Geertz.
>
> Given these considerations, I chose an ethnographic methodology and narrative as my means of reporting research data from my desire to describe writing teachers' lives rather than from an intention to develop or prove a theory of teaching. While these teachers' stories might prompt further research or might result in future theories of instruction, most immediately they will be worth listening to if they tell

us about our own teaching and our own writing classrooms. (summary of pages xvi–xvii, Bishop, 1990)

Elizabeth Chiseri-Strater describes her choice of research methods in her ethnography *Academic Literacies:*

> My initial research interest was to understand how students interpret the literacy demands made on them in academic settings; what it meant from their vantage point to be literate in a university. . . . An ethnographic design seemed most appropriate for my purposes because it is concerned with the informant's world-view. (1991, 184)

But Barbara Walvoord and Lucille P. McCarthy begin their methods discussion for *Thinking and Writing in College* by saying,

> Our questions, as we began the study, were broad ones about students' thinking and writing. They were the general questions that Geertz says are traditionally asked by ethnographers facing new research scenes: "What's going on here?" and "What the devil do these people think they're up to?" (1976, 224). We chose the naturalistic inquiry paradigm to ask those questions. (1990, 10)

In 1991, when I began teaching a research methods class focused mainly on ethnography, there were few book-length studies to read whose researchers claimed this approach. Now the number includes Chiseri-Strater's and Walvoord and McCarthy's as well as Robert Brooke's *Writing and Sense of Self* (1991), Robert Brooke and John Hendricks' *Audience Expectations and Teacher Demands* (1989), Christian Knoeller's *Voicing Ourselves* (1998), Bonnie Sunstein's *Composing a Culture* (1994), Anne DiPardo's *A Kind of Passport* (1993), Marilyn Sternglass's *Time to Know Them* (1997), Howard Tinberg's *Border Talk* (1998), Nancy Welch's *Getting Restless* (1997), and my own, *Something Old, Something New* (1990a), with others forthcoming from several composition presses.

During the same, relatively short period, books on composition research methods included attention to naturalistic and ethnographic methods, including those by Kirsch and Sullivan (1992), Lauer and Asher (1998), Mortensen and Kirsch (1996), and Kirklighter, Vincent, and Moxley (1997). And several collections concerning teacher research appeared, such as those by Bissex and Bullock (1987), Daiker and Morenberg (1990), Goswami and Stillman (1987), Myers (1985), and Ray (1992).

Ethnographic writing research would also appear to be thriving because it accesses and acknowledges some formerly repudiated skills, those of several generations of writing specialists whose education was formed in literature departments and whose critique of those departments has been buttressed by the rise of literary theory. Personally, I am inclined toward ethnographic writing research and critical narratives as a primary way of reporting writing research, even while being struck with the similarity of what I now do as a qualitatively oriented writing classroom researcher to what I do as I read and apply critical theory. And my students are quick to experience this similarity as well. As Devan Cook (1996) notes during the first week of her research methods class,

> Ethnography seems to seek (in this stage of my thinking) to rebuild any experience, setting, or world, in writing—as does any written communication. I'm tempted to believe that ethnography is an artful science.

In these journal musings, Devan joins a diverse group consisting of research methods teachers, research practitioners, postmodern anthropologists, and others who are trying to understand the limits and potentials of this type of research. By her fourth week of study in the research methods class, Devan continued,

> Interesting how as we go along things become clearer . . . or whether such matters only seem clearer to us because we are more immersed in our studies and not looking at theory quite so hard. Is this an example of the ongoing and productive oscillation between a project and theorizing about it, the oscillation which is in fact the process of doing ethnography? Yes, I think without the theorizing I might be doing research of some kind (all those notes and all that taping of interviews and classes must be something!), but it would not be ethnography.

Back to Defining *It*

Anthropologist Harry Wolcott (1987) claims, "There is something of the perceptive ethnographer in each of us . . . each of us must succeed as an intuitive participant and observer for sheer survival in a social milieu. Each of us must figure out how to cope with the world we encounter, the unexpected as well as the expected" (45). It is natural as humans to be intuitive participants in the everyday landscape, but to become successful ethnographers, we need further training.

Ethnography as an approach is difficult to define because of the sweeping concepts involved: culture, language, symbol. To undertake ethnography, however, novice ethnographers must begin to make sense of their domain, and that domain ultimately is culture. " 'Culture'," Harry Wolcott explains, "as an *explicit* statement of how the members of a particular social group act and believe they should act, does not exist until someone acting in the role of ethnographer puts it there" (1987, 41). Wolcott's assertion that culture is constituted contradicts the more prevalent view of research in general that knowledge—of the cultural or material world—is out there waiting to be discovered. Therefore, ethnographers, practitioners of a subjective process, have had to fight hard for prestige in academic communities that valorize the objective stance. Often the method continues to be regarded as nontraditional: "'Educating the committee' can be a real life experience for neophyte qualitative researchers" (Meloy 1994, 20), and on top of that, the student is often struggling to learn the approach herself: "If some doctoral students feel defensive about their decision to undertake qualitative research, then might it be less from the fact of their methodological choices per se than it is from the fact that they are inexperienced researchers and methodologists, less able to explain and argue their choices and less sure about knowing what they are doing and why?" (Meloy 1994, 21). This certainly seemed to be true for those methods students with whom I've worked. Nancy Reichert notes this struggle in her class journal:

> The readings and the interviews [conducted by our class] got me thinking right away. At first, in fact for quite awhile, I wasn't really sure what ethnography was. The authors that we read seemed to all have a slightly different answer to what ethnography was and what its purpose was. Several authors didn't seem to value ethnography all that much. They seemed to think that it was a good way to get thinking about a "real" research project.

Nancy rehearses major research arguments. Is ethnography science or philosophy? Is ethnography on a continuum of empirical methodologies, ranging from qualitative to quantitative? Is ethnographic work primarily prescientific, generating hypotheses for later, more rigorous testing?

Some composition scholars have found it difficult or impossible to define ethnography and are therefore hesitant to sanction it as a research process. George Hillocks (1986), in his meta-analysis, leaves qualitative research out of his story of writing. Stephen North (1987), in his research categories, separates ethnography from hermeneutical research and from teacher research—separations I would argue against—and ends up defining it as a practice that functions poorly, creating a research community with borders but no center.

Linda Brodkey directs our attention away from method and toward researchers' attitudes and alignments, distinguishing analytic ethnographers—who identify categories and sort data into those categories—from interpretive ethnographers whose "'themes' . . . might be described as arising out of 'breakdowns' in the ethnographer's understanding of particular phenomena . . ." (Brodkey 1987b, 31).

But inevitably, ethnography remains resistant to methodological definition by way of enumerating its constituent parts; that is, ethnographers may agree on required techniques in general—such as triangulation, field notes, participant observation, longitudinal investigation, recursive analysis, and so on—but they rarely agree on the quantities and ordering of techniques or the degree to which quantitative data are "allowable" and desirable. And the pluralism versus purity arguments that arise from such methodological distrust can make a novice researcher despair of getting any realistic advice about how to enter real writing cultures in order to conduct actual studies. Most simply, Harry Wolcott suggests that the ethnographic label "should be reserved for descriptive efforts clearly ethnographic *in intent*" (1987, 43).

These definitions set aside received advice ("The trick is triangulation" or "First decide on your questions and population") and describe what is more likely to happen. For instance, I studied retraining college writing teachers and the ways they modified their teaching after enrollment in a graduate pedagogy seminar, because I had taken that seminar two years earlier. I wanted to know more about such an experience. I began with a completely ethnographic intent, but knew I sometimes bungled my ethnographic practices—losing a taped interview or reading a transcript in an interested way—and learned I would need to weave fragmentary case-study data into satisfying research stories. It is more honest and accurate, I believe, to admit to our creations, combinations, adaptations, and inventions, because this is how we actually make knowledge.

To define ethnographic research, then, a new researcher must sort through definitions offered by other researchers; all are shaded by the originating discipline (such as sociology, anthropology, education, cognitive psychology) and the needs of the witness (his current project and situation within the humanities and/or social science professions). You might start with those I've collected here. I'll follow with abstracts taken from recent research listed on the ERIC document data base. (For more on using ERIC to help with your own research review, see Chapter Two.)

Anthropology-based Research:
An ethnography is a written representation of a culture (or selected aspects of a culture). (Van Maanan 1988, 1)

Education-based Research:
Ethnographers attempt to record, in an orderly manner, how natives behave and how they explain their behavior. And ethnography, strictly speaking, is an orderly report of this recording. Natives are people in situations anywhere—including children and youth in schools—not just people who live in remote jungles or cozy peasant villages. (Spindler & Spindler 1987, 17)

Psychology-based Research:
The self as we experience it, understand it, and act it out is a function
of the dynamic interaction between individual and social groups, so
to describe the self usefully we must investigate these interactions.
(Brooke 1991, 16–17)

Methods texts may define ethnography by constituent parts and in
opposition to other methodologies; for instance, ethnography may be
described as one point in the continuum of empirical research, which
moves from descriptive (at that far end, case study and ethnography)
to the experimental (at that far end, experiment and meta-analysis)
(Lauer & Asher 1988, 16). Others view ethnography in opposition to
experimental empirical research:

> Experimental inquiry is generally based on a positivist view of social
> behavior (Comte 1973; Durkheim 1956) that seeks to identify facts
> and causes. Ethnographic inquiry emanates from a phenomenological
> base (Husserl 1931; Schutz 1970; Weber 1947) that seeks to under-
> stand social behavior from the participants' frames of reference.
> (Kamil, Langer & Shanahan 1985, 71)

Most definitions identify particular methodological aspects of
ethnographic projects: Ethnographies generate hypotheses, focus on
context, are written up using thick description, require participant observation, and use multiple measures for data collection, that is, triangulation (Kantor, Kirby & Goetz 1981, 298; North 1987, 277; Lauer
& Asher 1988, 39). More recently, definitions explore case-study reporting and the dual roles of ethnographers in composition, who are
often teachers and researchers or teacher–researchers (Bissex 1987,
1990; Myers 1985).

> When illustrating what we mean by "qualitative research," we often
> refer to its most popular forms—ethnographic and case study inquiry.
> But we recognize that there are many other forms of qualitative re-
> search: oral histories, narrative inquiry, craft interviews, observa-
> tional-descriptive narratives, introspective reports, and more. (Kirsch
> & Mortensen 1996, xxx)

You'll find many of these terms in the following abstracts of recent
research. Each of these abstracts will include key terms that will require
further defining in subsequent chapters. At this point in our discussion,
they provide pointers into the language(s) of ethnographic research
communities.

**Hunter, Linda. "Reexamining Writing Requirements
across the Curriculum: Assignments and Assumptions."
ERIC Document no.: ED382970**

Abstract: A four-year ethnographic study was conducted at St. Olaf College and examined six assumptions about student attitudes toward writing. The study, involving administration of the Writers Block instrument, writing samples, and several interviews with three students over their 4 years in college, evaluated the following assumptions: (1) that once students learn the value of writing and revising, they will do it; (2) that emphasis on the process is more likely to produce the instructor's definition of good writing; (3) that revision is the site for growth in writing and learning; (4) that students will improve at identifying the rhetorical situation; (5) that students' confidence and competence will grow over time and practice; and (6) that students will come to find writing satisfying as they are successful. Several of the assumptions did not hold up to scrutiny from the perspective of these students' behavior. Preliminary conclusions suggest that in the face of student pragmatism, faculty will need to ask themselves what goals are for students in their courses. Do they want to learn to examine issues and data in the same analytical, inquiring mode they do, or are they more interested in having them look up information and produce "correct" academic writing. If the thought process is more important, then instructors need to look at what types of assignments are most effective.

—Paper presented at the Annual Spring Conference
of the National Council of Teachers of English
(Minneapolis, MN, March 16–18, 1995)

Linda Hunter conducts a four-year study. Traditionally, the longer the time in the field, the more *reliable* the ethnographer's account of the culture studied. We look for *longitude*. (Although some studies, as we'll see, can study a single learning event, most cover a school term, an academic year, or, in the more extensive project, like this one, a multi-year period.) Although the term of study was long, the number of students followed through the four years of college learning was small—three case-study students. The study also mixes *quantitative* and *qualitative* data-gathering techniques—administration of a Writer's Block instrument, a *survey* that can be counted, tabulated, and quantified—and a collection of *writing samples* and *interviews* that provide data that must be analyzed through words. This study also collects more than one kind of data in order to *triangulate*, that is, verify observations by confirming them, using more than one data source. Although ethnographic in intent, the researcher began with *assumptions* that are shared here.

Arnold, James C. "Telling an Impressionist Tale: Enhancing Our Knowledge of College Students." ERIC Document no.: ED375716

Abstract: This paper explores technical questions of ethnographic study and uses as an example an actual episode observing college students and the subsequent decisions and steps taken to produce a written account. In particular, the paper seeks the question of researcher subjectivity by examining some issues relating to the practice of incorporating a field worker's voice into research reports. The first section of the paper outlines some views on the field worker's stance taken from the fields of mainstream sociology and anthropology and then supplements these with ideas from a feminist orientation. Subsequently a first-person "impressionist" account is offered of an evening spent at a fraternity house by a participant-observer at a large, all-house party. The account includes commentary and interpretation informed in part by the author's own biography. A following section describes how the field notes were produced and transcribed into readable text. It also discusses his personal feelings about writing the material and sharing personal background material in the text, choice of tense, and how he inserted himself in the account while trying to minimize interrupting the story's flow. Final thoughts address how a story such as this is enriched by including autobiographical elements. Contains 19 references.

—Paper presented at the Annual Meeting of the
Association for the Study of Higher Education
(19th, Tucson, AZ, November 10–13, 1994)

This author examines research methods but also introduces important terminology. The author became a *participant–observer* at a fraternity house party. The term of study is short, but the author is assuring us that he became immersed in the culture—we can assume he partied as well as studied the party. Although a participant, he was enough of an observer to take *field notes* that were *transcribed* into readable text for further and/or later *analysis*. His analysis depends on *interpretation, biographical awareness* and a *theoretical interpretive lens*, in this case, using a *feminist* orientation. Finally, he reported his findings in a *story narrative*.

Moje, Elizabeth B. "Literacy in the Chemistry Classroom: An Ethnographic Study of Effective Teaching." ERIC Document no.: ED352624

Abstract: A study that described, analyzed, and interpreted the ways an effective high school teacher used literacy activities (reading, writing, and discussion) to teach chemistry to first-year chemistry students. The teacher selected was considered effective by peers and students and professed to intentionally use literacy activities as a means of teaching content. The teacher taught in a rural, midwestern high school located outside a mid-size university town. Field notes from classroom observations were informed by teacher interviews, as well as interviews with key student informants. Results indicated that: (1) literacy activities both depended on and fostered students' abilities to organize materials, concepts, and thinking about chemistry; and (2) the atmosphere of organization and active involvement was developed through the teacher's use of multiple literacy activities. Findings suggest that effective teachers choose instructional activities that foster direct student involvement, and that effective teachers develop teaching strategies that best suit their individual classroom contexts.

—Paper presented at the Annual Meeting of the National Reading Conference (42nd, San Antonio, TX, December 2–5, 1992)

This author investigates the culture of a chemistry class to investigate *literacy events in general*. She gives her grounds for choosing this teacher—he was considered effective and did use literacy activities to teach chemistry; in this, she is conducting the more focused ethnographic writing research of the sort I have been discussing in this chapter. She is not dropping down to immerse herself in just any aspect of another culture (as she might if she were whisked away to Morocco to study Berber life). Instead, she has initial interests (literacy in non-English classes) and looks for a promising environment (a class in which the teacher is likely to be teaching in a way that will allow her to make discoveries). She conducted *interviews* with both teacher and students and identified some students as more likely to provide information than others—these became her *key informants*. She observed the *entire class culture*, taking *field notes* for later analysis. We are not told clearly the duration of the study but assume it took place over the course of a full unit, a term, or a year.

Fey, Marion Harris. "Reader Response, Collaborative Writing, and Computer Networking." ERIC Document no.: ED364875

Abstract: Part of a larger ethnographic study, this investigation focused on the literacy development of a college student as he participated in the virtual culture of a computer-networked writing classroom where all instruction and communication occurred through the computer. The student was a member of one of two classes of adult students, ranging in age between 25 and 48, all employed in upstate New York. Data included transcripts of large- and small-group discussions, response writings and compositions, composition logs, focus group discussions about computer networking, transcripts of electronic mail communications, field notes, and student interviews. Results indicated that: (1) e-mail communication between the teacher and the student served as backstage support; (2) the relationships the student developed with members of the small group provided an anchor for his actions within the large group; (3) the student gained respect from class members, which may have been more forthcoming through computer networking than in face-to-face interaction where traces of the student's speech handicap might have caused resistance; (4) his writing demonstrated a closing of the communication gap through his strength of voice and his attention to clarity and coherence; and (5) the student acquired metacognitive knowledge about writing and valued peer response. Findings suggest that an electronic environment where readers' responses link feelings to thought and where responses are shared with ease can lead to more powerful learning for some students than in a traditional classroom.

—Paper presented at the Annual Meeting of the National Reading Conference (43rd, Charleston, SC, December 1–4, 1993)

This case-study report focuses on a *single student* who participated in a larger study. The entire study encompassed two computer-networked writing classes. Data for this student, presumably, would include his participation in *large- and small-group discussions*, his *writings* in class, background information from *focus group interviews* (he may or may not have been a member of one of these focus groups, convened, we assume, to talk about *particular issues* in computer networking), his *e-mail transcripts*, and the *researcher's class notes*, which may or may not have mentioned his daily class activities and attitudes. Instead of trying to capture complex interactions across many class activities of many students, this author uses one student's case to make points about how a writer experiences the electronic writing environment. We can assume that a write-up of the larger study would include more cases, perhaps *structured* in a manner similar to this one. When an author presents *multiple cases,* she often develops a more coherent worldview of the culture and creates a greater sense of *verisimilitude.*

Campbell, Elizabeth Humphreys. "Fifteen Raters Rating: An Analysis of Selected Conversation during a Placement Rating Session." ERIC Document no.: ED358465

Abstract: An ethnographic study investigated conversations during planning meetings and placement rating sessions for selecting and rating freshman composition placement exams. Planning meetings involved the administrative coordinator and two assistants selecting model essays, discussing the rubric, and confirming the final plans for the rating session. Fifteen instructors of first-year composition at a large, public, urban midwestern university holistically rated about 2,000 placement essays over a 4-day period. Conversations were tape recorded, transcribed, and analyzed. Results indicated that, while choosing the model essays, the planning team focused on an informal rubric; during the rating session itself, however, no mention of the informal rubric was made. Most discussions took place around problematic or puzzling essays; ones that fit clearly into a category did not require much discussion. Findings suggest that administrators of holistic assessment sessions should expect discussions during rating sessions to stray far from the terms of the written rubric as the raters struggle to work out the meaning of scores they assign.

—Paper presented at the Annual Meeting of the Conference on College Composition and Communication (44th, San Diego, CA, March 31–April 3)

This ethnographic study is short-term and event-oriented. Placement essay raters are convened for a short period of time—in this case a *four-day period*—convening a temporary culture of individuals gathered to be trained to read and respond to student placement essays. This author chose to study all *fifteen raters,* taping, transcribing, and analyzing their *conversations* as they trained for this event.

These abstracts raise issues related to all ethnographic writing research. Researchers are concerned with identifying an issue they want to investigate (from the training of holistic raters to the way a chemistry teacher uses writing to teach chemistry) and a population/environment/context to enter (a rating session, a high school or college writing classroom, a fraternity house discussion). The researcher has to decide how long she needs to stay to learn about the way individuals in this culture experience their lives and which data-gathering techniques give the investigator the best means of identifying patterns and themes and verifying those patterns and themes. The researcher may study the culture broadly, reporting on events, or study the life of one or more individuals inside the culture, whether key informants or case-study subjects. The researcher must decide to what degree her participation is necessary to elicit trust and information from members of the culture without "going native" (say, partying too hard at the fraternity party and not being able to read field notes the next day). Particularly, in the case of writing classrooms, she needs to be aware of power and authority issues (can a teacher and student both trust the researcher, both be key informants, and so on) and realize that data can later be analyzed using different theoretical lenses (in one case under discussion, by taking a feminist stance).

To end this chapter, I invite you to conduct the same type of abstract analysis on two versions of the same study and then on two separate, recent research reports (all listed in ERIC). What follows is an abstract of a book-length report and an essay-length report from Anne DiPardo's ethnographic study of basic writing students. What definitions does she use to convince you that her work is ethnographic; what questions do you have about her project, given the limited discussion available in an abstract?

Essay abstract:

DiPardo, Anne. "Nested Contexts: A Basic Writing Adjunct Program and the Challenge of 'Educational Equity'." May 1992. ERIC Document no.: ED354523

Abstract: Conducted at a public university that had long been overwhelmingly Anglo despite being located in a state noted for its linguistic and cultural diversity, an ethnographic study examined one adjunct writing program and the varied students it serves. Data sources were both numerous and varied—data were collected concurrently at the campus level and within the various layers of the program. Two concerns (about academic standards and about cultural separatism) emerged as campus administrators struggled to explain their mixed feelings about the "equity policy" (designed to promote the academic and social adjustment of underrepresented students). Tensions also surfaced repeatedly at the English department and the small-group leader levels. In interviews with writing program administrators, faculty, and small-group leaders about the role of the program, the same dilemmas surfaced again and again—Should small group leaders: (1) consider cultural and linguistic backgrounds of students as resources to be shared or as stumbling blocks to be overcome? (2) act as nondirective facilitators or as directive leaders? (3) provide nurturing, understanding support to students, or insistent, sometimes aggressive prodding? (4) understand that all students must be expected to approximate native-like proficiency, or consider such standards to be inappropriate to a linguistically diverse population? And (5) adopt a quizzical, reflective habit of mind, or offer specific strategies and techniques? The study offers two student portraits (a Latina and a Black male) that suggest some kinds of understandings that might have usefully informed the group leaders' work—understandings that extend beyond the urgency of the instructional moment to students' struggles to belong in the academy.

Book abstract:

DiPardo, Anne. "A Kind of Passport: A Basic Writing Adjunct Program and the Challenge of Student Diversity." 1993. ERIC Document no.: ED355525

Abstract: Focusing on culturally diverse students and the adequacy of efforts to help them succeed in college, this book presents an ethnographic study of the basic writing course, a central element of the adjustment between academe and nontraditional students. The research site, pseudonymously called Dover University for purposes of this account of the study, was a typical, predominantly white, middle-class institution newly committed to the goal of increasing services to, and enrollment of, minorities, but with uneven and unremarkable resources and with a faculty and administrators who were well intentioned but sometimes weighed down by entrenched attitudes and precedents. The first part of the book discusses the background and design of the study. The second part discusses the nature of the larger social contexts in which the basic writing adjunct program was situated, and the nature of the more immediate social contexts (at the level of the English department) as perceived from the points of view of the writing program directors, adjunct component coordinators, and instructors. The third section examines four focal students' backgrounds, their attempts to adjust to college life, their struggles with writing, and perceptions of the small-group component of their basic writing course. The concluding section of the book reflects upon the complexities of designing effective programs to serve the needs of linguistically and culturally diverse basic writers, and discusses the more general ramifications of one campus's often troubled attempts to provide equitable opportunities for all. Interview questions are attached.

For the final abstracts, I include the entire ERIC document listing as taken from my university data base so you can see what a full set of search descriptors looks like:

Search Request: *(a=bullion-mears, ann)* *Long View*
CITATION—Record 1 of 2 Entries ***ERIC (RIE) (1988 to date)***

Authors:
 Bullion-Mears, Ann
Title:
 Developing Collaboration and Teacher Reflection in a College
 Curriculum Class. / by Bullion-Mears, Ann
Pub.Date:
 Dec 1993
Pages; Fiche:
 17; 1
Document no.:
 ED367983
FOUND IN ERIC microfiche unless noted otherwise:
 EDRS Price—MF01/PC01 Plus Postage.
Abstract:
 An action research study examined a teacher's developing collaborative practices in her secondary curriculum development and instructional methods class. The class was composed of 14 women ranging in age from 21 to approximately 50 in a medium sized southwestern university. Data were collected through a reflective journal and from certain student generated artifacts: walking journals, a mid-course

evaluation, and the final required university course evaluation. Data analysis revealed two themes: the evolution of student voice and the redefinition of teacher voice. Data representing instances of student voice were sought when students were given opportunities to collaborate with each other or the teacher in the decision making process. Students were also given opportunities to engage in self and peer evaluation and final grades were negotiated with the instructor at an end-of-term conference. The reflective journal itself was important in helping the teacher to articulate her voice as a teacher. She had the greatest difficulty in achieving balance and control, determining if and when to intervene. Final reflection delineated the need for the instructor to scaffold students as they develop new collaborative learning patterns. (Author/RS)

Notes:
17p.; Paper presented at the Annual Meeting of the National Reading Conference (43rd, Charleston, SC, December 1–4, 1993).
Speech/conference paper(150); Evaluative/feasibility(142)

Publication type (kn=):
150; 142

Language:
English

Geographic source:
U.S.; Texas

RIE/CIJE issue:
RIEAUG94

Major Identifiers (type ks=):
Reflective Writing
Voice (Rhetoric)

Major Descriptors (type sm= or ks=):
Cooperative Learning
Methods Courses
Preservice Teacher Education
Teacher Behavior

Minor Descriptors (type so= or ks=):
Action Research
Curriculum Development
Ethnography
Higher Education
Journal Writing
Secondary Education
Student Evaluation

Search Request: (a=atkinson, dwight)   *Long View*
CITATION—Record 2 of 5 Entries   ***ERIC (CIJE) (1988 to date)***

Authors:
Atkinson, Dwight
Ramanathan, Vai

Title:

Cultures of Writing: An Ethnographic Comparison of L1 and L2 University Writing/Language Programs. / by Atkinson, Dwight; Ramanathan, Vai

Pub.Date:

1995

Document no.:

EJ511926

FOUND IN:

TESOL Quarterly; v29 n3 p539-68 Aut 1995

Abstract:

This study describes the contrasting cultural norms of academic writing and academic writing instruction at a large American university, comparing these differing viewpoints in order to identify difficulties that non-native-speaking undergraduates might experience in proceeding from English as a Second Language (ESL) to freshmen composition courses. (30 references) (MDM)

Notes:

Theme issue topic: "Qualitative Research in ESOL."
Research/technical(143); Journal article(080)

Publication type (kn=):

143; 080

Language:

English

RIE/CIJE issue:

CIJFEB96

If not avail. in your library or through ILL, for sale from:

UMI

Minor Identifiers (type ks=):

Nonnative Speakers

Major Descriptors (type sm= or ks=):

College Students
English (Second Language)
English Departments
Second Language Programs
Writing Instruction

Minor Descriptors (type so= or ks=):

College Instruction
Courses
English Curriculum
Ethnography
Freshman Composition
Higher Education
Program Attitudes
Second Language Instruction
Teaching Methods

ISSN:

0039-8322

Authors:
Tinberg, Howard B.
Title:
Border Talk: Writing and Knowing in the Two-Year College. / by
Tinberg, Howard B.
Pub.Date:
1997
Pages; Fiche:
112; 2
Document no.:
ED404649
FOUND IN ERIC microfiche unless noted otherwise:
EDRS Price—MF01/PC05 Plus Postage.
Abstract:

By intertwining narratives, journals, interviews, and traditional analysis and argument, this book offers an ethnographic account of a diverse group of community college faculty working together to revise
their writing center's tutor protocols and expectations for student writing. In doing so, it takes postsecondary writing teachers to the place
referred to as the "border"—the sometimes conflicted space occupied
by the two-year college, between high schools and universities, between academia and the workplace. In the course of the book, these
teachers, including nursing, statistics, history, and English faculty,
address many of the unique concerns facing two-year college faculty:
reconciling their specialized knowledge with the college's commitment to general and comprehensive education; initiating students who
have had little success in school into the academic enterprise; and
reconceiving their work to include both scholarship and teaching. The
book also engages in broader debates about the nature of good writing, writing instruction, and the educational mission of the two-year
college.

    Beyond its ethnographic account, the book offers insight into the-
oretical questions regarding authorship and evaluation and presents a
view of community college faculty as reflective and impassioned prac-
titioners. An appendix is entitled "What Each Discipline Wants—A
Conversation." Contains 63 references. (MKA)
Notes:
112p.
Viewpoint(120); Non-classroom use guide(055); Book(010)
Publication type (kn=):
120; 055; 010
Language:
English
Geographic source:
U.S.; Illinois

RIE/CIJE issue:
RIEJUL97
If not avail. in your library or through ILL, for sale from:
National Council of Teachers of English, 1111 W. Kenyon Road,
Urbana, IL 61801-1096 (Stock No. 03782-3050: $14.95
members; $19.95 nonmembers).
Institution name (type a= or ka=):
National Council of Teachers of English, Urbana, Ill.
Major Identifiers (type ks=):
Teaching Perspectives
Minor Identifiers (type ks=):
Academic Discourse Communities
Job Relatedness
Writing Thinking Relationship
Major Descriptors (type sm= or ks=):
Reflective Teaching
Student Needs
Theory Practice Relationship
Two Year Colleges
Writing Instruction
Writing Teachers
Minor Descriptors (type so= or ks=):
Ethnography
Interdisciplinary Approach
Language Arts
Postsecondary Education
Rhetoric
Teacher Student Relationship
Two Year College Students
Writing Workshops

Chapter Two

Understanding the Process
A Global View

> How well does the researcher follow the rules and achieve the standards of their chosen methodology? And, on a meta-level, the question for me is: How does the design of the chosen methodology serve to generate a useful answer to the questions being examined?
> —W. James Potter 1996, ix–x

In this chapter, I share portions of four graduate student research projects in draft stages—one thesis and three dissertations—to examine where each researcher situates herself on a continuum of naturalistic, context-based approaches or methods. At one end of an imagined continuum, we'll place researchers using *ethnographic techniques* to collect data for context-based studies, and as we move toward the other end of the continuum we'll see researchers undertaking work that is *primarily ethnographic* in intent. We'll look at each research design and consider decisions the researcher made, examining what is gained and lost by mixing quantitative and qualitative data, by researching one's own class instead of entering the culture of another class, by interviewing individuals outside the classroom on a literacy topic, and by conducting a study as a long- or short-term project. We'll consider ideal goals and practical research decisions that modify a project and usefully or artificially limit our angle of vision as we begin to produce a thesis or dissertation-sized project.

General Design Issues

To help keep these projects in mind, I will provide an overview of them here. I should note, that these researchers—Kim Haimes-Korn, Amy Cashulette-Flagg, Donna Sewell, and Devan Cook—taught me a great deal about research as they shared their work over the past five years. All four projects were successfully completed and defended.

Kim's Project

Kim's designed a teacher-research dissertation. In this one-semester study of students in a small-group, writing workshop class that she teaches, Kim and eight prefreshman writing students meet as a group for one hour a week, and she tutors each student for an additional thirty minutes per week. She plans to "study the ways students' talk and interaction with one another shape their identities within the group and how those identities are enacted in writing." Having taught this class before, she knows her students will come from several ethnic groups, have different cultural backgrounds, and have previously experienced school in varied and individual ways. Her class readings, which provide some direction for class writings, focus on the subject of experience, leading her to several central questions for the study, among which are

1. How do writers negotiate identities in a group?
2. How does the act of naming their experiences in writing affect students' identities?
3. What is the relationship between the social and individual in the class?

Kim takes the intentionally interactionist position of a teacher–researcher: "As suggested by other studies (Danis, Elbow, others) teacher presence and guidance of some sort is important to the successful functioning of the group. The vantage point I am suggesting involves me, as a teacher and a researcher, as an integral part of the group." At the same time, Kim borrows ethnographic techniques by deciding to include a participant–observer in the classroom (a fellow graduate student), because "this would help me see the class from a different perspective." Data sources for the study include

1. audiotaped group discussions
2. audiotaped individual student–teacher conferences
3. student class writings

4. teacher–researcher journal

5. field notes from the participant–observer

(Abstracted and quoted from Kim Haimes-Korn's prospectus draft.)

Amy's Project

Amy's thesis study is "a short-term, naturalistic project using ethnographic techniques." In her final thesis draft, she explains that she intended

> To create four contextualized peer groups of three to five students as they workshopped their first paper of the spring 1993 semester in ENC 1102 [second-term, first-year writing]. While this study uses ethnographic techniques it is not a "pure" ethnography due to the shortened observation (five weeks) and the fact that I was an observer (rather than a participant-observer). This study does involve other methods used in ethnographic research, as defined in *The Making of Knowledge in Composition: Portrait of an Emerging Field.* Stephen M. North explains the process of ethnographic inquiry in this way:
>
> 1. Identifying Problems: Finding a Setting
> 2. Entering the Setting
> 3. Collecting Data: Inscription
> 4. Interpretation: Identifying Themes
> 5. Verification
> 6. Dissemination
>
> (1987, 284)
>
> These are the steps I followed. First I identified small groups as an area and the first-year writing classroom as a setting, then I entered that setting as an observer. Data collection included observation, student and teacher interviews, and student surveys. As I discovered themes I was able to verify my findings with the teacher and students involved.

In this study investigating how teachers prepare peer groups to respond to writing, Amy allows the teachers to set the schedules for her class observations, and she attends only when the subject of the thesis is being addressed—preparation for peer group work. Some of the questions with which she begins are the following:

1. Are groups formed by teacher or students?
2. What happens during early group interactions?
3. Does the teacher model response styles with student texts and/or published texts?

Amy surveys all classes and all students, compares and verifies her impressions of group work with the teachers' and students' impressions, and chooses to report her final observations in the form of four case studies of four different writing groups. (Abstracted and quoted from Cashulette-Flagg 1994, particularly pages 12–13.)

Donna's Project

Donna develops her ethnographic dissertation after reading Elizabeth Chiseri-Strater's book *Academic Literacies* (1991). Chiseri-Strater's year-long study encouraged Donna to take a long-term approach to her work although her participant-observation activity took place predominately during a short, six-week summer session, as she learned with new first-year writers in their first writing course. During the next two semesters (fall and spring), Donna followed several students into other courses to see where their writing took them for the next year. In her own words, from an early prospectus draft,

> My dissertation focuses on the writings of first-year college students and hopes to begin to answer some of the following questions:
>
> 1. How do students use writing in their lives?
> 2. How do they define writing?
> 3. What types of writing do they do?
> 4. How do their uses of writing relate to literacy?
>
> I am doing ethnographic inquiry into one summer session of ENC 1101 and other classes the students take. In addition to studying this one class, I am following the students from this class the rest of the academic school year.

For potential data collection techniques, Donna lists the following:

1. Field notes from participant observation in Summer ENC 1101
2. An initial open-ended survey that asks students to spell out the types and purpose of writing for them
3. A journal kept by the students in which they write down daily the types of writing they've done that day and their feelings about the writing, and the amount of time spent on it

4. Interviews with all students within the first three weeks

5. A refined detailed survey for the students to complete toward the end of the semester

6. Interviews with students again toward the end of the semester

7. Photocopies of all the text artifacts produced by teacher and students

8. Interviews with teacher (three times: before semester, mid-semester and after semester)

9. Research journal detailing the process of understanding the community

10. Photocopy of all students' writing assignments from all classes

In this early draft, Donna finishes with the many questions she has for the project and moves to a preliminary literature review. In subsequent drafts, she adds refinements to the one-year follow-up, deciding to observe second-term classes for up to ten students as often as she can (fall term) and interview the teachers of those classes. During the spring term, she reduces the number of interviews and students but continues to track several students from the initial summer class, to discuss with them how they are using writing in their private and public school lives. (See the complete prospectus in Appendix A.)

Devan's Project

Devan's research takes place out of the writing classroom but relates to classroom learning as she investigates the ways writing and work lives interact, examining "students' lives in regard to the contexts that their work lives provide for their writing and writing classes." Among other things, she wants to know answers to the following:

1. What motivations and rhetorical situations do students who work face? How do these factors affect students' processes of writing?

2. Given that ideological formation takes place in writing classrooms and also in the workplace, how do student writers who work negotiate ideological differences between academic and workplace expectations? What about differences in the way meaning is made? Where do students position themselves?

Devan plans to interview ten students at four local institutions, Florida State University, Florida A and M University, Tallahassee Community College, and Thomas College: "Using a series of three structured but open-ended long interviews . . . participant will represent differing levels of undergraduate and graduate experience: from first-year writers at all four schools through upper-division undergraduates to graduate students who are not teaching." Devan is influenced in her design by the literacy work of Deborah Brandt:

> Brandt usually interviewed her respondents in their own homes from one to three hours each; since I study a cross-section of students in writing classes rather than of the general population, I will interview students at their own school. The numbers 35–40 for an appropriate number of respondents and interview items from 1–3 hours keep appearing in this literature, as well. Gesa Kirsch spoke to 35 women for 2–3 hours each using a questionnaire as a springboard for her investigations of women writing in academic settings. (1996, 3)

Data collection for this project included interview notes, audiotapes, a research journal, and a piece of writing of the student's choosing. In discussing the relationship of her methods to ethnography, Devan notes,

> Methodology for this research is based on open-ended case studies rather than classroom participant-observation and uses interviews and examinations of student writing and talk about that writing to construct narratives and interpretations of student experience with work and writing. Case studies . . . are part of what Patricia Sullivan calls "ethnomethodology," but they are not ethnography entire: rather, case studies are part of ethnographic methodology and are frequently used in educational research. In fact, they are often used in educational research that is not so much ethnographic as descriptive or teacher-oriented; mine, however, is ethnographic. (Abstracted and quoted from Cook's prospectus draft)

I now propose that we look at these four studies together, considering how each does or does not meet the criteria we might develop for ethnographic writing research, based on the definitions explored in the previous chapter.

- Ethnographic writing research is ethnographic in *intent.*
- Ethnographic writing research is participant–observer-based inquiry.
- Ethnographic writing research studies a culture from that culture's point of view.
- Ethnographic writing research uses one or more ethnographic data-gathering techniques.
- Ethnographic writing research gains power to the degree that the researcher
  - **a.** spends time in the field
  - **b.** collects multiple sources of data
  - **c.** lets the context and participants help guide research questions
  - **d.** conducts analysis as a reiterative process

Let's look at these four projects, using these categories:

Ethnographic writing research is ethnographic in intent.

Ethnographic writing research is participant–observer-based inquiry.

Kim's project is not primarily ethnographic, though she uses ethnographic techniques, including a classroom participant–observer (who functions, however, as a provider of triangulating data rather than as a co-researcher).

Amy's project is not primarily ethnographic, because she intentionally focuses on a small part of the classroom culture—preparation for peer groups—and she does not participate; she observes and interviews.

Donna's study is primarily ethnographic, particularly as she immerses herself in the six-week summer session class, completing the work the students complete, befriending them, and spending time with them before and after class at the dorms as invited. Her follow-up year is not as intensely ethnographic. Certainly, though, her continued interactions with case-study students intensify the commitment she and the students feel toward the project.

Devan defines her project as primarily ethnographic, although the "culture" she identifies is more diffuse than one found in a classroom— that of student writers who work—and, as such, her participant observation takes place through a commitment to each individual, as she seeks to learn that person's worldview through interviews. Devan is a participant and observer within the confines of the interview format.

Ethnographic writing research studies a culture from that culture's point of view.

Because Kim is the teacher of the classroom she observes, she cannot claim to study the culture from the culture's point of view, because she has the authority to convene and shape that culture. In this, her role is a recognizably different one than that of the participant–observer ethnographer. David Bleich explains the role shift this way: "Teachers with the quality of classroom experience on their minds lean toward *including themselves as members of the class.* Thus, they are not simply 'participant-observers . . . ; they are, rather, *interested parties,* a group (teachers) whose own interests largely coincide, in the classroom, with the interests of another group (students)" (Bleich 1993, 180).

Amy can study the cultures of four classrooms from the participants' point of view, but as a single researcher focused on a classroom aspect, she cannot expect to be welcomed into the cultures of four complete classrooms, because she is allowed in at the teachers' invitation and only on particular teaching days. Amy does not have enough time to create rapport with all (or even most) members of each classroom community, and she is focused anyway on observing a single response group from each classroom, limiting her view.

In the summer session of her study, Donna worked very hard to know all the students in and outside of the class. For six weeks, she saw more of the class than she did of her own family (or so it seemed to her), and she attended every class and undertook all assignments. Although she had access to the teacher, she was more often on the students' side of the classroom and saw much more of them. In her follow-up studies of students during the year, her project was more like Devan's—the culture she now entered was the general student culture of the university—but she certainly had only the limited glimpses of some activities and some classes as offered to her by her key informants, case-study students.

Devan's *culture*, as mentioned, was the more difficult to identify, enter, and analyze (and possibly represented a more real culture—students who write who also work and whose work might influence their attitudes toward writing). Not unexpectedly, her interview approach had a lot in common with that of a journalist like Studs Terkel, who collects life histories through interviews. Devan identified students who could tell her stories; she then added their stories together to gain the power to persuade us about this category of people she found compelling. In doing this, Devan found her project to be as much about the process of taking an ethnographic approach as it was about a culture. She had to learn how to identify such a dispersed category of people, and she ended up examining in some detail her own attitudes toward her research subjects and research journey (for instance, how she responded to students and teachers who did and did not care to participate, and so on).

Ethnographic writing research uses one or more ethnographic data-gathering techniques.

All of these researchers viewed themselves as qualitative researchers who used multiple, context-based methods of data collection to improve, correct, and confirm their observations. They were not content to study classrooms, peer groups, students as writers in and out of school, from a single perspective, and they were not looking to isolate a single variable. Kim, to understand how her students experienced her curriculum, consulted her own and another teacher's observations, students' interview responses, and student writings.

Amy, who was cutting a wider swath—looking at four classes and four groups to see how four teachers prepared groups for writing response—developed background "profiles" for each class through surveys, in an attempt to characterize classes that were artificially convened by the university registrar as being "equal" selections of twenty-five writing students each. She interviewed teachers and group members to compare their impressions of group work with her own observations.

Donna's design was the most ambitious. She collected classroom notes and print artifacts (student writings) and teacher and student interviews from the summer class as well as asked students to keep records of their composing. Across the year, she asked selected students to keep papers from their two most writing-intensive classes each term and then visited those classes, interviewed the class teachers, and the students about the writing that was undertaken in each class. Her data collection was intense in the summer—material for all students was gathered—and then more restricted across the year, but it took place for a sustained time period for each case-study student.

Finally, Devan's data-gathering techniques included two sources: interviews with participants and her own reflective field notes. The fact that her reflections generated nearly as much data as her interviews was in part what led this dissertation into the meta-analytic arena, being as much about the process of research as it was about the subjects of her research.

Ethnographic writing research gains power to the degree that the researcher

1. Spends time in the field: Kim spent one semester observing her class. Donna spent six weeks as a participant–observer and one year as a case-study researcher. Amy spent the initial five weeks of a term collecting data on peer groups. Devan spent two months in a variety of intensive interviews, some successful, some not when potential subjects simply failed to show up as previously agreed.

2. Collects multiple sources of data: Kim conducted interviews, kept field notes and participant–observer notes, and collected all classroom artifacts. Amy collected survey results, interviewed teachers and students, and read student writings. Donna conducted interviews with teachers and students, kept field notes, and read students' drafts and class writings. Devan conducted interviews and kept field notes.

3. Lets the context and participants help guide research questions

4. Conducts analysis as a reiterative process

All of these projects changed greatly in the process of data collection, analysis, and write-ups. Classroom realities, developing knowledge, waxing and waning energies, and developing perceptions of a culture influenced all four researchers to adapt and change their initial designs.

Kim spent two years on data analysis, focusing at the end on the subject of *experience* and taking an issues approach to reporting, with multiple case-study portraits used to illustrate issues, rather than a purely case-study approach. Ultimately, she found her participant–observer's data less important to the study than she had originally expected. Amy spent one year on data analysis and reported her work in four writing-group case studies.

Donna spent eighteen months on data analysis and found that her data collection techniques did not allow her to capture enough to draw conclusions about students' nonclassroom writing and general processes of writing (although she asked students to keep writing logs for the summer, she found that this data was not particularly relevant or reliable). She became more engaged in learning about the writing students did in college, often very little after the first-year writing classroom experience, and the way students' day-to-day living conditions affected their attitudes toward and performance in school.

And, in Devan's study, as I mentioned, this researcher moved from a focus on students who write and work to an examination of her own position in regard to this type of research approach, as she asked questions about what prompted her original research questions, her responses to interviewees, and so on. An efficient drafter, Devan spent nine months on writing and revisions, completing several large-scale reorganizations and re-visionings of her project.

In each of these studies, researchers had to balance *ideals* and *reals*, at times modifying their understanding of what would make excellent teacher research or ethnographic writing research. For instance, Kim studied her own classes because no other teacher she knew was investigating the ways students made sense of their experiences through writing in just the way she felt she did. Kim was interested in exploring a developing curriculum, but not interested in doing so in the clinical sense of asking two teachers to teach a certain way and then compare results. Amy, on the other hand, was undertaking a shorter term project, in keeping with the requirements of a thesis rather than of a dissertation. Although, like Kim, she began with a classroom question (how to improve writing response groups), she began from the premise that she herself was not always successful with these groups, though the use of such groups was advocated in her teacher-education classes. Amy wanted to look across several classes for commonalties, things that could be determined about group preparation and then possibly be applied in other classes.

Donna was more generally interested in writing students' lives and how out-of-class experiences might be shaping their in-class performances. In this investigative goal, she more clearly needed to move to a general ethnographic design, because she was neither exploring a

single curriculum or classroom treatment nor trying to look for commonalties across classrooms, as was Amy. Donna wanted to see how a
well-taught process-writing classroom played out in a student's general literacy experiences across a year or more of college. And finally,
Devan took a more autobiographical stance. She was a student writer
who worked and knew that such work had contributed greatly and in
complicated ways to her own development as a writer. She wanted to
see how that occurred for others like her (only not just exactly like her,
because she carefully balanced her recruitment of interviewees from
several schools, genders, ethnic groups, ages, and so on).

In each study, these teachers-who-became-researchers undertook
an exploration that interested them personally. Here again we see the
difference between the motives for ethnographic writing research and
the motives for the cognitive and clinical research of the 1980s, during
which researchers were developing a model of a writer's composing
process. These researchers wanted to know more about the world they
and their writers inhabited, and they did this by pursuing questions
that arose naturally out of their experiences as writing teachers and/or
writing students.

This overview should initiate you, as a new ethnographic writing
researcher, to some of the big questions you'll have to ask yourself,
among which are the following:

- What—theoretical, practical, and personal—is prompting your interest in this question, and how does that interest relate to your
  choice of methodology?
- How do you characterize the world of qualitative, context-based,
  naturalistic writing research, and the area of ethnographic writing
  research in particular? With what attitudes and philosophies do
  you align yourself that then guide your methodological choices?
- As you make choices that shift you across the continuum from
  ethnographic in intent to naturalistic using ethnographic methods,
  what are you gaining and what are you losing with each methodological choice you make?
- How will you know if the choices you make are useful or cause
  your research to become questionable? Another way to put this:
  How and to what degree can you, or do you need to, defend these
  choices?

Or, as one of the respondents in Judith Meloy's study of writers of
naturalistic dissertations explained, "Many of my colleagues at your
workshop [on naturalistic dissertations] seemed uncertain about what
qualitative research was. Until they know this, they will be lost, both in
explaining their work to others and in conducting the research for

themselves." Another respondent said, "Students should know the assumptions of both the qualitative and quantitative perspectives to better define and defend their own work" (1994, 21).

> Devoid of context, the data become sterile. One of the reasons teachers have rejected research information for so long is that they have been unable to transfer faceless data to the alive, inquiring faces of the children they teach the next morning.
> —Donald Graves, quoted in Lucy Calkins 1985, 127–28

Theoretical Issues and Design

This chapter is concerned so far with design decisions. Later chapters discuss choices a researcher makes in writing it down (collecting data) and writing it up (analyzing and presenting data), but the quality of *those* decisions rests on the quality of initial decisions made by an ethnographic writing researcher. Immediately, he decides what degree of affiliation is involved. Is he quantitatively inclined or qualitatively inclined, teacher–researcher or ethnographer? If he is an ethnographer, how does he derive his ethnographic approach, from what philosophical and/or theoretical angle?

> In descriptive case studies, subjects are asked to solve a carefully designed problem or to do a preselected task. . . . In ethnographically oriented case studies, researchers become participant observers in a natural setting, spending at least a semester (and often a year or two) as live-in observers. . . . In teaching case studies, the practitioner-researchers usually begin with tentative theories that inform their practices, and they observe the results of those practices.
> —Lucy Calkins 1985, 130–31

Kim, Amy, Donna, and Devan, each situated herself differently. All preferred qualitative methods. Kim chose a teacher–researcher stance (Calkins' teaching case studies), and Amy chose a context-rich comparison approach (Calkins' descriptive case study). Donna aimed to enter the students' summer teaching community and follow several during portions of their next school year (Calkins' ethnographically oriented case study), and Devan focused on collecting numerous, detail-rich interview narratives (which fall less surely into any of the three categories, pointing out the trouble with these and any of the categories I attempt to offer).

Beverly Moss (1992) uses Dell Hymes' category systems to provide some insight into these choices. She points out that Hymes

> identifies three modes of ethnographic inquiry: comprehensive-oriented ethnography, topic-oriented ethnography, and hypothesis-oriented ethnography. Comprehensive-oriented ethnography seeks to document or describe a total way of life. Few ethnographers claim to have done totally comprehensive ethnographies. . . . Topic-oriented ethnography narrows the focus to one or more aspects of life known to exist in a community. . . . Comprehensive and topic-oriented ethnographies lead to hypothesis-oriented ethnography, which can be done only when one has a great deal of general ethnographic knowledge about a community. . . . [E]thnography in composition studies is generally topic oriented and concerned more narrowly with communicative behavior or the interrelationship of language and culture. (1992, 155–56)

By Hymes' definition, each of the four studies I've discussed was topic-oriented. Each researcher had questions about literacy that could best be answered by engaging with learners in the context of the learners' lives and (often) classroom cultures. Kim wanted to understand how students negotiated their developing sense of identity in a classroom focused on discussions and writings on the theme of "experience" and in an intensely structured setting (small-group and one-to-one instruction). Amy wanted to know how teachers prepared small groups to work together and how students received such preparation. Donna wanted to know how instruction in a first-year writing classroom affected a student in subsequent academic writing situations. Devan wanted to know more about the way student writers who worked understood the demands, processes, and practices of classroom writing in relation to writing they did at work.

All researchers had identifiable topics. No researcher was prepared to undertake a comprehensive ethnographic writing research project nor a hypothesis-oriented ethnographic writing research project. All used some ethnographic techniques, but only Donna and Devan were interested in increasing the degree of comprehensiveness by intentionally positioning themselves as ethnographers: For Donna, this meant immersing herself in the summer training class, and for Devan, this meant a course of meetings with "informants" in sites of their choosing, under conditions they set, to the degrees that they were willing to accommodate her and complete the interviews.

Additionally, these decisions required a shifting of power and research space—from Kim's ability to convene and organize class and set up regular interview times; to Amy's less controlling but still teacher-structured intervention in class groups; to Donna's ability to invite discussion before, during, and after the classes without the students' teacher being able to control and set that agenda; to Devan's pursuit of interviewees across several locations (four college campuses) and times (several months).

We can see what these researchers decided to do as they began their projects. It's worth taking a moment, however, to see what they decided *not* to do. Let's try to recast each study as even more ethnographic, asking what would have to change, as well as what would be gained and what would be lost by such changes?

Kim found the course she was teaching compelling. It is unusual, in these days of rising enrollments, to find a pre–college-level class of eight students who meet together once a week and then are tutored individually by the same instructor. This is a college preparatory course offered through the Reading/Writing center for S/U credit. Kim believed that these students, like any other writing students, learn best by reading, writing, speaking, and listening together, working on full-text, exploratory compositions. She used a variation of the Bartholomae–Petrosky and Coles sequenced writing assignments on the topic of experience, often drawing from writings by African-American authors. (Her minor area of study is African-American literature, and many of the students in her section are also African-American.) At the most basic level, she thought "good things" happened in this course, that students used the readings and writings to name themselves and their experiences as they entered the academic community. She wanted to study these developments, ones she wasn't sure took place in other sections, similarly structured in terms of meeting time but not in terms of curriculum. Kim did not want this to be labeled a *writing center* or *basic writing study,* because she did not see these courses as limited or labeled that way. Rather, for her, these classes presented complicated and compelling learning communities.

Kim can argue this study in two directions, it seems to me. She can conduct teacher research—as we know she did—because she wants to understand more fully a curriculum she has developed. We could also look at her argument that the class size and organization is unique and worth studying, and we could suggest that she study two other teachers' sections as an ethnographic writing researcher. Although she might continue to be interested in how students make sense of their learning, she can't be sure those classes will be focused on the topic of *experience.* Other courses may be run as drafting workshops, or could be themed differently. (Writing teachers in our department often choose the theme of *authority,* and readings and writings investigate that or other key concepts.)

In any event, to study the classes of others, Kim would be looking, perhaps, to explore her sense that here is an unusual teaching approach—small classes, consisting of a small group community and one-to-one conferencing, which help these students make the transition from underprepared to prepared for first-year writing courses.

She could study one class, sitting in on all group meetings, asking the teacher to tape tutorials. She could increase the study size by observing more than one course, perhaps even all of the courses that are organized in this way in a given term. Say there are eight. She commits herself to eight weekly group meetings and the taping of sixty-four individual tutorials a week. Suddenly she has more data than a single researcher can reasonably analyze. She could look for co-researchers, although these are not yet sanctioned for dissertation research (though some would argue that this should be possible) and are difficult to recruit without grant funding. So, Kim has to back up and ask whether it would be preferable to study only the group culture of the classes, attending four classes regularly and interviewing a selected number of students from each class outside of class? Perhaps following only two students from each class through the conferencing phase of the course?

Each design decision, as you can see, makes the study potentially more ethnographic and more complicated. And is it really more ethnographic to study more communities, or is Kim better off entering and learning the culture of a single classroom community as a participant–observer? For instance, if she visits and writes as a student in one class, she is participating. If she studies four classes, will she be able to participate, and to what degree? Does she want to simply experience life in this close and intensive and—as I've labeled it—unusual writing community (given that our regular writing sections enroll twenty-five students)? Or does she have a yearning to experience life in several of these communities, and to what end?

The degree to which she is tugged toward comparison and contrast, she is tugged toward evaluating treatments and a positivist position. The degree to which she is content to describe, explore, experience, and transcribe the way it feels to the members of one classroom during one semester in time, she is taking the phenomenological ethnographic approach. You can see, perhaps, how Kim's decisions allow her to compromise (productively) in several areas. By studying (and writing with, as she did) her own class, she avoids the move toward comparison and focuses instead on describing students' experiences. By choosing teacher research, she can look at a curriculum she is interested in learning more about rather than studying the possible effects of class size. And finally, by adding the help of a participant–observer, she mediates, to some degree, her own subjectivity as a researcher.

Amy, as you recall, wanted to learn more about how to train writing response groups. She came to the topic because she was encouraged by the Florida State University writing program to use peer response groups, but these groups did not always work as well as she would have liked: "The most common problem I've seen in my classes is students failing to take up the role of active reader" (Cashulette-Flagg 1994, 4).

Amy was looking for ideas, methods, and, if not answers, ways to re-conceptualize her own pedagogy. Unlike Kim, she had no desire to study her own classes, because she already knew that some element or elements were lacking there. She worried that her groups worked on a hit-or-miss schedule. She had read theory. She had practiced. Now she needed more empirical data. She chose to cast her net widely and study groups in four classrooms rather than, say, four groups in one class-room. In making this decision, she assumed that the teacher's role was crucial, and as worth studying as the students' responses to training, a position confirmed by her review of the available literature on writing groups.

To take a more ethnographic approach, Amy might shift her questioning from *how* to *what*, looking at the life in one group-intensive classroom. In such a study, it would be essential that she choose a teacher who admitted to using peer groups extensively and to training them to some degree. No groups, no study. She would also want to increase the duration of her study, attending this class for fifteen weeks of the term rather than the five weeks of her actual study. She would not be simply an observer, but a participant–observer, working in one group (or moving each class period from one group to another group) and completing the course assignments to learn what the class required, from the writer's perspective, of writers and group members.

Amy could decide to study the entire classroom culture—audio/videotaping all groups—or she could focus on the experiences of being a researcher–member of one group all term long. She would aim to talk to students before, during, and after classes in a series of interviews or informal interactions. (As they are accepted as part of the students' community, classroom ethnographers will sometimes find themselves invited by students to dorms, to parties, and so on.)

Amy—working more ethnographically—would not just look at how the teacher trained the students for working in groups, but also aim to describe the effects of this training term-long, capturing their discussions, collecting their drafts, and so on. While she could try to do this in all four classes that her original study identified as group work–intensive, it is likely that she could not be an active participant–observer in all of the classes and that by studying them all in this manner she would be tempted to compare and contrast group, class, or teacher effectiveness, that is, to measure rather than experience and re-port on that experience.

More briefly, let's look at Donna's and Devan's already more ethno-graphically inclined studies. Clearly, Donna might have tracked student literacy more fully by choosing her case-study students from the sum-mer class that she did enter as a participant–observer, and then by at-tending *all* class meetings of those students during their second-term writing class and one additional class. (Instead, she sampled all classes.) Instead of the seven students she followed in the fall and the four students in the spring, using this sampling method, she might have, like Elizabeth Chiseri-Strater, followed two or four students, all year long. As it turned out, there was a dearth of writing taking place in classes outside of English, and Donna might have sentenced herself to endless hours of attending classes and writing about not writing.

Devan could have chosen a variety of different designs. She might have conducted initial interviews and then asked for permission to follow two or more student writers who also work in the course of composing a class paper and during a composing event on the job. This would have required that she make a far more in-depth commitment to fewer writers when she did not know, at the time, what she was looking for. In a way, her project then might have become a preliminary examination, leading to a more traditional ethnographic study. Early in her study, for instance, she identified a gap between a student–writer's willingness to name on-the-job writing as writing. And this gap could have been explored by more intensive case studies. In her study, Devan was looking to gauge and analyze attitudes toward and about writing where a more ethnographically focused study would have, perhaps, looked at practices to see how they connect to attitudes.

Now, let's review some of the practicalities of design decisions and what they may indicate about the project you're undertaking.

Mixing Quantitative and Qualitative Data-Gathering Techniques

There is nothing inherently wrong with doing this. Amy surveyed all students in the four classes she studied to get a sense of their general attitudes toward group work. However, surveys can only provide averages, typical portraits, and the goal of most ethnographic inquiry is to represent particulars. Still, quantitative data can provide a demographic, a context, a backdrop, a broad picture upon which to place context-specific description. David Fetterman, in *Ethnography Step by Step* (1989), suggests that survey data should be collected early in the study rather than later. Survey, in this sense, can be a quick form of standardized interviewing (if open-ended questions are used) or can provide general measurements (numbers of participants experiencing this or that).

Participant Observation

"To the present day, 'field experience' constitutes such an attribute [professional status] for anthropology, and the implicit requirement of fieldwork virtually suffices to distinguish the anthropologist from the sociologist," claim Jerome Kirk and Marc L. Miller in their monograph *Reliability and Validity in Qualitative Research* (1986). This attribute seems to hold true in ethnographic writing research and helps us distinguish our work from the also compelling, but differently situated form of naturalistic research, teacher research. Participant observation in composition—and actually in any forum—raises issues of authority and power. By what means does the researcher access the community studied? (Often, in the case of classroom research, we ask a peer or teacher, rather than the students, to allow us into the classroom. Or if students are consulted, to what degree can they make the decision to allow our inquiry or disallow it?) Are we researching on our own institutional home ground—as was true for Kim, Amy, and Donna—or are we making an entry into categorically familiar (other college campuses) but culturally diverse environments (as did Devan, and she found more difficulties in doing so)? Beverly Moss provides useful suggestions for self-interrogation in this matter:

> (1) What role does an ethnographer's degree of membership in a community play in successfully carrying out the study? (2) How does the role of the researcher affect the preexisting established relationships in this community; specifically how does her or his role affect how he or she is perceived by the community and how he or she perceives the community? (3) Will the ethnographer make assumptions about what certain behaviors signify or how meaning is established in this community based on previous knowledge or on the actual data collected? (4) Would an outsider attach more significance to observed patterns than the insider, based on the degrees of distance? (5) What issues might an insider face when writing up the ethnography? (Moss 1992, 163–64)

Triangulation

Finally, let's consider triangulation one more time. All of these researchers collected data from multiple sources. They surveyed and interviewed (sometimes audiotaped, sometimes took notes); they kept researcher's journals and field notes. They might have videotaped, and in at least one case, Kim photographed her class and included that picture in her final dissertation draft (reproduced in Chapter Three). Students' writings—classroom writing and private writing—were collected, as well as teachers' class handouts, participant–observers' writings, and any relevant print documents. Some researchers filled blue crates and others file cabinets full of transcripts, memos, notes, and observations. Initial drafts were written, shared with some participants, shared with other readers, reanalyzed, clarified, and rewritten. In "The Dance of Qualitative Research Design," Valerie J. Janesick reminds us,

"Triangulation is meant to be a heuristic tool for the researcher. Although the term was originally used by land surveyors to describe the use of three points to locate oneself at particular intersections, it is not to be taken literally" (1994, 214). Janesick reviews Denzin's four categories of triangulation and adds her own, a fifth method:

1. *data triangulation:* the use of a variety of data sources in the study

2. *investigator triangulation:* the use of several different researchers or evaluators

3. *theory triangulation:* the use of multiple perspectives to interpret a single set of data

4. *methodological triangulation:* the use of multiple methods to study a single problem

> I would like to add a fifth type to this list: interdisciplinary triangulation . . . the prevailing myths about aggregating numbers and, more tragically, aggregating individuals into sets of numbers have moved us way from our understanding of lived experience. By using other disciplines, such as art, sociology, history, dance, architecture, and anthropology to inform our research processes, we may broaden our understanding of method and substance. (Janesick 1994, 215)

In this sense, ethnographic writing research has already performed interdisciplinary triangulation as a method, deriving as it does, as I have argued in Chapter One, from an amalgamation of social science–like locations, cognitive research–generated questions about literacy, and anthropological methods of observation. Kim, Amy, Donna, and Devan all used data triangulation; Kim used investigator triangulation when she asked a participant–observer to join her class. Devan used postmodern, feminist, and Bakhtinian theory as a lens for developing and conducting her study, resulting in theory triangulation. And Amy probably used the broadest methodological triangulation as she studied the issue of training peer groups—observation, interview, and survey across four classes.

> . . . *contact zones.* I use this term to refer to social spaces where cultures meet, clash, and grapple with each other, often in contexts of highly asymmetrical relations of power, such as colonialism, slavery, or their aftermaths as they are lived out in many parts of the world today.
> —Mary Louise Pratt 1991, 34

Ethnography exists where cultures meet. Mary Louise Pratt's influential essay "Arts of the Contact Zone" has sensitized researchers to the complexity of the interactions that I have had to simplify in this

chapter in order to discuss them at all. The modern ethnographer cannot avoid or neglect to consider colonialism and asymmetrical power
relationships as they are inscribed in our cultures, for they affect our
studies. However, there is no research at all without our being willing to enter the contact zones, determined to learn how to conduct
our research with care. For as Pratt's title suggests, our work is both act
and art.

To write an ethnographic report is to embark upon a complicated,
reiterative journey. I have a poster from *The Body Shop* hanging on
my living room wall, and I'm sure I bought it because I had recently
completed my first ethnographic writing research project. It says (in
part), "reuse, recycle, rebirth, revamp, return, reuse, recoup, rethink,
recharge, redeem, reform, recreate, recover, rebuild." It hangs in my
house, reminding me to seek connection between past and present,
subject and object, theory and practice. We'll continue to do the same
throughout this book, returning to issues already raised while starting to design a new project, from the initial idea on, and then returning to the practicalities of *being there* as a researcher and then *being
here*, back on the page, as an author of a research report, discovering
how to generalize but not overgeneralize about what we see, say,
and do.

> If the truth be known, ethnographers, like the rest of us, make
> whopping generalizations from rather modest observations of a few
> cases. Their forte lies in knowing those cases exceedingly well and
> in recognizing a critical distinction between generalizing and over-
> generalizing. . . .
>
> —Harry Wolcott 1987, 50

Practical Issues: Actually Designing It

At this point, we leave Kim, Amy, Donna, and Devan's studies to consider the process of beginning your research. Soon, you will be con-
ceptualizing and commencing a project, realizing, as others have before you, that it is a complex journey of growth and development as
your ideas evolve and eventually are presented in written form. Judith
Meloy points to this complexity when she observes, practically and
metaphorically,

> It is only at the point of closure to a qualitative research experi-
> ence . . . that the complex, layered experience in which we engage
> begins to take shape as a sensible whole that can be—and indeed

has been—organized, interpreted, and perhaps, understood. Theses do not emerge all at once; if the thesis is qualitative, chances are it will not arrive head first. (1994, 12)

However, as potential parent to a qualitative child, you want to do everything you can at every point to assure a healthy offspring by taking care during the entire development—conception to birth—whether your data arrives head or feet first.

While your research interests are no doubt very different than mine, the steps we take in thinking through research are the same. We need to

- identify a problem, a research site, and a population or culture
- develop a conceptual or theoretical framework
- undertake a preliminary review of the available relevant research literature
- choose data collection strategies
- refine the research design
- embody that design in an initial research prospectus

To be practical, we need to set aside issues of philosophy and epistemology, discussions of postmodernism or narrative conventions, not worry excessively about ethics and authority, although I'm fully aware that those issues will arise for you even in the design phase of your own work, as they will be taken up several times throughout this book. Still, in order to make good design decisions, to even begin the process, we have to simplify for a while, assuming that classroom educational ethnography can and does take place and that our goal is to produce a strong version of such work.

What should a research plan include? Judith Goetz and Margaret LeCompte suggest the following:

1. The focus and purpose of the study and the questions it addressed
2. The research model or design used and justification for its choice
3. The participants or subjects of the study and the settings(s) and context(s) investigated
4. Researcher experience and roles assumed in the study
5. Data collection strategies used in the study
6. Techniques used to analyze the data collected during the study
7. Findings of the study and their interpretations and applications (1984, 34–35)

You can see how these points are derived from the classic scientific model of research. The conventions of the scientific method require that we formulate a question, review related research, decide on sample size, describe subjects, collect data after variable selection and hypothesis setting and often after conducting a pilot study, analyze data, and report our results. At a minimum, a qualitative researcher identifies a problem, enters the setting, collects and interprets data, and reports. But these steps are more complicated than a listing makes them appear, and they are particularly complicated for the ethnographic writing research approach.

Ethnographic researchers are concerned with how to enter the scene, make contact with individuals in the culture, and elicit information. After information is elicited, ethnographic decisions include deciding on themes or categories for data analysis (because the data with which we work is generally textual and requires interpretation as we move from the *etic* [observational data] to the *emic* [culturally meaningful data]), developing methods for verifying an interpretation, and so on. The preresearch decisions are no less complicated or important in qualitative research than in quantitative research; they are simply different.

Identifying a Problem

An ethnographic study begins not in the field but in the library. Others must have studied either this community or similar communities, and one begins by reading their reports. These reports give one a general picture of the community and tell one what to expect, what to look for, and where to look. The reports are necessarily somewhat false since the community must have changed since it was observed before, or a similar community must be different in some ways. If the previous observers are available one can interview them to get their anecdotes, half-formed insights and hunches, their glosses and background material on their reports. Sometimes an impromptu anecdotal account can give a livelier feel of daily life than a carefully polished written report.

—Paul Diesing 1983, 2

Like most researchers, you will probably start with a very general idea, scene, hunch, possibility, or general interest area and with a literature review, searching the data bases of your university library system. The on-line catalog will tell you what holdings you have on campus or in the state university system and the ERIC document system, which indexes resources in education, as in the samples you read in

Chapter One. ERIC ED documents are available in microfiche and provide copies of conference papers, from the CCCC annual conference and many other reading, education, and writing conferences around the country. ED documents also include individually submitted papers and copies of books from certain publishers, such as the National Council of Teachers of English. Researchers send in two copies of their work and give permission for ERIC to abstract and list this work. EJ numbers in ERIC represent abstracts from journals in education, writing, psychology, reading, and related areas. Copies of the journal articles or microfiches and paper copies of papers can be purchased directly from ERIC, although many libraries purchase the entire microfiche collection and have holdings of the major journals that ERIC reviews.

You would do well to search *Dissertations Abstracts,* to see what other researchers around the country have done most recently, both methodologically and in the same general content area. Finally, you can check three other sources for sources. You do this because indexes always point you to further information, as when you read an article and look at that author's "works cited" pages for the sources that the researcher used. By reading his or her citations, you'll intersect an ever broadening system of potentially usable information. The journal *Research in the Teaching of English* publishes a bibliography of research in writing in two of its issues each year, and the Conference on College Composition and Communication has supported a series of bibliographies in composition, available through Southern Illinois University Press. Finally, there are a number of e-mail lists for those in composition, and list members often poll their membership for ideas and sources and citations. In addition, the CCCC is increasing its on-line services, with the aim of making texts from and for the convention available in the form of abstracts and, in some cases, full papers. You can access CCCC through the NCTE website at www.ncte.org.

Also, authors often re-search or do further work in the same area, so perhaps by browsing, looking at one work, you'll find more work by those who have something to contribute to your project. Finally, as someone new to a methodology, you would want to search ERIC for information on research methods. I did this myself to provide ERIC abstracts to analyze for Chapter One. I have done it again several times while composing this book.

ERIC indexes are also available in paper format, and hand searching through these bound indexes can provide interesting associational browsing. My first introduction to the ERIC system took place this way. I moved to on-line searching as it became available. Currently, I'm able to access the library data bases from my home computer and modem. Many of my readers will be far more sophisticated than I in using these technologies, but the theory of what we're all doing is the same. We are searching in order to broadly understand *who* is researching *what* in this *area* using these *methods,* to find *relevant articles* that may offer *methodological advice* and/or *reports* that complicate our understanding in ways that help—eventually—to focus our own projects. We are not trying to see—as in a positivist-based project—if someone's already done our study, because we are the only ones who can enter a proposed culture, classroom, or community. Our study cannot have been done before, nor can it be replicated afterward. However, there is a lot we can learn beforehand about situating ourselves in field conversations about studying writing classrooms and about representing students' views. This is problematic for anyone who isn't a student to do, yet equally problematic for a student of ethnography to do.

Conceptual Frameworks

> A conceptual framework explains, either graphically or in narrative form, the main dimensions to be studied—the key factors, or variables—and the presumed relationships among them. Frameworks come in several shapes and sizes. They can be rudimentary or elaborate, theory-driven or commonsensical, descriptive or causal.
> —Matthew Miles & Michael Huberman 1984, 28–29

A conceptual framework can help the researcher sketch out possibilities. I often sketch several diagrams to help me see the factors I should consider—am I looking at the classroom community alone or the classroom community imbedded in the context of the university writing program and the university community? I explore these questions in Figure 1A.

Figure 1A
Listing Ideas/Connections

classroom	classroom
writing students	writing program
teacher	university
	student's living situation
	town

Figure 1B
Clustering Ideas/Connections

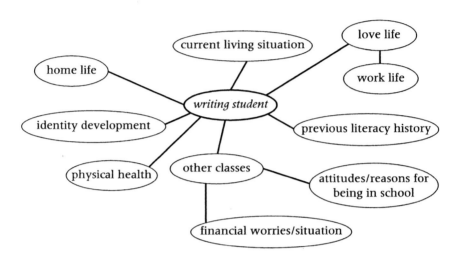

For example, I may want to understand more about the writing classroom from the students' points of view. I can start with the writing student and investigate forces that I know, or guess, impinge on her writing processes and progress through a class (Figure 1B).

At the least, a conceptual framework is a map or chronology that encourages you to think about your options as a researcher. It aids your thinking when you develop this framework as both a list and a drawing.

Developing Research Questions

As you begin to visualize a project, you also need to interrogate yourself, your developing ideas, your evolving sense of a study-under-construction. You can list your initial questions and then write notes that explore those questions. Reviewing your framework sketches, lists, and notes, you see your own developing direction(s). Then, you'll make more notes, sketching out possible data-collection strategies. Sondra Perl describes the process this way:

> As writers, we don't plan ahead of time everything we will say. More often, we discover what we want to say as we go along. So in ethnography, we don't enter a setting deciding ahead of time what events will mean, but we allow the meaning to emerge from our observations and

repeated reflections. We may enter with certain guiding questions, but we don't impose our answers. We allow them to emerge from the process of looking. (1983, 11)

Once you begin to understand your initial research decisions, the process begins again: You sketch, list, revisualize, and finalize your conceptual framework. Here's a revised framework for a study, from which the researcher hopes to access students' views of the classroom:

Before term: Identify and interview teacher, prepare class surveys, continue literature review.

During term: First week surveys, second/third week interview with ten students to choose four to five key informants, weekly interview with key informants, weekly copying of all student writings, field notes, and memo after each class and each student interview ($\times 4-5$ per week), completion of all class work, last week survey of class. Possibilities for out-of-class interactions with key informants? Hold weekly interviews in dorms, library, etc.?

Week after term: Interview teacher, copy any remaining class artifacts.

Four weeks after term: Interview key informants—consider a group interview for this.

Ten to fourteen weeks after term: Share initial data with teacher and key informants. Interview re: their responses to this material. Again, possibly a group interview.

At this point—at some point—you'll need to write an initial draft of your research plan, trusting the writing process itself to help you clarify the study. Generally, a naturalistic prospectus will answer as many of the questions it can of those I've shared so far in Chapters One and Two, and the researcher will include, at a minimum, the following (though your subheadings may be more narrative or general and less social scientific than these):

Introduction

Literature Review (on the research area and on your methodology)

Methodology/Study Design

 Research Question(s)

 Culture/Population

 Data Collection

 Data Analysis

Probable Reporting Procedures/Methods

Appendixes

Works Cited

A prospectus can be as short as ten pages and as long as fifty, depending on the level of detail required by you and by those reading it. As this chapter ends, I encourage you to review Donna Sewell's drafts in Appendix A to see how her initial writings, conceptual framework, and drafts of research questions became more refined over time as she revisited her purposes and evolving project. (I would also direct you to Appendix C of Judith Meloy's 1994 book, which presents the table of contents of five different projects for review and analysis.)

After your initial draft—I call it a full-breath draft, for at this stage it probably includes lots of promises and thinking aloud to yourself—you'll begin to feel you can dig into your project (for instance, by identifying classroom teachers who might work with you, and so on). But you'll also have raised new issues. Again, because ethnographic writing research is a process, some of these issues will be resolved after you actually enter the field and begin—no sooner. As I mentioned earlier, an ethnographic writing researcher has to have lots of plans and a high tolerance for ambiguity. The next chapter deals with creating some of these day-to-day plans, by reviewing particular methods for data collection and by sharing the advice of practitioners whose advice, of course, you will have to adapt to your own ethnographic site.

Chapter Three

Getting There and Being There in Person

So, what *is* it like to be an ethnographer? It is to deal with mountains of data and packed blue crates of information—and then make sense of them. . . . I soon discovered that I needed a system in which I could categorize my materials and have them available in a chronological sequence. . . . I moved to a three ring binder. . . . I know this might sound kind of trivial, to talk about my mini-epiphany involving notebook organization, but it really spoke to me about what it is to be an ethnographer. You have to see things in a different way. . . . Not only did I have to change the physical way I approached a class, but I had to try to see information differently—that is, instead of building on ideas I already had, I had to try to pull them back and make myself receptive to what might arise. . . . It is an interesting contradiction because the ethnographic process calls for strict organization, which is linear in nature, yet the interpretation calls for a more circular vision which is recursive.

—Kim Haimes-Korn

This chapter considers arriving and entering—gaining access to a community of study—as well as processes for participating and observing within that culture. Once you have arrived "in the field," you'll be endlessly involved with *writing it down*, in order to write it up, later, from the reflective distance of your author's desk.

Writing it down is the first major phase of the comprehensive textualizing project that results in your ethnography. Being able to convince your readers that you have been there is a double act. You must have actually been there (the concerns of this chapter—being there in person), and then later, you have to assure readers that these engagements truly did take place (being there rhetorically on paper, the subject of Chapter Five). In *Works and Lives: The Anthropologist as Author,* Clifford Geertz reminds us that the latter activity is less about facts than about presenting those facts, depending as it does on the ethnographer's "capacity to convince us that what they say is a result of their having actually penetrated (or, if you prefer, been penetrated by) another form of life, of having, one way or another, truly 'been there'" (1988, 4–5). However, having identified your research project, you still need to gain entry to a site, dwell there, and collect and "write down" your data before you can later "write it up" convincingly.

In this chapter, I consider gaining access in general, and then I overview the particulars of data collection—looking, talking, and collecting—through participant observation, interviewing, compiling field notes, and collecting field artifacts. To organize these discussions, I pose questions and suggest possibilities, much of this advice coming from other researchers who have "been there," too.

Getting There: Asking, Giving, and Receiving

I walk down the hall toward Dr. Ruth Mirtz's office. My thoughts move lazily through the possibilities of conducting a short (four week) ethnographic research of her first-year, first semester composition course. From the little I know about the process of gathering data for this—my first attempt at qualitative inquiry—I know I can video-tape the class proceedings, tape record class discussions, interview individual class members and/or the teacher, photograph or survey participants, write field notes as I observe the class, write belated journal notes, enlist one or more other researchers for a team approach, analyze what I see and hear and feel, and even ask the subjects of the research to write responses that will in effect become a sort of self-analysis of themselves as reflected in my observations. So while considering all or some of these as possible if not necessary for triangulation in an effort to approach some objectivity, I know I first have to gain access to the situation I want to observe. Lightly rapping at Ruth's open door, I see her bent over her desk. She greets me with a "hi" and what I've come to recognize, after one year of acquaintance, as her typical quizzical look when addressed.

Ruth is the director of the First-Year Writing program at Florida State University, and I am a third year ABD, Ph.D. student working under her supervision in the teaching of my own first-year writing courses. Perhaps she is wondering if I'm having a problem with one of my classes, or perhaps she wonders if I'm coming to get help for or to engage in conversation about my in-progress dissertation for which she is one of my directing committee of four. I don't think she expects my request, which is to become an observer in her ENC 1101 classroom.

Ruth graciously says "yes," and asks me if I intend to come the next week. I answer yes without having in mind to start so soon, but find myself rather pleasantly committed to beginning the mini-ethnographic study as early as her next class meeting. I agree to come Tuesday and impetuously tell her I think I might be interested in looking at how the real and the artificial play out in her class, to which she says, "great" or something like that. After promising her a copy of the project manuscript, I find myself back in the halls of academia with my lazy thoughts of how in the hell I'm going to do this.

—Sandra Teichmann

Sandra's narrative gives us a fine sense of what it feels like to embark on an ethnographic project. Having studied research methods, Sandra knows her data-collection options and she also knows an individual who will be likely to give her access to a site of study. Although she knows there are methods in general, she doesn't yet know what methods in particular will lead to reliable data collection for this, her first study. She has chosen the somewhat less conventional route of studying up—asking someone in authority for permission to study her class. And Sandra's initial request is met with an invitation to begin immediately, taking this researcher out of the state of possibility and plunging her into the reality of immediately needing to become an ethnographer, perhaps as soon as the next day. Her subject, Ruth Mirtz, herself a classroom researcher and an interested teacher, asks only for a copy of the final report, as many subjects or participants will, and Sandra promises it, before she has any idea of what that report will actually look like.

An ethnographic writing research project has begun. There are many questions that you'll ask yourself at just such a juncture.

What is your professional and personal relationship with the individual who gives you access to the community (if there is such an individual)? How do they feel about having a participant–observer in that environment? Of what power relations among individuals should you be aware, and how will you negotiate them?

What compensation, if any, do you need to offer these individuals?

> My data gathering officially started in the setting of Donna Qualley's Prose Writing course, which she volunteered to have me visit during the first week of classes (September 1987) to see if it would be suitable for my research. I came on the second day of her class and stayed for the entire semester. . . .
>
> —Elizabeth Chiseri-Strater 1991, 184–85

As reported in her book, Elizabeth Chiseri-Strater had the opportunity to "visit" a colleague's class and then remain and study one that suited her research interests. Not all of us will have that luxury. Many times, we need to identify a teacher (or a key individual within a work or learning community) we don't know and ask that person to allow us into a classroom or workplace. Usually, we initiate this contact before the study begins. We may do this by approaching colleagues and, in return for their letting us into their classroom, offering to provide them with a description of their course community. We may find, as did Sandra Teichmann, that an individual readily agrees to allow us to study because we've tapped this person's natural pleasure in being found worth researching (this can be true for colleagues in various work situations) or the individual also may be a researcher and knows what our request entails. Our contact person may become a key informant or simply be the person who puts us in touch with the person who helps us gain access to a site: "An intermediary or go-between can open doors otherwise locked to outsiders," David Fetterman reminds us. "The facilitator may be a chief, principal, director, teacher, tramp, or gang member, and should have some credibility with the group" (1989, 43).

Unlike what we saw in Sandra and Ruth's exchange, we may find that we make a contact nervous and have to spend more time explaining our project or trying to offer incentives that will encourage participation and allow our work to go forward. Incentives rarely take the form of cash, and usually only if we're asking for a long-term commitment. In this case, an honorarium may allow the individual to feel reimbursed for time to a small degree and—equally important—the honorarium may encourage this person to take the project more seriously. However, it's wise to offer to reimburse participants for any expenses related to the study, such as photocopying document artifacts for you. In addition, you should always volunteer your time for this work, not require the individual's time.

Some teachers-studying-teachers offer to work with that teacher's students in tutorials or work groups, to participate productively in a classroom, to allow the individual to research in their own classes, to conduct a class when the teacher is attending a conference, and so on. In "Engendering Ethnography," Roxanne Mountford reports that researcher Ellen Cushman "offered tutoring and counseling in exchange for the time and information of women in an African American urban neighborhood." Mountford continues, "An ethnography should reveal the nature of reciprocity and, most importantly, examples of when the reciprocity failed" (1996, 221). Each act of reciprocity, then, should be considered for how it affects the relationship(s) between the individuals involved.

In some cases, a teacher's reluctance to let us study may indicate a classroom well worth entering, but, more likely, it indicates a site that may be so unproductive, it is not worth negotiating to enter it. Teachers may hesitate to allow entry to their classrooms because they sense what researchers should already be aware of and be prepared to discuss: the power differentials inherent in such studies. In "Seduction and Betrayal in Qualitative Research," Thomas Newkirk pinpoints the problem:

> University researchers who study the classroom of public school teachers and subordinates (students and teaching assistants, nontenured faculty) have a special obligation to recognize the vulnerability of those they study. . . . In many cases, the teachers being studied feel some professional discomfort (no matter what the consent form says) in saying no. (1996, 5)

Most often, we tend to study horizontally, or down. Much more rarely do we study up. That is, we'll ask a peer to help us, or in the case of writing program directors who are researchers, we may ask a peer to let us observe his or her class or to act as co-researchers. In my study *Something Old, Something New* (1990a), I found teachers, graduate students in a program from which I was hoping to graduate, who were willing to act as key informants. I had had long-term interactions with these colleagues by having been a participant–observer in their teacher-education class via the sanction of their professor, who had been my professor for the same course in a previous term. These teachers knew that they would be conducting dissertation research themselves in the near future and perhaps asking other program participants for similar research assistance. It was in their interest to serve my research interests; as often happens, though, three teachers who initially agreed to work with me eventually dropped out of the study, leaving me with five case-study teachers instead of the eight for which I had originally planned.

Although it is legitimate and sometimes preferable to work with a friend, a peer, or a local contact person, there is much to be gained by moving beyond a known contact and arranging to enter a community of individuals who are not under the authority of or organized by someone personally known to you. In fact, some researchers strongly advocate this. In this event, you'll still probably work through a network of colleagues, talking to a fellow teacher at another campus or asking a worker in an organization to identify likely individuals to contact, because, as David Fetterman states, "A strong recommendation and introduction strengthen the fieldworker's capacity to work in a community and thus improve the quality of the data" (1989, 44). No matter who grants you access to a site, you should always work professionally at developing and maintaining these contacts. Even with a colleague or friend, follow up on a verbal agreement with a written letter confirming your participation and outlining your project. If they ask for a copy of the final report, as Ruth Mirtz asked of Sandra Teichmann, be sure that they receive it, even if only in draft form.

"No subject is a hero to the ethnographer—nor an ethnographer to the subject," says Mara. Concluding that it was inevitable that Shelley would reject her interpretation of the meaning of collaborative writing in her classroom, Mara wishes that they had both read Thorne's (1980) observation that the ambiguities in the researchers-subject relationship "make it easier for one's subjects to forget they are subjects, to think of the researcher *only* as a friend" (p. 291). Urging students not to study spouses or partners, prospective employers, colleagues or important friends and their sites, Mara and Neal propose that the possibility of conflict over observations and interpretations is likely to compromise either the study or the relationships or both, risks that can even end academic careers or relationships.

—Mara Casey, Kate Garretson,
Carol Peterson Haviland & Neal Lerner 1997, 120

If you are studying up, as Sandra Teichmann was when asking to visit her teaching supervisor's own class, you'll want to be sure to consider how participation affects the power relationship between you and an administrative superior or supervisor. Will studying your employer's classroom or your own workplace compromise your ability to present your findings? To what degree will you encourage or feel worried about this person's collaboration in your project?

Equally, the degree to which you align yourself with the teacher in a writing classroom will affect how the students in that classroom relate to you. If you are lucky, as was Taube Cyrus, the teacher you contact will also be conscious of the dynamics of your entry:

> Sheila listens to my proposal and consults a calendar, using her index finger to situate chronology. She has no problem with me visiting her class, but would like to discuss it with the students first, to see if they are in agreement. "Check back with me Thursday," she advises.
> Later that week, Sheila stops me in the hallway between classes. "They have no problem with it. In fact, they seem quite open to it." She seems pleased.

In Sheila Ortiz-Taylor, Taube Cyrus has encountered a teacher who is aware of the way a researcher may affect the quality of classroom interactions, and then takes the step of asking the community's opinion. Even if the students view this as merely an act of courtesy on the teacher's part, that action will smooth Taube's entry. Researcher, teacher, and students all know that the teacher has the authority to simply invite the researcher into the class, and while we'll never know if the students actually felt as if they could have refused, we do know the option was at least discussed openly.

What roles will you take vis-à-vis the individuals in the community?

Earlier, Sandra Teichmann realized she was about to become a participant-observer before she had anticipated. Here is her first impression of the activity; she notes the students' relative indifference and her own heightened sense of occasion:

> At 7:45 a.m. Tuesday, I enter the classroom. One or two students, already sitting in desks placed in rows, glance at me and then look away as if my coming into what is now their third week of class is nothing extraordinary. But I think my presence is extraordinary. New students do not usually become members of a university class as late as the third week, and students in first-year university writing classes do not usually look like I do: a beginning-to-gray woman who could be the mother of any one of the two young men and one woman sitting in the room. On a sheet of the handful of white paper I brought in with me (the only thing I brought other than a pen, my glasses, the watch on my wrist and, of course, my

```
clothing and the ever conflicting theories and ideas
about life and writing I carry around in my head), I
began noting that, as we wait for 8:00 a.m., one stu-
dent is reading from a text (not English), one student
is writing in a notebook, and one is organizing a
binder with papers from his back pack. To make sure
I'm in the right place, I ask those three, as a group,
if this is Dr. Ruth Mirtz's class. One of the young
men politely answers, "Yes," so I write that down too.
```

In the case of classroom research, you may gain entry via the teacher's permission, but you may be more interested in studying the viewpoints of the students in this structured culture, where teachers have power over the members of the classroom at large, no matter how they might choose to downplay or diffuse such authority. For instance, Elizabeth Chiseri-Strater's field notes include the notation, "[I] notice that I pay more attention to the students than to Donna [the teacher]," and this attracted her to the class. However, Chiseri-Strater's focus on the students and the students' apparent acceptance of her presence did not negate the fact that she was there by virtue of Donna Qually's "ability to present me as a colleague" and therefore optimize the students' acceptance of her in that role because she had been introduced that way: "As the semester wore on, students made occasional references to me as 'the researcher' or to 'Elizabeth's research'" (1991, 184–85). In fact, Chiseri-Strater talks of being a "family member" of the classroom, pointing to both the role she took and the roles that developed within that community (187).

Such a comfortable and integrated role is not always the result of "entering the field," because your entry and position are continually under negotiation. In a transcript from his interview with students at the end of a writing course in which he was the participant–observer for a quarter, John Hendricks' role is clearly not that of a family member. He begins the taped discussion this way:

Interviewer: Um, you've seen me sitting here probably for the entire quarter, some of you have noticed me and some of you haven't probably—

[General laughter]

Interviewer: Um, like the good news is you've all been aware that I was here, um, and I—I should explain to you what I've been doing. Um, some of you know, or have been told, that I have been doing research for my own class. I am an instructor at the University in the comp program. Um, and I have been teaching—and have been interested in this class, um, for my own purposes. But I've also been doing some research on this class as a class. (Brooke & Hendricks 1989, 104)

Hendricks' joke, the group laughter, and number of pauses hint that the interview is not completely relaxed.

During one term, many of the students who were conducting mini-ethnographies for my research methods course were graduate teaching assistants who allowed each other into their classrooms. Because of this, we decided to make general discussions about those projects off limits during regular class time, electing instead to work in small groups once a week so that teachers who were studying classmates' classrooms could discuss their classroom observations out of those teachers' presence. While our decision to study each other's classes seemed immediately to raise potential conflicts, we also realized that we couldn't practice ethnography without sites for study. In this instance, for learning purposes and due to the truncated nature of our studies, it seemed better to have access to a peer's classroom than to have no classroom to visit at all.

And the truth is, quite a few ethnographic decisions rest on access. As Mark Hankerson explains in the opening to his mini-ethnography:

> I decided to observe a computer section of first year writing (ENC 1101) at Florida State University for one month. The instructor of the class, Miles Watson, is a teaching assistant like myself. The simple reason I chose Miles' class was because the 10:10 time slot was the only time I had available in my jammed schedule.

Mark chose a class he could make time to visit, out of a relatively small offering of computer courses, and was lucky enough to find that teacher willing to let him attend that course at that time.

And there was learning to be found in these sometimes complicated interconnections, in which participant–observers were older, reentry graduate students who looked different than the student populations into which they entered or who were visiting the classes of fellow teachers, with whom they normally would share teaching questions and stories. Shifting roles forced novice researchers to reflect on their subjectivities and viewpoints, and these peer researchers found they had as much to negotiate (maybe more) in understanding their role as the members of the community they entered had in understanding why the researcher had arrived. "Call me Ethnographer," Mark observed wryly as he opened his report on peer Miles' classroom.

In his mini-ethnography, Ormond Loomis outlined his multiple roles:

> How many times had I sat in a classroom as a student? How many times had I stood in one as a teacher? Too many to want to count them in either instance. I

had even sat in classes to observe as an intern [stu-
dent-teacher]. I thought I knew the environment thoroughly enough to predict what I would find, but did I?
I had never approached a class as an ethnographer. To
test my assumptions about the environment and the
culture it contained, I determined to push my observational skills to the fullest.

And the subjective nature of our enterprise did not disappear simply
by studying the classrooms of those outside our course membership, as
Mark McBride learned. He chose to study an office-mate's classroom
and ended up worried about offending this office-mate when he found
himself sometimes feeling judgmental about her teaching and when his
focus moved from the students in a particular peer group (as he had
initially planned) to considerations of how this teacher had been trained
in our department writing program. He also found, to his surprise, that
this teacher who was giving him classroom access had "expectations"
about her involvement in and the returns she might receive from such
a project. He explained:

It was awkward with her [teacher] as an office mate because we'd talk about her class and I was torn between being a friend and a researcher. . . . She would
also ask me things: what was I finding, how did the
group go that I sat in?

Mark learned from this experience that he would have to negotiate his
researcher's position on several levels because he was in close daily
proximity to the very individual who provided him access to his site of
study—they shared an office—and also because the discussions between these teaching peers now as *naturally* turned to the project at
hand as it formerly had to teaching in general.

What permission do you need from individuals to use your observations in a later written report?

We talk about how to introduce ourselves: entering
the scene. We talk about permission slips all around
for everyone in the class.

—Devan Cook

Every term, I ask my writing students for permission to reuse their
work at a later date. Devan Cook, who had been both a writing student
in one of my classes and later a research student in a research class,
knew from this that collecting permission to share student work had
long been part of my general classroom strategy. I had learned that I
could never predict when student writing from one class could usefully

inform the learners in another class, so I made sure to collect permission from all of my classes. And then I learned, as an ethnographic writing researcher, that I would need to always study with my subjects informed consent. My informal consent form evolved into versions of this:

Date: _____

Wendy Bishop has my permission to use my work for educational purposes (for use in other classes as well as for illustrating textbooks, illustrating research reports, essays, professional talks, and so on). If my work is used, I would like to (circle one):

a) use a pseudonym
b) use my given name (print here, please)

Signature: _____

Permanent contact address: _____

In Donna Sewell's prospectus draft in Appendix A, you'll find a similar, informal consent form geared to her dissertation, which occurred before our university began to require more formal permissions from students who used ethnographic approaches in theses and dissertations. As a courtesy and to avoid having to describe your project endlessly, you may also want to give students or participants a short written description of your project and the role(s) they are agreeing to take in that project.

> Federal regulations require that any research that will be conducted on human subjects must be reviewed by a board charged with assessing the risks and benefits of the project. As qualitative research is usually of naturalistic design (i.e., there is no research intervention), and thus the researcher is not disrupting or increasing the risks of *everyday life*, such projects often receive expedited review.
> —Janice Morse 1994, 228

Social scientists have long been under the jurisdiction of federal, state, and institutional review boards, which review and regulate experiments conducted with human subjects. On a growing number of college campuses, writing ethnographers are required to submit their projects to these institutional review boards (IRBs). They were put in place to protect the rights of human subjects, and are a needed mechanism for doing so. However, some argue, as does Janice Morse in the preceding quote and as I do particularly about teacher research in one's own classroom, that the type of research we are talking about in this book does not manipulate "subjects'" environments or trespass on their "rights" in the way clinical laboratory conditions may sometimes be in danger of doing. Instead, ethnographers need to take the care that print journalists take, asking permission to tape or photograph or videotape individuals and to quote from the data collected. We need to be willing to go off the record at times and always to allow those with whom we work to review our data and our reports. We need to realize that when we ask for permission to study, we are asking permission to enter the environment, not to manipulate the scene. As visitors, we want to be sure that we are as fair and ethical in our later reporting as we can be and that our hosts have clear knowledge of how we'll use data collected on our visits. We need to consult with them about how we are representing them, and we need to observe the conventions of hospitality and collegiality.

Still, there is a growing argument to regulate research. Some institutions, like mine, allow for expedited IRB approval and do require such formal permissions be filed with the submission of completed theses and dissertations. The National Council of Teachers of English (NCTE), which supports several teaching journals, has moved to formalize its consent process for publishing student writing, and researchers such as Paul Anderson argue for more discussion in this area. He feels that composition and rhetoric as a field need to be concerned with the ethics of reporting what he terms "person-based" research because "our newly acquired research methods might require new ethical guidelines" (1996, 65). Given that we in composition, unlike social scientists, are not working from long tradition, Anderson also urges researchers to educate themselves about the function and purposes of IRBs and to familiarize themselves with issues of informed consent: "The NCTE and MLA policies requiring researchers to obtain permission from research participants should be reframed so they are consistent with the federal policy, and other journals should consider formulating such policies as well" (83). They can do so, he suggests, by contacting the Office for Protection from Research Risks' at <http://22.nih.gov:80/grants/oprr/oprr.htm> or their campus review board. Because we are already seeing an increase in the same, I have no doubt that discussions about the extent of permissions needed and the ethical issues involved in conducting naturalistic research will continue for as long as we conduct such projects.

The informal permissions collected for studying one's own class or for undertaking class-related mini-ethnographies are not, of course, legal documents. Rather, I see them as a promise to those with whom you work and as a written alert to them that you are a professional, conducting professional work. I always collect permissions as I introduce myself and my project, and I always make it clear that it will not be a problem if an individual chooses to withhold permission. In the case of my own classes, I mention on the first day that I always conduct research on and write about my classes and that I collect permission slips on the final day of class, making it clear that withholding permission will not affect a class grade because I don't check to see who signed the slips I requested until after I have evaluated final portfolios and submitted class grades (in fact, sometimes I don't need to refer to the slips for several terms, if ever). Students have felt comfortable enough with this system to withhold permission for personal reasons in each class; individuals in all formal research projects I've undertaken have chosen to do the same. Not everyone, of course, agrees that these permissions can ever be "freely" given when we continue to study, as I expect we will, within hierarchical institutions.

> Paradoxically, the measures devised to protect those being studied often aid the researcher in the seduction. An opening ritual is to sit down with prospective subjects and go over an "informed consent form" approved by the institution's committee on human subject research. Typically these forms provide a very brief and often vague description of the project, and then provide a number of assurances— that the subject can decline to participate and can withdraw at any point, that he or she will remain anonymous, and that results of the study will not affect grades in any course related to the research or be communicated to supervisors.
>
> —Thomas Newkirk 1996, 4

At a minimum, you need to be aware of the practical and ethical issues of obtaining and using any type of informal or institutional consent form and work with your advisor, grant officer, and/or institutional review board in order to meet state or federal requirements. You also need to be aware that journal editors and publishers will require written permissions before they can allow you to share your findings publicly.

If you apply for grant funding, however, you will need adhere to the grant-giver's regulations and preconceptions about research in general and often will be required to (or want to) go through formal channels of IRBs. Be prepared, also, to make a strong case for naturalistic research in general and ethnography in particular, because these models may challenge the prevailing definitions of research at your institution. If you are coordinating a large research project with other researchers under your direction, and are liable for all of their actions, you would naturally choose to go through formal reviews. Expect these reviews to require a fully developed research plan and to take time, because review boards meet at regularly set time periods.

> [W]riting about human-science research has actual or potential con-
> sequences for the lives of those with whom we create descriptions,
> narratives and interpretations. . . . We need to consider both our stated
> intentions and the possible effects of what we do.
> —John Lofty & Richard Blot 1997, 45

In a related issue, researchers have different attitudes toward naming research subjects—whether to report data by using an individual's
given name or an assumed name. When I began my research, it was
common—borrowing from the clinical tradition—to assume that pseu-
donymous research was somehow more "valid" and that those who
knew their identities were protected were more open and honest with
researchers. Our understandings of the situatedness of all research has
changed these assumptions. Today many researchers allow those they
study to make their own decision about whether they would like to be
named, and often those so consulted ask to be named.

Researchers also have moved from naming themselves "researcher"
when labeling interview transcripts, as I did in my study *Something
Old, Something New*, or "interviewer," as John Hendricks did in *Audience
Expectations* (Brooke & Hendricks 1989), to using first names, as my students tended to do in their own mini-ethnographies and as I currently
do in my own research and see peers doing as well.

How much of your project and your own life or research history will you share with participants?

If we gain entrance to a site on the premise of reciprocity, this approach suggests that we be open and sharing with our key informants
and, when possible, with many in the culture we are entering. Because
we take an ethnographic approach in order to learn about the community from the inside out, trying to influence the community as little as
possible, we often find it useful to remain general about our research
goals and questions. And indeed, our plans are most general at the beginning of a project and become more specific as the patterns of what
can be seen begins to demand a researcher's attention. By deciding on
your own researcher's stance, you set the stage for subsequent decisions
about your project.

```
At 8:05, Ruth asks me to introduce myself. I do, say-
ing I'm a graduate student at FSU and am beginning a
research project. Ruth then asks if anyone in the
class has ever been the subject of a Primary Research
Project. None have. (I haven't either, and to tell
you the truth, I am a little taken back by the words
```

```
"Primary Research Project" in connection with my in-
troduction. Part of the lingo I guess, and it does
give me a certain amount of authority which I swell
up and absorb.) Ruth continues to say that some quite
interesting material can come from such research.
(Oh boy, now my subjects are really interested, and
so am I.) By giving me this importance, Ruth seems
to be absolutely gracious and welcoming, but then
perhaps she is also building up what I'm doing here
as a means of justifying my existence for her and her
students?????
```
                                                    —Sandra Teichmann

It is likely that the novice researcher will err on the side of insecurity and fluctuating stances, as Sandra does here, moving between seeing herself not at all a researcher and then more than a researcher than she knows she is, yet. The experienced researcher may be prone to problems in the opposite direction, experiencing moments of hubris (the sense of swelling importance that Sandra touches upon can become an endemic state) and imagining they're taking a clearer role than is usually possible to negotiate. Still, you have to appear trustworthy to gain trust, and you have to share in order to be shared with. You also have to be willing to be disappointed, stood up, and taken less seriously than you take yourself, understanding that participants, however willing they appear, aren't always able to meet your research expectations.

What factors make it easy for you to "blend in"—do you need to protect against over-facile blending?

What factors will work against your integration into this community?

Have you taken into account your own personality and availability for entering this community? Do you need any preparation? Special introductions?

Though I consider myself something of an introvert, I enjoy the conversational demands of ethnographic writing research. You may succeed because you truly like to talk and listen to others; you may find that although you aren't normally talkative, your ability to observe and analyze what you observe is your strength and that you can make the more active contacts—scheduling and conducting interviews—that such research requires. There is no doubt, though, that yours will be a person-based project. And that who you are will matter to your informants. Respect and confidences have to be earned, and differences cannot be wished away. The ethnographic site is a social space. And you have to undertake many social negotiations.

> Fieldwork, like friendship, requires a number of social lies to keep interaction flowing smoothly.
>
> —J. Cassell, quoted in Mara Casey, Kate Garretson, Carol Peterson Haviland & Neil Lerner 1997, 119

You'll need to interrogate your own positions. You may also be let down because you make more of your situation than others do:

```
I felt a little self-conscious entering the scene,
but as I said in the ethnography, the students could
not have cared less, it seemed.
```
—Mark McBride

Sometimes your entry goes better than expected:

```
    Observing Sandra's first class seemed to go well.
I introduced myself with the rest of the group, and
took that opportunity to explain to the students why
I was there. I wasn't nervous at all, which, looking
back, I am surprised about.
    Later tonight I will transcribe some of the tape
and look over my notes.
```
—Ellen Schendel

And other times, you'll have to negotiate visible and/or dramatic differences, such as being of a different generation (as was Sandra, from both student and teacher, when she entered Ruth's class) or such as being a complete outsider—the traditional anthropological role, arriving from a different culture or class, (possibly) being of different racial background, speaking a different "life" language if not first language. These differences may be literal and/or metaphorical and will require that you translate yourself to and into the culture even as you work to understand that culture while you are there.

Being There in Person: Looking, Talking, and Collecting

> Despite the proliferation of terms and ideas, the qualitative approach essentially relies on three types of evidence-gathering methods: document examination, interview, and observation. The second and third of these, which identify people as the subject of the investigation, often show considerable overlap.
>
> —W. James Potter 1996, 95

Shirley Brice Heath's classic ethnography of the literacy learning in the communities of Roadville and Trackton opens with a description of her long-term participant-observation process: "In the years between 1969 and 1978, I lived, worked, and played with the children and their families and friends in Roadville and Trackton. My entry into these specific communities came through a naturally occurring chain of events. In each case, I knew an old-time resident in the community, and my relationship with that individual opened the community to me" (1983, 5). As I mentioned earlier in this chapter, the researcher first finds and enters a site, often via the intercession of community members.

Traditionally, ethnography gains power from the length—longitude—of the study, the depth of understanding we feel the researcher can claim through long-term participant observation in that culture. Most of us will not have anything near the nine-year residency that Shirley Brice-Heath describes in *Ways With Words,* and many of us today distinguish between macroethnographies and microethnographies. Macroethnograpies report research on multiple sites and involve larger or longer projects than do microethnograpies, which can report on the culture of the single classroom, the single learner, and even the single learning event. Although I won't label all the studies mentioned in this book *microethnographic,* most are clearly so when compared with a nine-year macroethnographic journey like Heath's. To avoid confusion with these terms, students in my classes conducted what I called *mini-ethnographies,* something between trial runs and pilot projects and actual microethnographies. These were brief person-based studies that encouraged them to undertake basic ethnographic practices: document examination, interview, and observation.

> "Writing it down" is an interpretive act. . . . Careful analysis, triangulation, and constant self-questioning will bring you to a reliable and valid understanding of another culture. Right? Well, not at all. It is hard to understand, at first, the degree to which "writing it down" is interpretive, that "what is written 'down' is treated as data in the writing 'up'" and that *both* phases of the work involve the creation of textual materials. (Atkinson 1990, 61)

No one else can step into the same river of our research project for a second time and return to the same situation we once encountered. Therefore, our work is beyond replication. No matter how carefully explained, no one can participate and observe in the exact manner of the primary ethnographic researcher because her consciousness is the study's primary interpretive tool. Postmodern critiques of research suggest the degree to which our work relies on tropes, researcher personas, and persuasions, that all research methods and research reports are rhetorical. All of us use the reliable triad of classical persuasion: *logos,* the appeal to reason; *pathos,* the appeal to emotion; and *ethos,* the appeal of personality or character. As in any persuasion, "these means we use will be partly determined by the nature of the thesis we are arguing, partly by current circumstances, partly (perhaps mainly) by the kind of audience we are addressing" (Corbett 1965, 37). While these issues will be foregrounded in Chapter Five, it is worth noting them now, for the degree to which you decide to participate and observe, as well as the duration of your study, will surely affect your ability to understand and interpret the community ways of the culture you are visiting.

Participant Observation

As a participant–observer, to what degree will you participate? Observe?

```
        The circle looks at me blankly. I'm beginning to
wonder if at times I'm too invisible, acting too
bored and thus contributing to the student's own
boredom, or if I'm too eager, causing at times too
much of a performance around me. Having no idea what
image I present and knowing that at times I feel ei-
ther extreme and often something in between, I sit,
during class, numbly considering my position relative
to this culture I've invaded, and wonder what indeed
is going on here: high drama or the basic business
of living? Toward the end of class when my group of
four have again assembled and are writing a memo to
Ruth answering questions Ruth has asked about the
first draft they are handing in, I photograph the four
students and Ruth. As we leave the classroom, Mindy,
having just received her portfolio back, confides to
me that she received only a grade of B and says she's
very surprised, upset and is going to get an A in
this course, no matter what she has to do.
                                    —Sandra Teichmann
```

Different researchers set different limits. Some observe more than participate, and some feel that participation is intrinsic to their accurate observation. At one extreme, you have the distant white-coated clinician, the spy, the fly on the wall; at the other extreme, you have the tainted site, where the researcher has disappeared into the community or culture, has gone native, has created obvious and often dubious fictions out of the potentialities of fact. These are considerations for "being there" on the page, but they are also considerations for being there in person.

Just as researchers need to decide how much of themselves to share with community members—their personal history and project design—they also have to decide how much they will participate as actors within the scene and how this will help or hinder their ability to observe. In his project, Ormond Loomis assumed an active and interactive role:

> I worked with Jeane, Karen, and Tres [in a small group setting in the classroom]. As we convened in the northeast corner of the room, I scheduled an interview for the next day. We silently read each paper; wrote responses to questions the authors had appended; and, after everyone in the group had responded, discussed the comments. Allen [the class teacher] allowed the students to leave as they finished working in groups. Jeane, Karen, and Tres remained longer than any others, talking among themselves and with me about the written responses. As Jeane was leaving, I heard her schedule a conference with Allen for the next afternoon, and knowing that she would be near my office, I scheduled an interview with her to follow her conference.

For Ormond, working with a peer group and staying late with this group (although it is certainly possible that the group stayed late and on task partially *because* of his presence), he was able to take advantage of a moment to contact an informant—Jeane—and set up a conference at a mutually convenient time.

James Potter divides observational choices into three: passive observer, active observer, and active participant (1996, 94). For some ethnographers, the first choice belies the methodology; for others, the latter makes careful analysis almost impossible. Most will opt for the middle road—that of active observer, moving into the scene, where it seems natural and polite, and moving back to observe more carefully when that also seems functional. Some ethnographers prefer the active stance, because the ethnographic moment is often slow to occur and cohere—sometimes it is not even noticed until later, when the researcher textualizes all the events and analyzes them for recurring patterns. Here, while writing a wry end-of-class analysis–parody, Ron DePeter captures the slow side of such work:

> Observing was tiring. It was like something you didn't want to do. It was in the afternoon, after my other classes (I take two classes of my own as well as teaching three sections), and you just feel like sleeping, or going home to watch General Hospital. But you know you've got to sit there and observe.

Participant–observers can find themselves unexpectedly disappointed by their subjects' seeming lack of involvement. Teachers may see us as "simply" a class visitor, or put us to work if we are taking up class space. Key informants can lose their initial enthusiasm. This can go beyond forgetting appointments to treating our (by now precious) research reports with true indifference. Sandra Teichmann was surprised to find that a student she studied was totally uninterested, beyond "school politeness," in the report of her study, which she had tried to share with him:

> 9 a.m. Thursday, I'm waiting on a bench outside Ruth's classroom. Remembering my promise to give a copy of this ethnography to her at the end of the semester, and now worrying about what she will think, I'm startled to see Josh come down the hall, dragging his feet, my manuscript draft in one hand. He smiles and hands it to me saying, "I didn't get time to finish reading it."
>
> I say, "Did you write any comments?"
>
> "No," he says and moves on toward the closed classroom door carrying his purple textbook and a manila folder.
>
> I follow him and ask, "What did you think about what you did read?"
>
> He says, "It was different."
>
> I press him, "Do you think it was the truth?"
>
> He says, "Yeah," moving to turn the knob on the classroom door, "yeah, I guess, but I didn't read it all. I had to study for a quiz." Before I can ask more, he passes, sixty minutes late, through the door into Ruth's classroom where I can see students sitting in a circle quietly writing. The door closing behind him, I'm left standing, disappointed in the hall.

Field Notes

How will you take field notes? During or after the events? Will you use a tape backup and write during the events? Will you participate and tape and then transcribe later? How much later? Will you mainly keep retrospective accounts?

How often will you review your notes?

The first choice facing a participant-observation researcher is what to record. Of all possible features of classroom interaction, which ones

> find their way into the researcher's notebook? I suggest that the na-
> ture of this choice is a form of selective description. The researcher
> tries to describe what occurs, but at the same time chooses which fea-
> tures to record based on some motivated sense of what might later
> prove significant.
>
> —Robert Brooke 1997, 15

Note-taking practices are as varied and individual as handwriting.
In fact, in these days of notebook computers, notes may not be taken
by hand at all. Most of us will want to combine sketching—literally—
noting the speakers in a scene (as in the sample in Pat Hendrick's mini-
ethnography in Appendix B). Some researchers develop checklists and
grids to tabulate regularly recurring activities. Some indicate speaker
and turn taking using personally developed shorthand. Some spend
several days trying to capture the general scene and then, as Robert
Brooke suggests, motivated by their research questions and a sense of
what may develop into usable data, focus on such elements of the
scene. As Ron DePeter explains, class notes have much in common
with a writer's journal notes; in his mini-ethnography, he realized that
he tapped the same skills he tapped as a creative writer when looking
for scenic detail:

> I took notes. I always do. Sometimes I go out for
> a quick meal and I take a piece of paper and pencil.
> I write things down. I notice things. I'll notice a
> girl feeding French fries to her boyfriend. You try
> not to be too obvious because you don't want them to
> feel conspicuous. Sometimes I just write what I'm
> thinking, and don't observe.
> The notes I took in the class were trying to link
> things. Like when I saw them having a discussion, I
> tried to look at how the women talked, or the men
> talked, or what they said. Or when they read their
> essay aloud, I looked at who paid attention. It was
> mostly the women looking. The men would lay their
> heads down, but the women would look at the reader.
> You see things. But like I said, you don't know what
> to do with them.
> We observed a group. There were five people in
> it, but a lot of the times one or two was absent. You
> became close to them in a way. You got to know Josh
> as the big guy. At first I thought he was obnoxious.
> You make first impressions, and they last. . . . Josh
> was carefree. He would hop over the table like over

a pommel horse when the class was over. . . . We had
to interview the students. I did two. Bryan and
Michelle . . . People are not the way you imagine
them.

I've found myself filling seemingly empty classroom observation moments with lists—I've listed shoes students are wearing and T-shirt inscriptions and later found this helps me understand the students' activities and preferences. Likewise, I find that quietly noting "under-life" behavior can prove useful—off-task talk about parties and dorm fire alarms can tell stories behind stories of why drafts have not been prepared for that class day. Equally, noting physical characteristics, whether student and teachers interact in close proximity or position themselves in predictable and recurring patterns, can lead to researcher insight.

> The author of fieldnotes (who will also be a reader of them on multiple occasions) should be aware that he or she is just that—an author. The work of observing, participating, listening, and writing is different from that of a stenographer. One is not attempting to transcribe from memory all the many and varied observable and memorable sayings and doings. The notes of the experienced ethnographer will also go beyond an inconsequential listing or jotting of random fragments.
>
> —Paul Atkinson 1992, 17

The participant–observer is often multitasking. Some prefer the backup of a tape recorder; some prefer to observe and make notes after the fact; others prefer to keep running notes, which they amplify right after the site visit.

Field notes made on the spot are essential; I'm
finding myself very comfortable with them, and uncomfortable at the same time. Is this what I'm supposed
to be doing, noticing what people look like so I can
know them? Will there be significance there? I always
think there is significance in these things—when four
people in a class show up in black tee-shirts, they
have passed around an e.s.p. message and have some
kind of extra-conscious link though I can't say what
that link might mean: there are so many things it
could mean.

—Devan Cook

Field Memos

How will you conduct ongoing field analysis when you are generating data? How often will you review your field notes?

Will you memo yourself? Will you need to memo others— co-researchers, research directors, and so on?

Will you transcribe tapes as the research goes on and write memos of those, or will you listen and write memos of key sections to which you might return?

Will your memos help you modify and refocus your research questions and/or directions? Why or why not?

As she conducted her three-semester dissertation ethnography, Donna Sewell met with me at arranged intervals to discuss her progress and analysis. She found it useful to provide us both with documents for those discussions, generated from her field notes and including a section, "Questions for Wendy," that she used to remind her of points she wanted to discuss.

For his mini-ethnography, Ormond Loomis, who came to composition with a degree in folklore, which I expect usefully informed many of his research choices, kept a double-entry journal, amplifying his class notes with several levels of researcher commentary. In the left-hand column, he noted class activity and discussion, recording turns taken by the teacher, Allen, and students in class. In the right-hand column, Ormond noted the activities going on: "Allen refers to the text on the blackboard." As the discussion continued, the right-hand meta-commentary included researcher reflection, indicated in his final text by italicized thought: "A number of students are still arriving. *There's an empty chair next to me on the left. I wonder if any of the late arriving students will take it, or am I intimidating perhaps.* Mary comes in and takes the chair on my left."

Whether choosing double-entry, during the observation, or post-observation retrospective note taking and recording, all ethnographers have to cope with their multiple roles and with several levels of observation data. Looking at excerpts from other studies will help you to see the range of possibilities and pick methods that suit your observation and/or participation style and research project.

Most of those who are entering new territories, both of methodology and writing cultures, will want to analyze where they've just been and plan where they will go next, as Jennifer Ahern does here:

> Looking forward to my next visit: I felt like a bonafide ethnographer. I went "There." I took copious

notes. But I felt uncomfortable as an observer—There were no other observers there. Matt referred to me as the "Spy" and wanted to know what kind of information I was looking for. So I'm on the margins from the beginning. My position in the culture is clear (non-participant observer/outsider), and I wonder how honest my key informants will be if I'm not their idea of a team player. . . . Was I surprised at what I saw? Yes. I was impressed by the academic surface, tutors, students, papers, books, academic conversations were everywhere. . . . I noticed that football players were the dominant force in the study hall, and I wanted to know why. I went back to my original research question: What happens in the student-athlete study hall and refocused: How do the football players influence what happens in the study hall and how are they treated?

Informal Surveys and Questionnaires

What are you asking and why?

Throughout this book, I'm using the term *survey* primarily as a verb—to look over—in the nonstatistical sense. Naturalistic surveys collect general information from members of your community. To do this, you may construct a questionnaire, one or more pages of questions that each individual in the study is asked to complete. These survey sheets will most likely be reviewed and analyzed to provide a project baseline, a review of general information about those involved in your study. This review may include informal coding procedures or simply be reflected in narrative tabulations.

When I was beginning my ethnographic work, I entered then-current discussions about the value and possibility of mixing qualitative and quantitative data—words and numbers—in naturalistic research. Since that time, a brief ten years, there seems to be a more general acceptance that surveys and questionnaires can help the naturalistic researcher. Such work can provide a useful preliminary overview of a population and help identify possible key informants. While some qualitative research is still grounded in statistical surveying and/or analyses that are checked by trained co-raters (see Christian Knoeller's *Voicing Ourselves*, 1998), most humanistically trained writing researchers these days are not stopped by not having a quantitative research background. They may be aided by doing so; insights as to what such training can contribute can be gained by reading James Potter's book, which looks at qualitative research from a quantitative researcher's perspective. Many ethnographic writing researchers begin projects by conducting informal surveys and counts to assess general tendencies. In this sense, surveys function as quick group interviews and cultural overviews.

In the sample here, as he opens his mini-ethnography, Mark Hankerson reports the result of his initial class survey:

> The questions on the survey were: (1) Why did you register for a computer-based ENC 1101 course? (2) Do you have prior experience with computer word processing? Little? Some? Extensive? Explain briefly. (3) What do you hope to gain from this course?
>
> Afterwards, I learned three things from the students' responses:
>
> Almost half of the students did not originally set out to register for a computer section of ENC 1101. Nevertheless, more than two-thirds of the class classified themselves as having at least "some" computer word processing experience. More people than I expected (about one-third of the students surveyed) stated that they hoped to become better writers—and did not mention the "bonus" of learning more about computers or merely receiving an "A" or simply fulfilling a course requirement.

For his project, Ormond Loomis combined a questionnaire that provided baseline information about the class participants and also allowed him to assess their willingness to be key informants, available for interviews, and general research participants. Like Ormond, you may find surveys very useful (and to that end, we'll discuss possible question designs in the next chapter) or, like Mark McBride, ultimately not of great worth:

> The questionnaires from the entire class proved, in the end, somewhat useless, mainly because after reviewing the three students' revision processes, I no longer trusted their self-perceptions.

Mark's observation reminds us that surveys are only one method of providing triangulation and that the researcher still needs to verify survey-developed impressions or counts of general tendency and self-report. Researchers may find that surveys often loom large as they begin projects—as part of the process of defining and refining research questions and directions—and then equally often recede to the status of confirmatory data along the way, as in this instance.

Co-Researching

If you work with others, what roles will each of you take?

What are the drawbacks of co-researching?

What are the benefits of co-researching?

How will each researchers' contributions be represented in your final written report(s)?

We may value collaborative writing research for some of the same reasons we advocate co-researching in the writing classroom. Conducting ethnographic writing research this way is process-oriented, just as most of our contemporary writing classrooms are, and the more eyes and ears we have discussing and analyzing complex classroom interactions, the more we may expect to learn. Even the isolated anthropologist was often accompanied by a generous helpmate (a research assistant or, as was often the case, a spouse, who functioned in this role or was also a credentialed researcher). Clifford Geertz's essay, "Deep Play: Notes on the Balinese Cockfight," begins this way: "Early in April of 1958, my wife and I arrived, malarial and diffident, in a Balinese village we intended, as anthropologists, to study" (1993, 224).

Kim Haimes-Korn included a co-researcher in her teacher-research project described in Chapter Two. Kevin Miller sat in on her course in two roles: to conduct his own mini-ethnography for my research class and to aid Kim in her dissertation data collecting. From the same course, Ron DePeter and Devan Cook shared data they collaboratively collected in Sandra Teichmann's writing classroom, but they chose to write up their observational reports separately. A look at some of Devan Cook's notes indicates some of the problems that can arise when co-researching (interestingly, the same problems often arise for student writers in collaborative writing groups in the writing classroom, like the one these two collaborating researchers studied). Working together can improve our sense that what can be seen has been seen, but it can also slow the research project. Collaboration takes time and negotiation, and sometimes, accommodating another researcher can slow one's process more than support it.

```
     [Research Methods Class] Group Time: Ron and I
talk: Dawn isn't here, but that's OK since Ron and I
need to talk. I ask Ron what we're doing. In the in-
terview, it was like we're studying Sandra—we're
curious and interested in Sandra's teaching. I am
stubborn and only interested in what I'm interested
in but I didn't realize Ron was that way too. . . .
We decide to work on a survey—Ron has questions
```

which we'll refine by administering them to my class on Wednesday and then give to Sandra's class on Thursday. That ought to give us a chance to see if any of the questions are extraordinarily dumb. We also decided to study and interview the students in Group 5. . . . All this negotiation takes an hour.

Ron and I finalize our interview questions:

1. Do you think your writing has changed in the last 8 weeks? How? Do you feel you were able to write about what you wanted? (Follow up)
2. Tell me about the day your group ran class. (Follow up.)
3. What do you think of Sandra as a teacher? What's she up to?

We discuss whether or not we need to ask exactly the same questions. I realize this was my idea, that maybe I'm pushing Ron around. Maybe he wants to know different things than I do: but from what we've said to each other, I don't think there's much essential difference.

Co-researchers not only have to negotiate entrance to the community they are studying, but also have to negotiate their own relationships to each other. Sometimes, often in fact, co-researchers have different levels of authority, which also must be negotiated during the data gathering and later during analysis and authoring. Are they truly co-researchers and co-writers, or is one—by mutual agreement—assisting the project of the other? And, in each instance, how do those decisions affect the co-researcher's roles?

For a graduate student in the field of composition studies, the invitation to do collaborative classroom research with the director of freshman English seemed almost too good to be true, except for one small detail: many of the actions under scrutiny would be my own . . . my classroom identity would be fully exposed to someone who played an important role in my professional development. I took my first graduate course in the field from Russel. He guided one of my research projects; he acted as my academic adviser; he wrote my recommendations. His title was "Director of Freshman English" and mine was "Graduate Assistant." . . . As usual, Russel would supervise and respond to my professional performance. But in this situation, he was a "partner" who first watched and scribbled notes in a yellow legal pad—then returned to his office to render "my experiences into text."

—Russel K. Durst & Sherry Cook Stanforth 1994, 61–62

Just as Russel and Sherry had to negotiate their institutional relationship, Robert Brooke and his colleague Joy Ritchie reconciled their collaboration by deciding to have Ritchie contribute a chapter to a book otherwise authored by Brooke. Problems related specifically to university credentialing arise when the research in question is conducted for an M.A. or Ph.D. degree. Although there is discussion these days at professional conferences about alternatives to the solo-authored dissertation report, these alternatives are not yet in evidence for a variety of reasons, some of which are raised in Chapter Six.

Interviewing

What is the nature of the interviews in your project?

Are they adding confirming or disconfirming data, or are they at the center of the project?

Where will you interview and under what conditions?

As James Potter points out, observation and interviewing often overlap. Interviews range from on-the-spot informal questioning of a member of the culture to arranged and organized discussions. Interviews can be conducted face to face (notes taken or recorded at the time or remembered and recorded retrospectively), via a detailed questionnaire or a simple writing prompt, or from a distance, via phone or the Internet. Key informants can be identified who help the researcher verify impressions. Groups can be interviewed together to provide a dialogic investigation of an interview (as in the John Hendricks quote in this chapter). Life-history interviewing may be crucial or central to a study of nonacademic literacy, as it is in the work of Deborah Brandt, who has been listening to "the accounts of ordinary Americans recalling how they learned to read and write" (1998, 167), but less important to a researcher interested in understanding observable classroom interactions, as when Robert Brooke (teacher) and John Hendricks (participant–observer) each kept notebooks on the same class for regular comparison. Even in this case, though, Hendricks did conduct interviews with some class members.

Interviewing immediately raises the question not only of what questions to ask, but also of how to capture, save, and retrieve the responses to those questions. Tape recorders can run out of batteries, so the wise researcher will have backup plans. Equally, interviewees can run out of enthusiasm and begin avoiding the interviewer:

```
I call Mindy first. She's busy but says she'll call me
back. She doesn't. I call again and leave a machine
message. She still doesn't call. I call Jennifer. She
```

isn't home, but I leave a message with her roommate
who will have her call me back. She doesn't. I call
Josh. He isn't home. I call Tiffany, who, when I ask
if I may record the conversation, says, "Sure." I ask
her to talk about the process of writing one of her
papers.

Sandra Teichmann vividly captures the phone-tag involved in
setting up interviews with busy subjects who may agree to work with
us in (due to?) institutional settings or due to momentary goodwill,
but later prove problematic to track down. After completing the mini-
ethnography quoted in this chapter, Devan Cook conducted the inter-
view-based dissertation project described in Chapter Two. She found
that her working-class students were often unable to keep intended appointments or that many indicated a willingness they really didn't have,
which resulted in a melange of mysterious no-shows. And, even when
subjects do show—or are part of a classroom group—technology is often liable to breakdown.

Visual Records: Videotape and Photography

**What are the benefits and drawbacks of using this more
invasive technology?**

Do you have adequate access to necessary equipment?

Many of the researchers in my classes obtained permission to
photograph the research site and sometimes the participants. Because
they often used traditional narrative techniques to open their reports,
and because ethnographic data analysis can take years, a photographic
record can prompt the author's memory, allowing her to recapture precise details. However, requests to obtain visual records can sometimes
threaten the comfort of participants and also misrepresent the scene.
Sometimes what is taking place outside the frame is as interesting,
more interesting, or as significant as what is shown. For instance, in my
study of college writing teachers, I could not follow five teachers back
to their home institutions after I participated in a summer teacher education class; instead, I asked these teachers to videotape for me those
classrooms several times during the term. Kind key informants that
they were, they did so, and the resulting videotapes were both infor-
mative and flawed: They ranged from a fixed tripod that never included
the teacher in the frame to student-run filming sequences to filming
done by campus educational specialists. These tapes did give me a sense
of the teachers' students and classroom facilities, but they could not in
any significant way offer me insight into the classroom cultures those
teachers and students were co-creating.

Figure 2

Instances of research informed by photographs can be found in Sondra Perl and Nancy Wilson's study *Through Teacher's Eyes* (1986), in which each case-study teacher is pictured as each chapter begins, as well as in Ellen Cushman's and Janis and Richard Haswell's *College Composition and Communication* essays (1996 and 1995, respectively). Publication of these photos and the increased use of WEB-based technologies in writing classrooms and writing research suggest that we'll be encountering more images in forthcoming research reports. These developments underscore the need for obtaining adequate permissions to share such materials. You can see the power of these visual images in the photograph (Figure 2) from Kim Haimes-Korn's dissertation:

> The following preliminary sketches represent my impressions after my first meeting with the students; I draw from questions on an introductory questionnaire (Appendix 4) administered the first day of classes and our first introductory conferences. In these short sketches I give my initial, somewhat narrow impressions of the students before I got to know them better throughout the semester. However, I feel the written snapshots provide good background information and give a good sense of their preliminary attitudes about writing and the writing class which they were about to enter. Although the case studies focus primarily on five of the students (Romeo,

Tiffany, Joel, Latisha, and Cindy), the others come
in through class discussions rendered in the piece.
—Kim Haimes-Korn 1996, 40

Equipment in General

Do you have funds and expertise to use the equipment for your project?

Do you have backup plans in the event of technological problems?

> Thursday: I enter the classroom with my newly-
> put-together ethnographer's bag. Hanging from my
> shoulder are my mini-tape recorder, extra batteries,
> extra tapes, a manila folder full of blank white pa-
> per, two ink pens and a sharpened pencil, extra film,
> and a camera loaded with fast film so I won't have to
> use the flash.

As Sandra Teichmann makes fun of her ethnographic image, she is also invoking cultural images of pith-helmeted anthropologists even while she alerts us to the real expenses that may be involved in our projects. While the simplest ethnographic bag contains pen and paper, many of us become sudden owners of microcassette recorders and transcribers. We can end up buying cassette tapes in bulk, and we can feel like we should have invested in the stock of the local copyshop as we end up making copies of documents for later review: students' drafts, classroom syllabi, program reports, and so on. Researchers who used to have to budget for library computer literature reviews now may need to upgrade their computers.

Indeed, the thesis and dissertation process is fraught with immediate costs and with hidden costs, from long-distance phone calls to major professors to buying an interviewee a double-latte. "Mara wishes someone had warned her when she was designing her study that audiotaping every class session, conducting seven interviews with Shelley . . . and interviewing each of the fifteen students in the class three times . . . would cost her about $3,500 in transcription fees alone. With such warning, she could have modified her inquiry to involve more manageable taping and transcribing" (Casey et al. 1997, 118). At the least, it is wise to decide whether you will need to save money and expend your own hours transcribing (and there are benefits from doing so) or optimize your time and spend wisely for interview transcription. Or, some researchers will do as Mara wishes she had done, design a more economical study or take running notes by hand or on a notebook computer.

When I asked case-study teachers to send me class materials, I provided tapes for videotaping, mailing envelopes, and money for postage and photocopies. Had I been on-site, I would have also given them my time—making the copies for them and for myself. Books have to be located and sometimes purchased, and copies of reports have to be made and returned to participants; some researchers pay assistants and/or audiotape transcribers; some treat fellow researchers to lunch in return for participating in a data coding session. Writing researchers may study cultures outside their home institution, town, state, or country, requiring extended stays elsewhere. Long-term, thick-description, person-based research can cost.

> To tape each of the eight student-led class discussions, I utilized a single, centrally located microphone. When recording, I joined the teacher and students who sat arbitrarily at desks in a circle. Identifying the sequence of speakers in the field notes proved a crucial step when later transcribing the tapes, since it was necessary to distinguish from among twenty-five voices and often between overlapping [speech] turns. I personally transcribed and edited all transcriptions, since proper identification of speakers was essential to the analysis.
> —Christian Knoeller 1998, 45

```
My tape recorder didn't record very well because
the kids were so spread out, you couldn't get every-
thing. Sometimes they got into small groups and you
could tape them. But you couldn't hear everything
then either, there was so much talk in the room. But
you hear things, you remember them. You hear them
talk about Beavis and Butthead or a fraternity prank
they saw.
```

Ron DePeter's observations remind us that tape recorders will not, for most purposes, supplant the participant recording along with the most fool-proof research recorders possible—human ears and hand and paper. Kim Haimes-Korn explores the frustration a researcher can feel in a normally noisy institutional setting, like a writing classroom or writing center. She finally realizes that the problem was not mainly her self-consciousness as a teacher recording her own teaching site but a problem with equipment. Here you see, again, how additional research dollars can suddenly be expended.

```
I am still annoyed with the taping process. I
originally thought it was my transcriber, but I found
out it was my tape recorder when I borrowed Kevin's
last group tape (mine was inaudible). This weekend I
```

```
bought a new tape recorder with a multidirectional
mike. I hope this makes a difference. I practically
lost a whole week of data (I will have to really
struggle to capture it). Again, the logistics of this
kind of research are not something you anticipate at
the onset.
```

One firm piece of advice: If you invest in audiotaping, invest in a tape transcriber for you or your transcriptionist to use. Nothing breaks a tape recorder or a researcher's spirit faster than starting and stopping the playback and rewind buttons by hand. Students in a methods class can't reasonably be expected to purchase a transcriber, but eventually a serious ethnographer will have to invest, and here's where researcher collaboration can be truly useful: Purchase one machine as a group and/or borrow it from your department or university.

Storage: General Data Management

How will you organize your data as you collect it?

How much data reduction will you undertake during the field experience?

Have you scheduled in time for reviewing, storing, and verifying field data (making sure tapes have recorded, etc.)?

Ethnographic approaches are notable for the ongoing data analysis they involve and for the amount of data they generate. Here, Ormond Loomis reviews a questionnaire immediately after having the class complete it, in order to pick his next interview participants:

```
In my office after class, I reviewed the [second]
questionnaires. Twenty-three students responded. As
their "sources of information" for the [University
Discourse] paper, they said they would use bathroom
graffiti (1), a campus zealot (2), the internet and
computers (1), media advertisements and flyers (1), a
tackboard (1), a trashcan (1), and campus newspapers
(14); three were undecided about what to write on.
In addition to having been among those who chose dis-
tinctive sources Jeane, Karen, and Tres had indi-
cated a willingness to serve as an informant. I made
plans to interview each.
```

Ethnographers provide such catalogs for themselves and for their readers. First, no report could include so much data, so the data are indexed. Second, such an index allows readers of ethnographic reports to gauge the amount, kind, and thoroughness with which data were collected. Certainly, too, these lists perform a rhetorical function as the researcher, as I did in my study and Elizabeth Chiseri-Strater did in hers, uses such a catalog to say, more or less: Trust me, I was there, in person, writing it down, then carefully saving it to analyze. I've come to you now, an expert, to tell you my story.

> I developed a continuous record-keeping procedure so that all material was collected and filed for future use. Methods included: labeled and alphabetized file folders for all print data, from survey questions to learning logs to seminar papers to the student papers in the case study teachers' own classes. By the end of the study, I had amassed print artifacts that filled approximately two, four-drawer file cabinets. . . . I typed daily field note summaries and, often, reviewed and elaborated notes. I collected 157 pages of handwritten class observation notes and typed 74 pages of field note summaries during the five-week period of the second summer session. During the fall of 1987 and the spring of 1988, I kept analysis/writing notes on the microcomputer as I transcribed tapes, entering observations and sorting out themes and ideas.
>
> —Wendy Bishop 1990a, 152

> In all, I collect 114 typed pages of coded field notes on the Prose Writing classroom, which I keep in a salmon-colored loose-leaf binder.
> —Elizabeth Chiseri-Strater 1991, 190

After having kept my three file cabinets full of ethnographic data during the course of the study, I moved this data with me from Alaska to Florida and it faces me in an institutional cupboard where it remains, ten years later. The ethnographer in the field attempts to be inconspicuous and to move lightly through the community; ironically, the author of an ethnography is burdened by data and drafts. In fact, when conducting research methods classes, I found it simplest to carry a blue plastic filing crate to classes with me—particularly one term, when the entire class was acting as a research team. I'm still known for carrying those crates around the halls, and students have told me that when they go to purchase their own file crates, they always seem to gravitate toward the blue ones. I don't advocate particular formats or organizing methods, crates or crate colors, but you do need to be aware that you will need to log in material, maintain it even in the midst of furious bursts of messy drafting, and then retain that data for some time as you share your research reports with readers. Organization can lead to insight; disorganization can lead to discouragement:

```
My first experience in class, I took notes like a
human seismograph machine, and I'm looking at the
bloat—piles of notebook paper stacked in little
piles all over my office. Data overload! If only I
could split myself down the middle, Doppleganger-
like, and have the other me doing all the field work.
```
—Taube Cyrus

A *Data Overload Ahead* bumper sticker would sell out at an ethnographer's convention. The purpose of careful research planning, as outlined in Chapter Two, should be apparent now: A good design helps you to keep your project (somewhat) manageable. Even so, you will constantly be asking yourself how to make pragmatic on-the-spot decisions about how much you should and can do. In Chapter Four, as we look at some particulars—developing and administering surveys and conducting interviews—we're doing so with an eye toward moving to initial data reduction. The ethnographic writing researcher needs to begin to start to reduce the data almost immediately, looking for developing patterns and initial units of analysis. Like Kim Haimes-Korn, whose observations open this chapter, your researcher-self will include a mix of linear and circular thinking, and like Taube Cyrus, you'll have to accept the limits of one human's energies and abilities unless you have a friendly doppelganger (who likes to research, too) at hand. So perhaps the bumper sticker should read: *Data Overload Ahead; Bring Your Doppelganger Along!*

Chapter Four

Understanding the Process: Local Views

> What are normally called data—journal entries, field notes, photographs, and so on—are, for us, better thought of as field texts. They are texts created by participants and researchers to present aspects of field experience.
> —D. Jean Clandinin & F. Michael Connelly 1994, 418

It is essential to begin your ethnographically oriented writing research with careful planning and to continue to center your work via ongoing self-questioning, as I encouraged you to do in previous chapters. It is another thing indeed—both more concrete and more lonely—to sit down at a table to list and to refine possible interview questions or to sit down yet again to analyze answers to those questions once collected from a population of teachers or students or literacy learners in any context. To pull meaning from the cascade of data you have generated as interested researcher, as researcher in search of a narrative thread, you will be working to organize, categorize, thematize, and textualize yet again in order to make meaning out of your developing understandings of who you were, where you went, what you saw, what you think you thought you understood, and what meaning you think your reader might make with you from those experiences.

```
    Let the data talk to you; don't put your own spin
on it.
```

Devan Cook reminds you, as I reminded her, after I had been reminded the same way, often and usefully, by my own quantitatively trained-but-moving-toward-qualitative methodologies dissertation director, Don McAndrew: Design a good project, collect field texts to the best of your abilities, and then look at and listen to what you've found. Allow the data to lead you into new knowledge instead of forcing the data into stories you already expected to tell.

Metaphorically, you listen closely, you put your ear to the conch shell of material collected and start to search and sort and itemize and make sense of it—as humans so naturally and so often ably do—but you also have to respect it as not-you, as having a life of its own now that you have textualized it.

Like so much in context-based research, it is at just this point that the "listen to" metaphor breaks down, for as ethnographer, you are always listening to *a version* and that version is mediated by who you are. You designed the study, you made initial decisions that allowed you to collect this and not that data or detail. You must justify not collecting or not observing something else. You will continue to make analysis decisions—looking for metaphors and analytical lenses close to hand (based on experience) and farther away (say, one found by reading another's research study) that allow you to create a reasonable and reasoned interpretation of what you have fanned out on the analysis table before you. Your aim is to create a sense of trustworthiness for the researcher persona you ultimately present on the page. The best, most honest, most pragmatic way to do that, of course, is always to do everything you can to earn the trust of colleagues, culture, informants, and readers.

> Trustworthiness, many have argued, is a more appropriate word to use in the context of critical research. It is helpful because it signifies a different set of assumptions about research purposes than does validity. . . . One criterion for critical trustworthiness involves the credibility of portrayals of constructed realities.
> —Joe L. Kincheloe & Peter L. McLaren 1994, 151

You focus on presenting trustworthy aspects of your research endeavor, because, no matter how well you design, document, and detail your work, you cannot assume that replicability can ever be attempted or achieved. Due to the phenomenological grounding of your study, the context-based version of a once convened but now changed or evolved or dissolved culture that you entered, no other researcher could conduct your project again. Your project design, decisions, units of analysis, and narratives of having been there are presented to elicit trust and to provide insight, not to validate your practices. It is the essential nature of the ethnographic enterprise to be situated in time and place and culture and researcher(s) perceptions.

> Reliability is the degree to which the finding is independent of accidental circumstances of the research, and validity is the degree to which the finding is interpreted in a correct way. . . . In the case of qualitative observations, the issue of validity is not a matter of methodological hair-splitting about the fifth decimal point, but a question of whether the researcher sees what he or she thinks he or she sees.
> —Jerome Kirk & Marc L. Miller 1986, 20–21

Although you are using criteria different than those applied by positivist researchers, you are not in any sense being less rigorous: You are trying to refrain from "spin" even as you know that a certain amount of the same is inevitable. As readers, our belief in you is supported by the degree to which we judge that you have been as precise in your methods of analysis as possible and, at the same time, aware of the limitations of all you undertake.

Aiding you in that undertaking—particularly as you interview, survey, and begin to analyze your data—is the prime purpose of the discussions in this chapter.

> The constructivist or interpretivist believes that to understand this world of meaning one must interpret it. The inquirer must elucidate the process of meaning construction and clarify what and how meanings are embodied in the language and actions of social actors. To prepare an interpretation is itself to construct a reading of these meanings; it is to offer the inquirer's construction of the constructions of the actors one studies.
> —Thomas Schwandt 1994, 118

Interviewing in Some (More) Detail

Perhaps you read the *Rolling Stone* interviews or perhaps some of Studs Terkel's interviews in his well-received oral history, *Working*. When your TV or National Public Radio station is on, you hear journalists interviewing each other about current events or interviewing celebrities who precipitated some of those actions. Interviews are woven into the fabric of contemporary life; they are ubiquitous. Because of this, we might think we know all about interviews until we sit down to do them, especially if we have never been (comfortably) interviewed and/or if we consider ourselves introverted or not personality oriented. Not unexpectedly, the person who isn't himself a "personality" is often a fine interviewer, because successful interviewing rests much more on interest, intuition, and the ability to listen to and follow cues and opportunities than it does on outgoing behavior. Certainly extroverts can be fine interviewers, too; I simply want to encourage the quieter individual to realize that there are advantages in such a social orientation.

Week One: Student Interview Questions— Writing Background

1. What's your schedule this semester?
2. What kinds of writings will you be doing in your other classes?
3. Do you think of yourself as a writer? Why or why not?
4. How much writing do you think you do?
5. Do you do a lot of reading? What do you read? (ten more questions)

Week Three: Student Interview Questions— Social Life and Writing Workshop

1. How did you feel about sharing your draft of essay two in class?
2. Did you refer to the handout Thom [teacher] gave you?
3. Did it help you respond to the other students' papers?
4. How many comments did you typically write on their papers?
5. Did you get a lot of comments on your papers? (twelve more questions)

How will you construct your sets of questions?

It's fairly easy to skim over another researcher's interview questions, as you have just done. It takes more time to slow down and ask yourself questions about questions. As you reread these, think about their content, sequence, and number. Imagine why Donna Sewell chose the foregoing questions, asked them in this order, and at this length and level of detail. How does a researcher decide which questions are appropriate, in terms of content and in terms of number that can be included in an interview session? And how does she decide whom to interview, when, and where? Choices like these can greatly influence the direction of an ethnographic project.

In a sense, ethnographers are constantly interviewing—informally as they contact members of a community, identify key informants, clarify observations by asking questions about what they have seen or understood from an interaction, and again as they share observations with community members for confirmation or further elucidation. In addition to all of the informal and unstructured interviewing, researchers, as Donna Sewell did and as you probably will do, can set up formal interview sessions with members of a community. These interviews in turn can be either unstructured or structured, occurring before the community convenes, during field work within that community, or retrospectively as the researcher revisits informant(s) and research site(s).

So one answer to "How is an interview script developed, ordered, constructed, and applied?" depends to a great degree on researcher and research goals. The analogy to drama is useful: Your script can result in a scripted play, with questions asked in certain ways, and with—at least on the part of the interviewer—actor(s) being guided through the performance; or the script can be used as a loose guide and a discussion prompt, with interviewer and interviewee improvising on the pre-selected cues and questions.

Informal questioning and interviewing rely on your skill at thinking on your feet, and such skills will be enhanced if you keep careful field notes and review your data regularly in order to list questions to be asked if or when the opportunity arises. By week three of her fifteen-week study, Kim Haimes-Korn decides,

```
After each week of class has been transcribed, I will
bind the transcript as a double-entry journal along
with Kevin's [participant-observer in Kim's class]
field notes. In this form I can go back and respond
to their words with a little distance.
```

Regular collection, coordination, and reading of data like this helps a researcher formulate questions that need to be asked at the next opportunity. And decisions on interviewing directions can be aided by regular consultation with and refinement of initial and overarching research questions.

David Fetterman describes four main types of interviews: structured, semistructured, informal, and retrospective, although he emphasizes that these categories are not as distinct as category making causes things to appear to be (1989, 48). Judith Goetz and Margaret LeCompte identify three different forms of interviews: key informant, career or life histories, and surveys (1984, 119). Andrea Fontana and James Frey offer a broad definition that underlines the complexity of

distinguishing between types of, purposes for, and processes of interviewing:

> The most common type of interviewing is individual, face-to-face ver-
> bal interchange, but it can also take the form of face-to-face group in-
> terviewing, mailed or self-administered questionnaires, and tele-
> phone surveys [we can now add e-mail interviewing to this list].
> Interviewing can be structured, semistructured, or unstructured. It
> can be used for marketing purposes, to gather political opinions, for
> therapeutic reasons, or to produce data for academic analysis. It can
> be used for the purpose of measurement or its scope can be the un-
> derstanding of an individual or a group perspective. An interview can
> be a one-time, brief exchange, say five minutes over the telephone, or
> it can take place over multiple, lengthy sessions, sometimes spanning
> days, as in life-history interviewing. (1994, 361)

Clearly, you'll need to decide on several aspects of interviewing:

- Number (one-to-one or group)
- Medium (verbal, written)
- Purpose (to understand an individual; to explore group dynamics)
- Duration (one time; cyclical; after the fact, retrospective)
- Type of questions asked and under what conditions (formal or in-
  formal, structured or unstructured)

There are other aspects of an interview to consider as well, including establishing rapport, understanding silences and omissions, reading
body language, being aware of gender influences on interviewing interactions, and so on.

These aspects should be investigated as they relate to your primary research question(s), researcher's goals, researcher's skills, and
resources. For instance, a group interview would not seem appropriate
if you are not able to conduct this interview in person (because so
much of the group's dynamics would be unavailable on an audiotape)
or if the focus is on the life history of a single individual (because you're
not likely to gather that individual's family together and interview them
en masse). Equally, e-mail interviews, while tempting for the degree of
immediate textualization they provide and the control they appear to
offer to the interviewee (who can find time to answer questions according to his own schedule), may also eliminate important opportunities
for providing you with the context clues that would be available face to
face as you watch how the interviewee responds and as you try to follow up on verbal leads that could prove highly productive. Additionally,
self-report, especially self-report without the perhaps sobering presence
of the interviewer, can sometimes encourage self-deception or the presentation of a "preferable" self on the informant's part.

> By nature, interviews are densely textured layers of narration . . .
> narrations themselves can change during successive interviews: be-
> ing questioned about their writing experiences led some writers in
> this study to reexamine their assumptions and change their narrations
> during second and third interviews. Finally, as interviewer and inter-
> viewee establish a relationship, conversations become more candid, a
> common vocabulary is established, and the depth and length of con-
> versations vary.
>
> —Gesa Kirsch 1993, 39

Finally, the researcher has to consider how much is enough and how much is too much: Can the data be accessed and analyzed? Two hundred unanalyzed hours of interview data can broadly inform the researcher who has listened to (as well as, hopefully, cataloged and memoed himself about) the contents of those audiotapes, but they cannot truly aid the textualization process if the researcher hasn't the time or energy or ability to render and reduce those accounts to manageable data displays. In this event, the researcher's memory (selective or inexact) of the interviews might not meet our trustworthiness goals for effective ethnographic analysis and reporting.

What basic advice will help produce successful interviews?

Rely on your own common sense to guide your interview process. First, choose key informants carefully and tactfully. You might enter the field and observe individuals for as much time as possible before you ask permission for interviews. You might, as Ormond Loomis does in the interview questions listed in the last chapter, collect general data on participants by using an initial survey that also asks for volunteers.

Second, make interviews nonthreatening and convenient. Find locations that are likely to put your informant at ease (the classroom after class or a nearby coffee shop). Schedule interview times at an informant's convenience (near where they have to be next; when it fits into their schedule rather than yours). Be clear about times, including offering to remind and then actually provide reminders about interviews. Be early rather than late. Be prepared (if taping, make sure your equipment is working and that your tape is labeled and in the machine). Obtain necessary permissions before you begin.

Third, don't wear out your welcome. Keep interviews to preagreed time schedules (ask yourself how much time is reasonable and also ask your interviewee; then stick to the prearranged time slot). Work to develop rapport, but don't overwhelm the interviewee. To create rapport and encourage sharing, you may want to respond to questions about the project, but don't dominate or take over the interview. You are trying to make that individual's experience understandable, not create a forum for your own. Provide a cup of coffee, for example, but don't overwhelm the interviewee with inappropriate or uncomfortable suggestions, such as offering them a full meal, which could make the interviewee feel bribed or, more basically, keep her eating rather than conversing. Thank the interviewee; answer her questions; set up continued interactions if they are needed and if your informant is willing. Never force a follow-up interview; never continue an interview if the situation begins to become uncomfortable for you or the informant. When appropriate, send a written thank-you or a copy of the transcript for the individual to review.

Finally, and perhaps most importantly, field-test your interview skills. Try out your interview questions and techniques on a friend. In addition, learn what it feels like to be interviewed. Put yourself in the interviewee's shoes: If part of a class, let yourself be interviewed by someone else, or ask the friend who is participating in a mock interview with you to turn the tables and interview you.

What are the benefits of structured interviews, sequenced interviews, long interviews, and follow-up interviews?

If unstructured interviews allow you the opportunity of following a lead (you might think of the newspaper interviewer who pursues a breaking story), it also potentially provides you with a wandering and digressing set of data to analyze after the fact. As Harry Wolcott wittily reminds those in the writing phase of a project, "The critical task in qualitative research is not to accumulate all the data you can, but to 'can' (i.e., get rid of) most of the data you accumulate" (1990, 8). Any well-designed study will quickly begin to produce data at compound interest, and unstructured interviewing can rapidly produce a massive stockpile of audiotapes or interview notes.

Structured interviews—questions are planned and designed before meeting with the informant—can focus your data collection in two significant ways. Structured interviews reground your work because designing them requires you to consult and refine your preliminary research questions in light of what you are learning as you construct the questions for the next interview. Structured interviews are efficient, using potentially scarce informant time to elicit the most essential responses. Structured and sequenced interviews ask questions in a prescribed order, with each new question building upon and/or enlarging upon the previous question.

It is important that you keep your list of questions to a reasonable length, given your informant's involvement and the time available.

You'll notice that I did not list all of Donna Sewell's questions earlier. In fact, fifteen questions is a relatively lengthy list. Open-ended questions (the answers to which may cover a great deal of territory and are commonly used in qualitative research) and close-ended questions (by which a respondent quickly chooses from a few options or even answers a set of yes–no queries and which are commonly used to collect baseline and demographic data) take very different amounts of completion time.

Most of the educational interviews that my students and I have conducted have ranged from thirty minutes to an hour, and include about four to twelve questions. Kim Haimes-Korn's data collection chart in her dissertation logs her individual interviews at thirty minutes and group interviews at seventy-five minutes. These are necessarily rough estimates, but the researcher courtesy conventions suggest that you not wear out either your interviewee or your welcome. Sometimes this is hard to do, though, because most interviewers arrive at the first interview overprepared with questions and find themselves astonished to find that each interview develops a pace and life of its own, and certainly that some questions prove well designed, while others fizzle unexpectedly. One question primes an interviewee for a ten-minute monologue, while another plunges the session into silence.

Most of us find that even structured interviews are most rewarding when we approach them flexibly, comforted by a script but willing to deviate from it. This suggests that you should prioritize your questions, at least in your own notes, in case you need to speed up your sequence and drop some unproductive questions (unless your research design prohibits doing so, which is more common in less naturalistically oriented inquiry). One of my dissertation committee members, Patrick Hartwell, offered me a very useful open-ended question: to ask my respondents at the end of an interview to reflect on the questions I had asked, and to tell me if there were something I had forgotten to ask or that the informant had expected to be asked.

Schatzman and Strauss divide questions into five groups: (1) reportorial questions that elicit a respondent's knowledge of factors in a social situation, usually preceded by interrogatives such as who, what, when, where, and how; (2) devil's advocate questions that elicit what respondents view as controversial; (3) hypothetical questions that encourage respondent speculation about alternative occurrence . . . ; (4) posing-the-ideal questions that elicit respondents' values; and (5) propositional questions that elicit or verify respondent interpretations.
—Judith Goetz & Margaret Le Compte 1984, 126

You might develop your questions initially by brainstorming about everything you would like to collect at this interview point. You'll rapidly gather more questions than one interview can encompass, so you'll want to categorize your collection of questions, asking which are like each other (can you come up with topic-oriented groupings?), which are premature, which are unanswerable, and so on. After you've reduced the number of options, consider how each question might be phrased and posed and which questioning method will lead to a rich and useful response.

Check your wording for bias, infelicities, potentially insulting language (however unintentional), and predetermination. Don't try to get the answer you want or predict; allow the informant to inform you. There is a distinct difference between formats when asking a female student these questions about gender: "Does it affect the class atmosphere that teacher X is a man?" and "Does gender—either teachers' or students'—seem to you to be an issue in classroom interactions? Please explain."

Easier said than done. For practice, you might try rephrasing another researcher's questions to create what seem to you to be better versions. When, at a later date, I looked at interview questions from my dissertation, I could find instances in which I was leading an interview despite my good intentions or in which I had neglected to follow up on a promising conversational opening. Once you're sensitized to these issues, you'll find that you also read published interviews with a more learned eye.

A structured interview session can consist of a single question, though this is more often the case in life-history interviewing or follow-up interviews. For instance, Marilyn Sternglass, in *Time to Know Them*, interviewed college students for a six-year longitudinal study of their writing in college. Although year-three and year-five interviews consisted of structured, sequenced interviews, at the end of the students' spring semester of their fourth year at college, she asked a single, open-ended question: "In what ways do you feel you are a different person from the person you were when you started City College? Why?" (1997, 311). A grand open-ended question like this reminds us that the interviewer's primary task consists of getting the discussion going in the area of the research topic. In fact, Elizabeth Rankin, in *Seeing Yourself as a Teacher: Conversations with Five New Teachers in a University Writing Program*, opens her book by pointing to the overarching question for her project: "In the beginning, I ask them all the same question: 'When you think about last year, if you close your eyes and look back on that whole year of teaching, what images come to mind? What do you see?'" (1994, 1).

When constructing a set of structured, sequenced interview questions, it may help to think of your work as similar to that of creating a script for a survey (discussion follows). However, remember that many such surveys are filled with yes–no questions and forced-choices options: "Did you receive a GED or a high school diploma?" This sort of question will immediately stop the interview flow as the informant waits for your next question. For most ethnographers, and particularly for postmodern ethnographers who seek to involve the informant in dialogue and co-construction (sometimes in co-authoring) of a research report, the unstructured interview will be, by far, the preferable format because it encourages discovery and dialogue and supports interviewing as a mode of community interaction.

For those expecting to compare and contrast or sample several focal groups' or key informants' positions or points of view, sequenced and structured interviews help to organize this event, even though we have to remember that, in doing this, we are already artificially (although usefully) reducing data and making the informants' opinions, as elicited, appear more similar than they might actually be. In *Academic Literacies,* Elizabeth Chiseri-Strater felt that structured interviews would allow her to collect similar data for her two key-informant, case-study students, but even more, that the interviews provided "the major source for my understanding the students' perspective on their own literacy" (1991, 191). It is clear that in this study, structure fostered preparedness, but it also gave way to unplanned interactions, providing a general map rather than a rigid itinerary.

In *Women Writing the Academy,* Gesa Kirsch points out the way interviews

> have a number of constraints: they formalize conversations, emphasize a question and answer format, imply a hierarchical relation between interviewer and interviewee (because the interviewer determines the issues to be discussed), position the interviewee as an object of examination, and can predetermine answers through the assumptions, categories, and word choices reflected in questions (1993, 33).

Despite this useful warning, it is also true that the interview is the second most common tool—after participant observation, which itself has elements of an unstructured interview—in the ethnographer's bag.

Several variations on interviewing can be useful. Informants can be asked to answer interview questions without the researcher being present—through either e-mail or the use of audiotapes; either alone or in a group. Informants have to be trained to conduct the interview to obtain the data you hope to capture, and, of course, you need to provide them with taping equipment or computer access if they don't have their own. Although I mention the drawback to this method, sometimes it has to suffice. For instance, in my study, *Something Old, Something New* (1990a), I asked teachers at five different institutions to video- and audiotape their classes to provide me with at least minimal insight into those far-flung communities as a follow-up to my initial participant observation of these teachers in their own summer, teacher-education classes.

In *Thinking and Writing in College,* Barbara Walvoord and Lucille McCarthy included student logs and taped outside-of-class interactions as part of their data-collection plan. They asked students to keep think-aloud tapes, which they found to be "rich and varied" and to "reveal much about the affective conditions under which students work. They were, for example, distracted by personal problems, interrupted frequently by the phone or by roommates, worried about exams in other courses, or anxious about their writing ability. In addition they wrote when they were hungry, fascinated, tired, bored, or enthusiastic" (1990, 29). In short, this narrative shows you that allowing subjects to self-interview can sometimes have the unexpected benefit of telling more about their lives than you had thought to ask or hoped to find out.

You may gain your initial introduction to and overview of your interviewing choices by reviewing the terms used here to describe interviewing practices and by reading in greater depth about the issues and choices found in the work of authors I have cited. At a minimum, you should consider these:

- Structured or unstructured
- Formal or informal
- Documented by audiotaping or note taking, or both
- Comparative, representative, conversational, dialogic, interactive interviews
- Open-ended or close-ended questions
- Grand-tour questions (obtaining the participant's overview, sometimes via a literal physical tour)
- Demographic interviewing (gathering quantifiable data) or life-history interviewing, or oral-history interviewing
- Directive or nondirective
- Exploratory or confirming
- Individual or group interviews
- Nonverbal observation to accompany interview—silence and speech patterns, intonation and volume, body movements— "Looks, body postures, long silences, the way one dresses—all are significant in the interactional interview situation" (Fontana & Frey 1994, 371).

As in everything about the ethnographic approach, you have to consider all of these issues, alone and together, before, during, and after; that is, make and document your decisions and do your best to learn along the way.

What are the benefits and drawbacks of transcribing taped interviews yourself?

Because computer technologies are advancing rapidly, word processors continue to affect the writing process, and some software is available to help researchers code and analyze qualitative and naturalistic data:

> . . . I grew accustomed to putting data on 5 × 8 papers easily typed or handwritten, easily stored, and easily sorted. My little stacks of cards or papers may seem archaic in a computer age, but I describe them to help others visualize processes partially hidden by modern technology. I marvel at software programs like THE ETHNOGRAPH, QUALPRO, OR TEXT ANALYSIS PACKAGE (TAP) designed for data management with personal computers. . . . Keep in mind, however, that most programs are attuned better to the almost limitless capacities of microcomputers than to the finite capacities of human researchers.
>
> —Harry F. Wolcott 1990, 34

The anthropologist's notebook has been joined for some years in educational research by the ethnographic writing researcher's notebook computer and tape recorder; audiotape machines have shrunk in size while improving in quality. The ethnographer's bag now often contains a microcassette recorder, and the ethnographer's study is often furnished with a head-set and tape transcription machine, which helps a transcriber slow or replay the tape while typing a transcript. University researchers may transcribe their own tapes for accuracy (it's easier, usually, to get this result because the researcher knows or remembers the context of the interview), economy (especially true for students who research), and/or because transcribing can speed the analysis process by allowing the researcher to begin classifying and thematizing data and to make initial decisions about what needs to be textualized (how many tapes and to what extent).

This work is speeded along if you have kept accurate interview notes, labeling tapes, organizing them in files (indexing related field notes and copies of interview questions), and so on: that is, back to the blue crate, or as Harry Walcott suggests, a drop file. Walcott suggests that all writers write the report before researching it (that is, plan it out—imagine it, outline it, prepare a chapter outline of what you expect the report to look like; more on this suggestion in the next chapter). After this, you create a file for each chapter and store relevant materials there. If you foresee a case-analysis organization for your written report, you may choose to store data and interviews case by case. At a minimum, you'll file all materials chronologically after thoroughly labeling and memoing yourself about the contents of each interview and its connection to collected textual documents (class handouts, writings that informants share with you, and so on). Time spent this way, as well as time spent on transcribing, may save you *writing it up* time later.

Audiotaping, videotaping, transcribing, and copying mountains of data can push precariously leveraged graduate students into economic collapse. Particularly for first-time ethnographers, the impulse to record, transcribe, and copy everything is a sound one, but it comes when their economic support is often thinnest—at the end of years of study when monthly checks to the therapist are nearly matched by those to the transcriber. A single study can easily consume several thousand dollars of recording and transcribing, in addition to the cost of renting or buying recorders and transcribing machines.
—Mara Casey, Kate Garretson, Carol Peterson Haviland
& Neal Lerner 1997, 117

Without a doubt, research costs. However, if you have research funds, are running out of time, are working with co-researchers, or simply find you're not good at it and can talk someone else into trading work, having someone else transcribe your audiotapes can be a viable option. Expect them to hit patches of incomprehensible tape; expect them to ask you odd questions about what you are doing or were thinking. Make sure to have backup copies of your tapes in case this individual leaves the job more abruptly and less professionally than expected. Expect to be involved in their transcription process fairly actively to assure a good-quality transcription. Also, be sure to spot-check the transcriptions for accuracy and to set up your transcription conventions ahead of time so that the transcript manuscripts appear as you need them to appear. The best way to do this is to transcribe an initial number of tapes yourself so that you can predict some of the special issues your transcriber might encounter and can estimate how much time each transcription session might actually require. Also, be aware that poor-quality tapes and/or tapes of group sessions, in which different individuals need to be identified, will probably require your personal attention. Christian Knoeller explains:

Identifying the sequence of speakers in the field notes proved a crucial step when later transcribing the tapes, since it was necessary to distinguish from among twenty-five voices and often between overlapping turns. I personally transcribed and edited all transcriptions, since proper identifications of speakers was essential to the analysis. (1988, 45)

What are the textual conventions for representing taped conversations?

In practice the reporting of informants' talk is as dependent on textual convention as any other element of the text. Any and every method for rendering spoken language is found to be conventional. There is no such thing as a "natural" mechanism for the representation of speech. Orthography, punctuation, type-setting—these are all textual methods through which speech is reconstructed and rendered accessible to the knowledgeable reader. In fact, ethnographers have used a very wide range of styles to represent their data. Each has its effects on the reader. Each may be used—consciously or unconsciously—to convey different interpretative connotations. The different conventions may allow the author to construct informants in quite different ways.

—Paul Atkinson 1992, 23

Transcripts are always edited transcripts. Researchers, especially ethnographic researchers, decide how to frame the session and how to represent the discussion in printed form. If you look at Robert Brooke and John Hendricks's appendix of interviews for *Audience Expectations and Teacher Demands,* you'll notice that they used brackets for interpretive commentary—[General assent] or [laughter] or [long inaudible passage]; duration was indicated by (pause) and emphasis by underlining the word or phrase: " 'Or is Robert just <u>really good</u> at hiding what it is he wants?' the interviewer asks" (1989, 115). *Yeahs* and *um-hums* are included, yet sentences are punctuated for reading ease and everything is spelled correctly.

Interview transcripts range from the journalistically familiar question-and-answer reporting session to transcripts that indicate intonation levels and duration of pauses and silences, asides and interruptions, background sounds and activities, and so on. It may help to consider how one researcher reviewed transcripts before continuing on to discuss what needs to be represented in a text. Gesa Kirsch says,

The cycles of analysis consisted of listening to audio tapes repeatedly, reading transcripts, comparing transcripts and audio tapes, identifying thematic topics within and across interviews, comparing the identified

themes with another reader (usually the research assistant working
with me), and consulting with several participants about the importance they assigned to themes that were identified. (1993, 35)

In this instance, two or more individuals reviewed a reported 590
single-spaced pages of interview transcript. We can imagine—particularly because speaking volume and intonation or speech patterns didn't
matter as a focus of this study—that these were plain transcriptions.
And in fact, they are reported in the book as block quotes, rather than
in a Q & A format, marking either pauses or commentary that has been
elided, while certain words and phrases are italicized to indicate speaking emphasis. Elizabeth Chiseri-Strater makes it clear she is mainly interested, as was Gesa Kirsch, in what was said: "Since I am not a lin-
guist, I never intended to enter the territory of discourse analysis: I
never intended to count male/female turntaking in transcripts of group
work as I eventually did" (1991, 195). Still, she did eventually count
who spoke, how often, and in what order, but again, she had little need
for analyzing speech patterns or voice levels, as have some researchers.
Whichever method you choose, you'll want to explain your choices to
your readers.

> Most of the quoted passages in this manuscript are drawn from tran-
> scripts of recorded interviews with the five graduate students in my
> study. Although I have not tried to capture every nuance of these
> conversations—every pause, false start, interruption—I have tried to
> maintain the flavor of the spoken voices. In some cases passages have
> been edited to delete irrelevant or repetitious material, such places
> are marked by ellipses. Except for isolated instances where a word is
> italicized for emphasis, italics indicate passages excerpted from writ-
> ten texts.
>
> —Elizabeth Rankin 1994, vii

There is also an issue of fairness in representation. I've had teachers review transcripts and say, "I never knew I said 'uh' so often." While
I transcribed pauses by my own system, using different length ellipses
to roughly indicate pauses and to capture vocal hesitations and place-
fillers like "uh," I eventually took most of those out, leaving only a
flavor of speech and honoring the teacher's preference for being portrayed in conventional interview language. This can be particularly
important when there is—as there so often is—an authority differential. Unless dialect or pronunciation or timing is an element being
examined by the researcher, there is no reason not to default in an
interview transcript to an informal, but lightly edited presentation of
speech. Kim Haimes-Korn and Devan Cook—whose projects I review

in Chapter Two—were particularly concerned that they represent their first-generation college students and working-class students in a way that *rendered and respected* their speech patterns.

Those interested in specialized and detailed transcription practices will want to consult the research in this area in composition, particularly the work of cognitive writing researchers who have a literature on collecting think-aloud protocols of students who are trained to narrate their writing processes verbally as they are composing. And all of us will want to remember that consistency in applying transcription procedures leads readers to trust the way that we frame and report the interview event.

What role do you have in the interview?

What role(s) are you willing to offer to the interviewee?

The metaphor of a frame—what is included and what excluded by framing—allows us to see what is involved at every step of the textualization process. As we transcribe and textualize interviews, we become ever more involved in issues of representation. When we conduct a structured interview, we decide what can be asked and what can't; we frame the transcript even before we transcribe it. Even in informal and unstructured interviews, we are active de-limiters of this textual space, for without our convening the interview, most interviews would never have taken place. As with most other issues in qualitative research, a spectrum of positions are available and chosen and championed, from the near-clinical interviewer (imagine a job interview) who asks questions and volunteers little to the conversational, friendly, perhaps even overinvolved interviewer (imagine moving to the community and becoming best friends with the town gossip).

> The researcher, again, according to traditional techniques, should avoid getting involved in a "real" conversation in which he or she answers questions asked by the respondent or provides personal opinions on the matters discussed. One avoids "getting trapped" by shrugging off the relevance of one's opinions (e.g., "It doesn't matter how I feel, it's your opinion that's important") or by feigning ignorance (e.g., "I really don't know enough about this to say anything—you're the expert").
>
> —Andrea Fontana & James Frey 1994, 371

This traditional stance, as Fontana and Frey point out later in their discussion, has been challenged by feminists and by poststructuralists. It has long been a part of the anthropological tradition to learn by doing and interviewing: One learns how to construct a Navajo hogan by helping to do so and in the process asking questions about how the house-builder knows what he knows, why he does what he does, why the community chose an eight-sided structure, and so on. Educational ethnographers also learn by doing. Shirley Brice Heath collected data "while minding children, tending food, or watching television with the families" (1983, 19).

And researchers like Donna Sewell and Elizabeth Chiseri-Strater, who moved out of the classroom to study writing students' experiences with literacy over longer than single-term time periods, develop and evolve in their relationships. Sewell found herself invited to students' dorms to conduct interviews, and Chiseri-Strater says,

> Our relationship develops over time from that of researcher and student in an office setting with tape recorder whirring in the background, to friends and confidantes in a variety of encounters: I order books from her, many of them about art history or women's studies, at the local "alternative" bookstore where she works; we have tea and muffins or coffee and bagels—depending on our mood—after her avant-garde art class; or we walk along together after classes with her dripping ice cream cones. I write her letters of recommendations . . . I drive her to her apartment in a spring thunderstorm. . . . (1991, 34)

Not only does a mix of roles take place, but it is reported. Sewell, Chiseri-Strater, and others are offering us, as readers of their texts, the option of deciding how to read the materials they have framed for us. We will want to evaluate our response to these stances, which actually take place on a spectrum of involvement: disinterested to interested interviewers, cooperative to disengaged informants. We also have to ask ourselves, as many of these researchers encourage us to do, about the relationships as portrayed. It is not just research report interpretations to which our informants may take exception; they may also object to the initial framing and portrayals of themselves as found in interview transcripts and early analyses.

Brenda Brueggemann finds that "there was no way by the end of my fieldwork that I felt I could neatly separate out my personal and professional roles and feelings, or my positions as participant and observer. I had come to claim what Donna Harraway calls 'feminist accountability' and 'feminist science' that which 'requires a knowledge tuned to resonance, not to dichotomy'" (1996, 31). And, although rarely reported, role conflicts can result in respondents who feel . . . well . . . *framed* in a negative sense of the word: "At least two informants were confronted with 'bad news' in the narrative, and their reactions indicated that my representations of them may have been problematic"

(1996, 46), says Cheri Williams. Hers is a rare report that admirably ex-amines some of these ethical problems in more detail.

The current turn is toward participative research when possible—wherein interviewer and interviewee consult and collaborate on inter-view directions and reports—and toward autoethnography, which pro-duces a "text in which people undertake to describe themselves in ways that engage with the representations others have made of them" (Pratt 1991, 35).

Constructing Surveys and Questionnaires

How have you developed and tested your survey questions (do they ask what you think they ask)?

I'm going to move lightly in this section for two reasons. First, most of us are survivors of surveys; we are regularly asked to fill out forms, providing baseline demographic data for employers and schools, for marketing or political surveyors. We know some of the demo-graphic categories by heart or can find them readily on the website of the U.S. Census Bureau. Second, the advice I have given earlier on con-structing interview questions is in general what I would suggest for surveys as well. And third, unless you have qualified through a statis-tics course, which I haven't, and define your research as more quanti-tatively and less phenomenologically based than I have been doing throughout this book, you will not be using standardized instruments and conducting statistical analyses of survey data. You will be using questionnaires to get acquainted with a culture, population, or person. You will be using them for broad comparative purposes or to "set the scene." You will be analyzing them for recurring themes or focusing on a particular response category and creating a chart, showing a range of answers, or you will be undertaking informal coding procedures.

I say all this with quite a bit of respect for the way a survey can help you gain a needed distance from a community, especially one you may know too well to see clearly; for instance, surveying an entire first-year writing staff will show you all is not what you might assume it is from the vantage point of being a member of or director of that staff. A sur-vey can also help establish rapport with a class or group. Although sur-veys can save you certain types of data-gathering time, they can also mislead you. You may find yourself compiling contradictory informa-tion—if the survey is poorly constructed—or you can alienate a popu-lation when your time would have been better spent establishing con-versational rapport without such an "authoritative" calling card. So, some basic advice, briefly.

Keep it short. And adjust your survey to your culture. Young children will need to be surveyed using fewer questions and an accessible vocabulary. Any individual needs clear directions and needs to be asked to complete a limited document in a reasonable amount of time. How a survey is presented can vastly affect responses, especially to open-ended questions. Asking a harried teacher to survey his students, providing him with confusing directions and a survey that takes too long or that he finds ludicrous or impossible to explain when asked about by students—well, you see the problems. It's best if you can administer the survey yourself. It's best if you can collect the results immediately. Surveys taken home often fail to rematerialize, especially if they seem long to respondents (one page, back and front, is always more welcome than many pages stapled together). If surveys need to be handed out and collected later, be prepared to follow up; be prepared with spare surveys to replace lost ones; be prepared to be promised returns of forms that never arrive. Be prepared to tap into some cultural frustration at feeling oversurveyed.

All that said, you will still encounter individuals who appreciate the chance to think over and construct their answers, as well as teachers who will be glad to offer you the first or last portion of a class for your purposes and who will encourage their students to support your work and/or will support it themselves by offering you all the information you need.

How do you know what you need? Construct the survey and try it out. Look for another, similar culture and try out (field-test) the survey. You might do this with members of a research methods class, or you may be able to ask fellow thesis or dissertation writers to help you revise your survey questions and try them out. Answer your own survey, timing yourself to see how demanding it is. Attempt an initial analysis to see if you can reduce the data you collect in a meaningful way; if you can't, don't collect it. If even you tire of the questions, reduce the number; and if your friends start to argue with you about what exactly you mean when you phrase a question that way, simplify it, create a better question, or drop the question. Overall, you don't want your subjects to be asked to be taken off your list for further surveys; if they don't, you've succeeded far better than the phone solicitors who phone my house far too often.

Are you using any standardized materials? Why and how?

Are you designing your own? How and why?

I can't vouch for all novice researchers, but I read research to help me design my materials. Because I wanted to consider teachers' attitude changes, I looked to similar studies—the few I could find—and looked at the surveys they used and with what results. I saved time by going where others had gone before, particularly as I was moving from a quantitatively based research orientation to a qualitative orientation. I was not intending to run (and didn't) reliability tests on individual questions or attempt to norm and validate a survey instrument; but I learned, as you will no doubt learn along the way or already may know, about the vast resources available in the world of sociological research and recent composition research.

I found and used the Daly–Miller Measure of Writing Apprehension (1975), and I found even more useful B.M. Thompson's 1979 research report questionnaire, listed in the appendix of *A Theory of Teacher Change Developed from Teachers of Writing*. Reading it helped me design a survey and develop interview questions of my own.

My professors directed me to the journal *Research in the Teaching of English* to see how other researchers used and reported surveys, and in doing so I learned about collections such as Fagan, Jensen, and Cooper's 1985 *Measures for Research and Evaluation in the English Language Arts* in my own field. This book led me to other resources in education and sociology. You may find yourself interested in and/or required to follow the same sort of route. You may find it useful to consult with a colleague in another department, to take a quantitative research methods course, or to learn how to run basic computer statistical analysis packages. You may take these routes, unless you move, as I have moved and as I've seen composition writing research move, toward a more holistic, context-based, observation-based, postmodern theory–based, naturalistic paradigm, in which your research questions, in general, drive the survey and questionnaire construction, as they have in most of the projects I report on in this book.

Coding, Data Reduction, and Data Displays

Charts and diagrams offer other ways to give our thoughts embodiment. They invite us to sort and categorize data, to explore what goes with what, and to contemplate how seemingly discrete data may be linked in previously unrecognized ways. Researchers who think spatially work through their charts and diagrams in order literally to "see" their studies before them, whereas most of us are constrained by the regimented vision of prose. Some qualitative researchers conceptualize and work systematically through their studies with huge charts and diagrams drawn on inexpensive newsprint spread across their walls or floors.

—Harry Wolcott 1990, 63–64

Our mantra here is data reduction, data reduction. But data reduction is for a purpose. Michael Huberman and Matthew Miles explain that data analysis and management result from three linked processes: data reduction, data display, and conclusion drawing/verification (1994, 428–29). We follow this process to learn what we know before we show what we know. Of course, researchers actually use these processes—outlining and overviewing, coding and reducing, collecting and connecting—throughout the length of a study, from inception to presentation.

I remember still sharing my initial ideas for my dissertation with Don McAndrew, who listened carefully, for a while, then swept me into a classroom next door to his office and attacked the chalkboard, drawing a diagram as we talked. We continued to modify the diagram, to talk, to draw. And before I left that day, I had a "picture" that turned out to be surprisingly true to the study I eventually undertook. I carefully copied our final diagram into my notebook and, bouncing a little with excitement, left the department building. A humanities-trained reader, it still took me some time to learn the value of sketching, of amplifying narration with charts and figures. Once I learned to stop assuming that all data displays had to have numbers and realized that they could help me think through and visualize and then better re-describe a problem, I started using them in my own work.

Even more, I found myself begging dissertation writers to help me understand the "forest" of their drafts by drawing a summary, here and there, and then there again. I remember Kim Haimes-Korn coming into my office one day in triumph, saying, "Wendy, I brought you a diagram," and that became a code-joke between us to let me know she had worked hard to condense data into a more reader-friendly form. Along the way, she too became convinced that data summary charts could help her and her readers understand data. At the least, charting out types and varieties of responses can save you narration time, and increase your trustworthiness, as readers are allowed to look over your shoulder, so to speak, as you reduce your data and prepare an interpretation. Also, as Wolcott (1990) points out, material laid out in order in charts allows you to make sense from a seemingly senseless barrage of detail. It works.

I should have realized it would be this way (although if I had, I might have faltered before the project), but writing this textbook has been much like writing a dissertation. I have collected voices of other researchers; I have pre- and postoutlined. I have amassed more data than I can use, and I have constructed drawings and charts and literally littered the house with books, papers, photocopies, and reminder notes to myself as I draft. When I want to review interview questions, I make lists of types of interviews. Then, like an ethnographic writing researcher, I continue.

Will you code your interviews, surveys, and/or questionnaire?

> Why code data? One explanation might be that division and classifi-
> cation are strategies people commonly use to organize their experience
> of the world. On the other hand, the impulse to divide and classify is
> not shared equally by all cultures. Sondra Perl (*Coding the Composing
> Process*) argues that using a coding system allows the researcher to de-
> pict what writers are doing from the moment to moment as they
> write, and coding the composing process in this way avoids having to
> rely on the retrospective accounts of the writers themselves, accounts
> that might be subjective, short and inaccurate.
>   —Keith Grant-Davie 1992, 272

Coding your data to look for emergent themes is one way to protect yourself from some (but never all) of the frailties of memory and
biased assumptions. Analytic coding procedures are used more regularly in quantitative projects and are not rigorously required or applied
in most qualitative projects. We heard Elizabeth Chiseri-Strater explain
that she eventually counted and analyzed turn taking in interview
transcripts, but she does not display these counts in her text. And Gesa
Kirsch described reading and rereading her transcripts looking for
themes. According to Devan Cook,

>   Data are—raw material to be studied. Coding is—
> dividing and classifying data, but there's no such
> thing as raw, and selection of data implies some
> prior category. In Sandra's classroom, I write down
> what interests me. Dividing and classifying are in-
> terpretations: reading, making meaning. Validity and
> reliability are problematic concepts; therefore,
> coding can help us read but perhaps not interpret in
> the way other than any reading does or can. For
> example: transcription of syntactic, episodic, or
> functional units? To what purpose? Are our codes
> adequate to our data? Reliability and objectivity
> are two will o' the wisps: one does not imply the
> other.
>   Appendices with examples can provide a kind of
> polyvocality, perhaps a place to show where inter-
> pretations come from and where the data being read
> have been pre-read to even be selected for reading.

As Devan points out, researchers now include this data as appendix
material that shows the researcher's analysis decisions.

In *Voicing Ourselves*, Christian Knoeller takes a more formal approach
to coding and data analysis because it is the best way to approach his

study questions. He wants to identify voicing in student discussions of literature; by *voicing*, he means the ways students used the discussions of others in their discussions. He explains his coding: "I first identified voicing during discussions and coded transcripts of classroom discourse accordingly. I define voicing as any part of an utterance, whether or not explicitly marked, that is attributed (or directly attributable) to someone other than the present speaker" (1998, 47). He continues for some pages to describe and defend his units of analysis and his coding process, which included creating a category system of four levels of coding and then verifying that coding: "Inter-reader reliability procedures were performed to ensure the integrity of the coding system. After I had coded transcripts of all eight student-led discussions, a second reader coded two randomly selected transcripts, that is, 25 percent of the student-led discussions" (1998, 57–58). Coded discussions are then presented in table form and displayed throughout his report.

In some cases, the material may not turn up in your main research report but may lead to a separate article, as a coded analysis of group journals did for me. I used my detailed analysis to help me better understand the five case-study teachers in my main report.

> To better understand teachers' log *response types* and *subjects,* I coded thirteen learning logs which ranged from 25 handwritten pages to 105 handwritten pages. . . . To analyze and draw conclusions from this wealth of data, I focussed on three, three member learning log groups and the nine logs they compiled and shared. I chose to code the logs myself following the practice described by Lucille McCarthy in her study "A Stranger in a Strange Lands: A College Student Writing Across the Curriculum." McCarthy used her knowledge of the writers' context to analyze data, looking for "confirmability" with other naturalistic data rather than agreement among raters (241). Equally, in the case of this project, codes were intended to provide a general analysis of teachers' writing by response type and subject . . . analysis confirmed my observational impressions that not only did individual teachers have a priority of concerns when entering learning log responses but also that groups developed particular response focuses and ways of discussing the pedagogy seminar.
>
> Overall, in *type of response* categories, log writers spent the majority of their time: RECORDing, RESPONDing, or QUESTIONing material.
>
> Overall, for *subjects of response* categories, log writers focussed on seminar READINGS, TEACHING, or themselves—SELF-ANALYSIS.
>
> Often these focuses were somewhat exclusive. . . . The log analysis, then, yielded a rude thumbprint of the log writer's interests or what Norman Holland calls an "identity theme." Three models of entries developed: 1) those in which the log writer focused on seminar issues and readings; 2) those in which the log writer focussed on a his/her own teaching, home institution, or general feelings about the

teaching profession; and 3) those in which the log writer shared entries across several subjects, usually reading, teaching and the individual. (Bishop 1991, 218)

Although the journal coding I conducted and reported on in this journal essay did not appear in my dissertation-turned-monograph, *Something Old, Something New*, I did provide a sample of and discussion of my log coding and analysis in the book's appendix (1990a, 155–58), because these learning logs greatly influenced my discussions throughout both the dissertation and the book.

I was interested at this point in how teachers' discussions seemed to echo, amplify, and support each other's learning, so I "divided learning logs into T-units and coded them with a set of codes developed from the [teacher's] instructions given to the participants" (1990a, 155). I continued on in this discussion to explain T-units, to defend solo coding (based on the example of another research study conducted by Lucille McCarthy), and then shared my codes and a sample coded log. And, although tables from those coding sessions appear in the essay and the dissertation but not in the monograph, I provided an audit trail so that someone curious about the coding could move from the book to the dissertation for charts and further discussions.

In my language and Knoeller's language, you will hear the influence of social science research: integrity of coding, interreader reliability, sample coded log, coding session, T-unit, participants, audit trail. This assumption of proof is giving way in ethnographic writing research to an understanding that reporting analysis this way is primarily a rhetorical convention; both types of reports present a plausible interpretation to a reading community of peers. A careful reading and note taking and rereading of transcripts, such as that reported by Gesa Kirsch, is no less useful or meaningful than my numerical tabulations and is often much more accessible to readers.

> [Context-sensitive text analysis] relies openly on *plausible interpretation* rather than on any kind of proof. Given its ambitious scope, context-sensitive text analysis cannot possibly be a highly formalized and testable scientific endeavor. It cannot control for all possible variables and it cannot insist on any one interpretation of findings. It can only try to assemble enough evidence to make a strong case for a certain point of view.
>
> —Thomas N. Huckin 1992, 89

The context-sensitive researcher is more likely to analyze in order to render, and this ability often results from researcher experience and intuition. Reporting on her dissertation study in Judith Meloy's *Writing the Qualitative Dissertation* (1994), Helen Rolfe observes, "I suppose the process of analysis I used should be called intuitive; it was certainly not mechanical. Although throughout the study there were strong indications of themes within and across sites, the process remained a mystery, revealed only as it happens" (66). Although Rolfe claims mystery, I think she was following recognizable research procedures, for she immediately reports further: "I constantly read and reread notes and interviews to steep myself in the information" (66). Coding and charting can help the less intuitive or the researcher with a less categorizing type of mind (or simply a less flexible memory) to find the themes that Rolfe found surfacing as she read and reread (and we can imagine she did this by reading actively—making notes, memoing herself, and so on).

> Even those researchers who claim to account for the context must disregard or decline to report most of what they record. So the issue is not who strips and who doesn't strip but how each strips to create accounts, narratives that gain the assent of readers. The issue is not which is more Real, but how each creates, through selection and ordering of detail, an illusion or version of Reality. The issue is not one primarily of methodology and objectivity, but of authoring and the cultural values embedded in various narrative plots.
> —Thomas Newkirk 1992, 133

To code or not to code? Your decision once again rests on your research goals and energies for moving from notes, summary sheets, and memos to more regularized analysis, which can include the following (this list compiles suggestions from Huberman & Miles 1994, 430; Goetz & LeCompte 1984, 172; and my own experiences):

- Noting patterns and themes
- Clustering by conceptual groupings
- Making metaphors
- Counting
- Speculating
- Making contrasts and comparisons
- Establishing linkages and relationships
- Shuttling between data and larger categories
- Noting relationships

Well then, why doesn't everyone code? First, it is time consuming. Second, it is unclear how highly variable, context-dependent materials, textualized or not, should best be coded and displayed. Third, if the human mind of the ethnographer is the main instrument for analysis, it makes sense that that instrument should be "fed" data in the way that best suits it. Some of us, as analysts, thrive on numbers, some on words. Some of us are good at making sense via metaphor, and some require spatial analysis opportunities. I know, for myself, that it can be over-whelming to analyze even the most basic of open-ended survey ques-tions. While we are all familiar with demographic presentations—"50% were male and 50% were female," "30% were second-generation col-lege students and 70% were not"—it is harder to make sense of even sixteen answers to a question like, "When did you decide to become a writing teacher and why? To understand those answers, I was able to group them into statements in a cell of a summary table (Bishop 1989, 561) in this manner: "to correct poor teaching in my own past history"; "to teach lit. but realized comp. skill more impt."; "did not decide, was part of my job"; "enjoyed or was a TA." Once summarized, I could scan these statements immediately to get a sense of why students were en-rolled in the class I was studying. I could also return to a one-page sum-mary later in my analysis to describe the teachers' antecedents and rea-soning if I needed to. Often I did, and I could do this without opening up a drop file containing sixteen, three-page surveys of raw data. Even-tually, I reduced those surveys to this single paragraph. The process shows the strengths and weaknesses of data reduction—eventually data can be reduced to near nonsignificance:

> The average, summer 1987, doctoral program participant was return-ing to academic degree work. Most often, she was an employed teacher with an M.A. degree who had not been pursuing graduate level stud-ies during the last three to twenty years. Approximately 80%–90% of the participants taught at the pre-college or college level or worked as administrators. All had completed M.A. degrees at other institutions, often in English with a literature emphasis. Many extended this pro-gram due to the *summers only* option which allowed them to remain employees while working on a higher degree. (Bishop 1989, 84)

What this average portrait hides, of course, is the male, unemployed, academic-year student who did not have a literature M.A. And there was one such participant.

> Coding systems help us read data, but they do not interpret for us.
> —Keith Grant-Davie 1992, 285

Coding may be less crucial or even less useful for microethnogra-phies than for macroethnographies. Those conducting large-scale proj-ects with multiple researchers may code and share matrix displays of data because they have the resources (interreader reliability takes more than one reader, for example), but also because analyzing data from multiple sites via agreed upon practices (and coding) can lend cohesion to the discussions and, hopefully, to the results. Individuals who intend to code and in other ways formally analyze data will want to consult other resources. The essay from Keith Grant-Davie, from which I quote here, is a necessary first stop.

> It appears that, to be credible, a coding system should be shown capable of working to some extent mechanically and predictably, independent of its creator. If proven reliable, a coding system acquires added authority, the implication being that it describes, rather than interprets, what is in the data. A high reliability rating thus suppresses the subjective, interpretive nature of coding and endows the system with the appearance of impartiality, making it seem a "true," more "scientific" instrument of analysis. . . . What reliability tests really do when they yield high rates of agreement is show that the researchers have successfully created a small, specialized community of readers who have been "normed," or trained to interpret the data in the same way. This kind of reliability does at least demonstrate that the coding system was applied to the data consistently within that community.
> —Keith Grant-Davie 1992, 282–83

Sharing Data with Informants

Will the person interviewed be reviewing the transcripts?

> To the charges that the researcher brings her own biases, qualitative feminist researchers would reply that bias is a misplaced term. To the contrary, these are resources and, if the researcher is sufficiently reflexive about her project, she can evoke these as resources to guide data gathering or creating and for understanding her own interpretations and behavior in the research. . . .
> —Virginia Olesen 1994, 165

Most of us would agree that the ideal ethnography would be one in which we can continuously reground our observations with the help of those we study. We also quickly realize, as ethnographic writing researchers who often work within institutional settings, that the scope for doing so is limited. That shouldn't, of course, keep us from trying. The longer our study and the more interactive (the more we participate rather than observe) and the more we are able to stay in touch with informants and community members after the initial phase of the study ends, the more we can reground our impressions, collect and correct our vision, and speak to and with the community about what we found there. This is the *ideal* scenario, but often it remains difficult to reduce the distance between researcher and researched, subject and object, seeker and the one sought, listener and speaker.

> When we construct texts collaboratively, self-consciously examining our relations with/for/despite those who have been contained as Others, we move against, we enable resistance to, Othering.
> —Michelle Fine 1994, 74

First, we often don't have much time, as our cultures evolve and dissolve, sometimes at the convenience of the university registrar, the needs of a worker to leave the workplace, or the disbanding of a literacy site when a project we are studying is shut down. Second, sometimes our informants flat-out aren't interested, as in the example in Chapter Three, in which Sandra Teichmann offered a student a report, which—somewhat to her dismay—he returned unread, not because he was upset with her representation of him but because he simply wasn't very interested. Sometimes informants will do us the favor of sharing their insights; you'll recall my earlier observation that many people are flattered by the invitation to be interviewed; however, our outcomes are of very little use or interest to many others. It's the same lesson some of us have to learn as teachers: Students loom large in our lives, but we often move like vague ghosts through theirs.

> Foucault invites researchers to explore the ways in which discourses are implicated in relations of power and how power and knowledge serve as dialectically reinitiating practices that regulate what is considered reasonable and true.
> —Joe L. Kincheloe & Peter L. McLaren 1994, 140

> Gayatri Chakravorty Spivak (1988) contends that academics/researchers can do little to correct the "material wrongs of colonialism." . . . Like bell hooks and Joan Scott, Spivak asks that researchers stop trying to know the Other or give voice to the Other (Scott, 1991) and listen, instead, to the plural voices of those Othered, as coconstructors and agents of knowledge.
> —Michelle Fine 1995, 75

So, as ethical discussions and postmodern theories of feminist collaboration and efforts to reduce subjective–objective polarities push us toward sharing and disclosure, practicality and actuality often keep us from doing so. That we try is important, how we try is important, and that we communicate our efforts and reports of such efforts is also important.

Just as I've said that sometimes what we try to share doesn't matter, I need to suggest how much it also *can* matter. Following are two stories that illustrate this point.

One of the teachers in my dissertation study seemed an unlikely candidate for a case-study follow-up project. Her journal entries led me to understand that she felt she already "knew" what was being covered in her teacher-education course; she was not likely to change her pedagogy as a result of the seminar I was observing, because she felt that the change had already taken place. I had trouble—I felt—finding out what she thought: Her answers often seemed evasive or self-serving. Six months after I finished data collection, she sent me a letter to my home address (which I had provided to all of the teachers in the class, asking them to contact me if they thought of anything they wanted to share). Her letter confirmed my reading of her journals; in it, she said that, thinking back on our interviews and her first term of teaching since I had seen her, she realized she had been less than frank in her responses to interviews and generally unreceptive to the summer course and now regretted that. I included her letter in the appendix material to my dissertation. I included her story to show how much we can sense but not know about informants. And then there was another story—this one, less satisfying.

As I completed my dissertation, I sent the chapters I had constructed to each case-study teacher as I was flying from Fairbanks, Alaska, where I lived, to Indiana, Pennsylvania, where I had studied, to defend my dissertation. When I returned home, I found a letter from one of the teachers; she had written to me immediately and told me that she had learned a great deal from the portrait I had composed of her learning and teaching.

Four teachers had not contacted me by the time I had filed the final draft. However, I did not contact those nonresponding case-study teachers again. I was rushed. I had sent them chapters. And I think now I was somewhat afraid. One case in particular seemed fairly unflattering. I was not surprised that the first teacher had written to me, for she was the teacher who responded most strongly and positively to the pedagogy I was studying; she was the teacher who exhibited the most change in a study looking at change. The teacher, in my researcher's opinion, who changed least, as you can pretty much guess, was the teacher who claimed in interviews that he was transformed and enlivened—a claim I did not find supported by the data I collected and analyzed.

In "Seduction and Betrayal in Qualitative Research," Thomas Newkirk explores this issue: "Because we present ourselves as completely well-meaning [when gaining access, proffering consent forms], we find ourselves in moral difficulty when we write 'bad news' in our final rendering" (1996, 3). Reader, I confess, I was somewhat less aware of it at that time, but I'm now fully aware that I did not call this latter case-study teacher to talk it over because I was mired in the dilemma of being a bearer of bad news.

Would I do things differently now? Probably. But I would also design the entire study somewhat differently at various decision points, and this was a major one. At the same time, I also didn't then realize that two other case-study teachers felt disturbed by their portraits: One told a mutual friend a year or more later that she didn't know she would sound that way in print. Two years after the study, when the book-length version was in circulation, a second case-study teacher told a mutual friend that she felt misrepresented to a degree. She didn't believe I had fully understood her classroom. And, indeed, I had only "studied" it via phone interviews, print artifacts, and one very homemade classroom video. I've since talked comfortably with this teacher about general teaching issues, but we have never really addressed that told-to-a-friend confidence, which was also told back to me in confidence. If this sounds more like social negotiations and gossip, it probably is. Still, I would do things differently, now, ten years later.

Now, a final tale: I have had a classroom mini-ethnography cause consternation to a colleague who had allowed one of my students to study him. Consent forms were signed. Classroom reports were drafted and commented on and shared: novice work, much learning. The teacher who was portrayed in the classroom study was—with some reason—much dismayed to read his portrait. I was able to assure him that the student had no intention of publishing that work. (He didn't, particularly after talking to the teacher, whose work he actually admired no matter how his report played out, and he had even less intention of doing so when he realized his informant was upset.) The professor, the student, and I (as director of mini-ethnographies) learned a great deal that term.

You may not be surprised to learn that several books that raise and consider these delicate issues have been published recently by composition presses. Writing research ethnographers are not paparazzi, nor are they pith-helmeted explorers. But they are part of a world that has made cultural capital in providing us with stereotypical images of journalists and anthropologists, with such a resulting trickle-down effect that you'll need to explain what it is you do and try to interrogate your own assumptions about these pursuits. I end this chapter by suggesting that the following quotes might function as koans—meditation pieces— for those considering the relationship(s) they hope to have with members of the communities they enter. These authors provide some vo-cabulary for undertaking thinking in this area: active co-participation, researcher and subject reflexivity, the creation of a vocabulary of under-standing, critical narratives, action research, liberatory social research.

> For example, Gergen and Gergen (1991) sketch an interactive ap-proach to inquiry called the "reflexive elaboration of the event," in which the researcher and participants open a sociopsychological phe-nomenon to inspection and through dialogue generate a process of continuous reflexivity, thereby "enabling new forms of linguistic real-ity to emerge" (p. 88). The overall aim of this approach is "to expand and enrich the vocabulary of understanding."
>   —Thomas Schwandt 1994, 128

> The project at hand is to unravel, critically, the blurred boundaries in our relation, and in our texts; to understand the political work of our narratives; to decipher how the traditions of social science serve to inscribe; and to imagine how our practice can be transformed to resist, self-consciously, acts of othering. As these scenes of transla-tion vividly convey, qualitative researchers are chronically and uncom-fortably engaged in ethical decisions about how deeply to work with/for/despite those cast as Others, and how seamlessly to represent the hyphen. Our work will never—arrive—but must always struggle—between.
>   —Michelle Fine 1994, 75

Personally, while I aim for ethical decision making in my own proj-ects, I've also been there, in that uneasy space where good intentions have gone awry or been misconstrued. These issues will return in the next chapter as I talk about how you might talk about what you saw and what you understood in the field from the safe haven of the writing desk. Clearly, more than good intentions are required. Equally clearly, ethical paralysis would keep you from ever arriving in the field site of your work.

You might think of the wry truism, "You are what you eat," right about now. We are, as researchers, the sum of the many ethical or un-ethical decisions we make along the research trail. We are trustworthy if we strive to choose the best course as we understand it. Sharing our work with our informants as often as is feasible and as interactively as possible will not only enrich our cultural understanding, involve us in triangulation as process, but also allow our readers to know what we did and why it worked out that way—which is also the subject of the next chapter.

Chapter Five

Writing It Up

> The ethnography is uniquely shaped by the sensibilities and style of its individual author. The ethnographer is, we know, the "research instrument" par excellence. The fieldwork is the product of a personal and biographical experience. Moreover, the text in which that fieldwork is finally (or provisionally) reconstituted is an authored work. Inevitably, it reflects the "literary" style of the individual sociologist or anthropologist.
>
> —Paul Atkinson 1992, 29

In some ways, the subheadings for this chapter could be stated quite telegraphically:

- Deciding what to write
- Deciding how to write it
- Deciding when it is sufficiently well written

As if it were that simple, but of course, it's not. Returning to Donna Sewell's researcher's notes allows us to see that these three issues become increasingly urgent within weeks of data collection. Even when she is well launched (research plan in hand, actively participating and observing) and thinking already about some day ending, Donna finds that certain data won't be available for weeks, that a brochure she expected to provide her baseline data doesn't exist, that her field notes are getting cumbersome, and that the students in her study don't seem to be completing the self-audits of their writing as she had asked them to do.

She determines that she needs to begin "writing it up" by composing initial character sketches that will help her retain and organize the sense she has of these students for later narrations. She already feels time pressures: The six-week course, her field site, has only three more weeks to run, so she wonders about her chances of confirming the character sketches with students to see if they agree with the way she is representing them.

```
Week 3
Problem Areas
```

1. Office of Admissions claims no data compiled on early-admission first-year students, must wait to check students against fall admissions data

2. No separate brochures on Landis Hall—the summer dorm for first-year students

3. Need to rethink field notes; they're bogging me down

4. Need to rethink [students'] writing logs
   Focus for next week

5. Check on obtaining background information on these students (SAT scores, high school GPA, etc.)

6. Develop character sketches in progress of three students

7. Obtain course descriptions and syllabi for students' other summer courses

8. Obtain permission from Thom [course instructor] and students to keep their portfolios and journals

9. Memo students about writing logs

```
Dear Wendy
```

1. What about having students read the character sketches before they leave for the summer? Isn't that a case of testing research against participants in the field?

2. What other areas should be addressed in interviews this six weeks?

One Eye to the Future: General Writing Issues

One does not expect all one's notes to appear, of course, but in principle one recognizes that they will not remain entirely private documents. I suspect that many fieldworkers have found themselves thinking something like "These notes will make a great example," or "I can use this incident to make a good story one day," or "This will go into my autobiographical confessional in due course." I know that I have sustained myself through the drudgery of fieldnote writing with consolations of that sort.

—Paul Atkinson 1992, 20

Starting, Stopping, Finding Time, Space and Support

Let's be honest (as Paul Atkinson just was). We're all looking toward the end, the payoff, the final product. We just don't know at this point how to get there. Why, if we did—because there is a wonderful sense of completion and accomplishment in the heft of a finished research report—we'd already be there.

Some of us delay getting going because we'd like to have written already, and some of us hesitate before we plunge in, from a general fear of starting. Others of us like getting into the water but get lost on the way back because we are uncertain of where we should or could come to shore. Still, we daydream the end and we work toward it: The knowledge that we will leave the field, finish the project, reap the rewards (and they are multiple) of our endeavors is part of what gets us through our sometimes tedious work. "Although she enjoyed her field work, as she faced her 32 binders of data day after day, Mara often felt as though she were trying to turn straw into gold, with no Rumplestiltskin around to ease her isolation" (Casey et al. 1997, 124).

New researchers may feel isolated every time they sit down to write it up, for no one can tell you precisely what to look for or how to know you have found it. One researcher's anecdote of sense making can look like so much nonsense to someone new to the data-reduction game or to someone without the researcher's access to the scene—that is, at times, to almost everyone else:

```
How do you know exactly what to look for in your
data? What does it mean to [Donna] Sewell that stu-
dents spend fifteen minutes a week making lists, two
hours writing letters, and thirty minutes doodling?
What kind of conclusion can she draw from that data?
I guess my real question is, will I know what I'm
```

> looking for when I study my own data for my own mini-
> ethnography? . . . Maybe when you read over your
> data, you just kind of know what is relevant. Or
> maybe it all kind of connects in your mind, and you
> can see a pattern or trend. Or maybe you have to de-
> cide what exactly indicates what before you study the
> data, although this seems less naturalistic and more
> experimental in approach—like proving a hypothesis
> instead of having questions and coming to a better
> understanding of something.

Although she doesn't realize it at this point, Ellen Schendel is already a careful reader, which is what, after all, a data analyst is. Ellen has guessed that researchers probably follow lines of interest or they wouldn't be researching at all. If this impulse is justified in launching them on a long-term project, it is justified, I believe, in helping them through their data analysis.

Sometimes it is not confusion that stops us from starting, however, but an unwillingness to embark on the journey:

> We can't do data reduction confessions [as asked
> for in a methods class]: the fact is that we're not
> there yet. I'm still flipping lenses, trying to find a
> pair to work in. We [the co-researchers] still have
> journals to code, transcripts to curl up with, "one
> more time" read-throughs, conversations and negotia-
> tions. Since to some extent the recorded data has been
> selected accidentally (we can't understand the tape)
> or randomly (I'll write down whatever I can, my hand
> moving as fast as it can, but somehow I select ac-
> cording to the things I ordinarily am interested in,
> too . . .), I feel like I've been through the hopper
> of data reduction once, and I'm not ready to re-hop.
> —Devan Cook

While I don't want to sound only discouraging notes, I share these generally-not-shared new researchers' observations here because it can help you continue on sometimes to realize that you're not actually alone, trying to turn straw into gold without notice or support. Feelings of confusion and aversion are part of the process just as excitement and enthusiasm and intellectual expansion are also a measure of the ethnographer's experiences.

Ironically, once started, it can be hard to stop writing. I can attest to this (and to the fact that endless drafts do indeed test a dissertation chair's patience) from the experience of having composed a 636-manuscript-page dissertation. Immediately after "getting done," I convinced myself to undertake a massive and sometimes painful "weight-reduction" plan that was required in order to fit this material to the requirements of a monograph series proposal, resulting in a slimmed down, far more readable 167-page published report. And the summarizing continued. Eventually, at one conference, when two colleagues and I were mistakenly given ten-minute spots on a research forum to report on individual book-length projects, I learned how to reduce my report to three minutes of explanation with the aid of a one-page summary chart of my five case studies (see Figure 3 on page 130).

But the report does not always get reduced (though it often moves in that direction). In fact, you don't dare forget that the dissertation or book-length report requires a certain type of textual support (usually in the form of appendices; enough, but not too many) to show that the novice (or even the expert) has undertaken the approach in a trustworthy manner, to provide an audit trail *or the sense that a trail exists.* Text gain and text reduction are often undertaken as you work to fit the publishing requirements of the field, requirements that were often developed for the more svelte quantitative research report, with its stylized reporting conventions that point to the common assumptions on the parts of readers and writers of those reports (more on these issues in the next chapter).

In ethnographic writing research, conventions are far from fixed, and our reports sometimes fit very uneasily into the space of the twenty-page journal essay or twenty-minute conference presentation slot. In fact, I continued to use sections of my original data later, adding and subtracting, shaping and reshaping them in order to submit portions of the project as journal articles: subsections on teachers' classroom metaphors, teachers' learning logs, and teachers' goals for continuing their education.

Harry Wolcott suggests that we write up the project before we even begin. The prospectus is certainly part of this prewriting process and, as the grant application or complete research plan, functions in a similar manner for the experienced researcher: *"Write a preliminary draft of the study. Then begin the research.* I did not say to show the draft to anyone, but I earnestly believe you cannot begin writing too early" (Wolcott 1990, 22). A prospectus has already required that you plot and assume, explore and anticipate, and consider not only findings, but also likely forms and formats for sharing those findings.

Wolcott also suggests that you draft a *detailed* proposed table of contents—either before you begin to collect data or as you begin to analyze it (or both). Ethnographic reports—just like ethnographic methods texts—lean toward the unwieldy even as your proposed reader will be hoping for a report that is succinct and convincing. Nevertheless, thick-description and professional data collection lead us anywhere but toward succinct. Continuous outlining can help. For instance, my out-lines for any book-length project are copious: I choose and abandon structures and organizational patterns; I pick metaphors to help guide me and my readers, find that they don't or that they overdetermine di-rections, and so look for and find others that work better, and continue on. There is a lot of fussing involved in getting it right, and outlines help organize that necessary fussy thinking. In another context, Wolcott has claimed, "Ultimately there is only one test of ethnography: The satis-factoriness of the complete account" (1987, 42).

An in-advance table of contents, then, can help you answer the perennial student question of "How long should it be?" with a realistic reminder of just how little reporting space is available, especially in proportion to the amount of data you have been urged to collect. Few readers will be able to process chapters of more than thirty manuscript pages—and reports of more than three hundred pages—just as few first-time book-length writers can undertake projects of much greater length without wearying and wandering and testing their readers' pa-tience or taxing their own energies and budgets.

Prewriting and pre-outlining can help you discover direction and detail. They also help you to keep the whole in mind—the entire data set—while allowing you to address manageable chunks of data at any single analysis session. This can be done by forming drop files (men-tioned in Chapter Four) and of course, you always need to keep audit trails. In the same manner as you compile bibliographic citations, quote your data precisely *from the beginning* so you don't have to search for a lost and barely remembered quote at a later time.

All writers need good workspaces, but the ethnographic writer needs a big workspace. You'll want to sort, reshuffle, and fan out text artifacts where you can see and organize them. Reference books stay in stacks close at hand. I sometimes feel like I live in a house of paper. A house filled with paper. For this vast composition, you need significant spans of work time and plenty of space to follow leads, to encourage insight, to uncover moments when the kaleidoscope patterns of your project suddenly shift and click into a recognizable pattern, providing an encouraging design and direction.

Of course, we rarely get enough space to spread out (and stay spread out), but having it can help. We also need time. If you find yourself not writing, you may need to take an ethnographic spring break or contract for a self-sabbatical. Seldom discussed is the guilt that can be generated by involvement in time-intensive, longitudinal work. It is no small in-vestment of human interactions and paper and ink to have boxes of data in an office or storeroom, filling a livingroom, or spreading across the kitchen table. While data collection must take place within the studied

Figure 3
Overview of Case-Study Teachers—Susan, Rosalyn, Peg, Nick, and Julia

	SUSAN	ROSALYN	PEG	NICK	JULIA
BACKGROUND Years Teaching	14	5	6	9	16
Level	College & WC teacher trainer	College	Community College	Community College	High School (8) Administrative (5); College (3)
Current Institution	Four Year College	Four Year University	Community College	Community College	Four Year University
State	Oregon	Virginia	Florida	Pennsylvania	South Carolina
Professional Memberships	CCCC, WCR/LA	CLA, CCCC, NCTE	None	NCTE	NCTE, MWSC, PRSA
As writer (self-report)	Writes regularly for work and school purposes	Average writer but doesn't write much	Writes little but does well when she writes	Likes to write but not for professors	Fluent writer and free-lance journalist
RESPONSE TO Ph.D. Program	Positive	Positive	Positive	Positive	Positive
Teaching Basic Writing Course	Slightly resistant	Positive	Positive	Positive— models on TBW instructor	Positive
MAJOR PEDAGOGICAL CONCERNS	The reading/ writing connection and WAC	Issues of standard English and dialects	To try every new activity she can	Being less dramatic and in control of the classroom	Issues of standard English

ATTITUDES TO STUDENTS	Supportive but feels students need structure	Views students as "soon to be peers"	Wants an affective relationship but disappointed by "weasel" students who don't work hard enough	Enjoys humor as a way to relate to young students	Sees students as "kids" but changes to seeing them as peers
FALL 1987 TBW Most used activities from Teaching Basic Writing Course (TBW)	Paired student response; revisions; small class size; teacher in conversations with pairs of students	Peer groups; teacher conferencing; revisions; grammar work sheets; student journals with teacher marking grammar; teacher shares writing; sentence combining	Teacher/student conferences and peer groups; student-chosen topics; drafting and portfolio evaluation	Journals; teacher-led discussion; student-chosen topics; teacher shares writing; drafting and folder evaluation	Peer groups and teacher/student conferences; journals; teacher shares writing; drafting
Least used activities	Student journals; teacher sharing writing	Sentence-combining	Sentence-combining; teacher shares writing	In-class conference; less peer group work than others	Sentence-combining
Primary Teaching Method	Individualized and structured	Groups with teacher; conferencing	Individualized—teacher conference is primary; groups are secondary	Teacher-led (structured classes) even during group or journal sharing	Peer groups primary; teacher conference secondary
Change Pattern	SUB-TYPING of TBW information (stores info. for later use)	BOOKKEEPING—broadens and adds to previous activities (but keeps old too)	INTENTIONAL CONVERSION—old methods are temporarily abandoned	VERBAL CONVERSION—based on affec	MULTI-FACETED CONVERSION—integrates old and new

culture—providing the researcher with built-in classroom or workplace schedules that organize and regularize data collection—data analysis takes place in the cluttered spaces of the researcher's life. Without paid research time, teacher–researchers, in particular, will find themselves reading data at extraordinary moments and in unlikely locations, or find those pleasures too often deferred to imaginary summer holidays.

Don't let yourself feel like you're spinning straw into gold alone. Find, or form, a writing community. Don't work in isolation. The dissertation writers Judith Meloy consulted were unanimous in their need to talk about their writing *while writing*. Sometimes they needed listeners, sometimes readers. Sometimes they needed to read someone else's text; sometimes they needed help seeing their own texts through others' eyes.

> Just as rhetoricians may imply invention heuristics, so too must the ethnographer follow certain exploratory methodologies prior to writing up an ethnography. [Robert] Brooke points out that what one chooses to explore is selective. His interest in Erving Goffman's underlife, along with his readings in anthropology, philosophy, and developmental psychology, all contributed to what he focused on while observing a classroom. Brooke eloquently explains that foregrounding the rhetorical forces that shape our ethnographies makes us more critical of how we represent ourselves as well as others within our studies.
> —Christina Kirklighter, Cloe Vincent &
> Joseph M. Moxley 1997, x

And finally, as a way of adding dialogue to your project, continue to look for readings that help your writing. Consult your initial "works consulted" list again as you start to write it up. Reconsult the ERIC data base and Dissertations Abstracts; sit down and thumb through the last five years of your professional journals and you'll find that relevant essays that you "didn't see" at the beginning of your project now jump to hand and provide you with ideas. As you are synthesizing your data, you will find it useful to look once again at the work of other researchers and to revisit methods books. Terminology, suggestions, applications that were incomprehensible to you before will speak to you more clearly now. Jane, another of Judith Meloy's respondents, points out, "It has been very useful to go back to various methods books now, as I work on data analysis. Although I had read them before, tidbits are much more meaningful now that I'm into it. I guess that's true of any learning: it's meaningful when applied to a context" (1994, 76). Returning to theorists who have a relevance for your project will continue to prove generative through every phase of it.

Initial Drafting: Data Analysis as Invention

Anywhere you begin, you at least begin. Start with any process that helps you get a handle on your data. Many writers with whom I've worked seem to find it useful to sketch—in words. Whether you compose participant sketches based on demographic data or based on initial impressions (or both), as Donna Sewell does with all of the potential case-study students for her project, like Cara P____ in the following extract, doing so involves you in data reduction and general text planning. By sketching, you regularize your impressions and also begin looking for analytical lenses, metaphors, and narrative strategies; you compile a sketchbook of starts.

Donna's initial sketches were composed during the fourth week of her six-week participant observation of a writing class. One of these sketches is followed by Kim Haimes-Korn's character sketch of Joel Lalog. This finished sketch appears in the introduction of her dissertation to orient the reader to the case-study student and her project as a whole. You'll notice that Donna's sketch has the spontaneity and informality of a field note (which, in this version, it is). She appears to be combining observation data with interview data, but she doesn't label her sources. Kim's portrait of Joel, on the other hand, provides a stronger sense of the researcher's process for triangulating data: quotes from the student's interview and a report of his own observations about himself. Kim's sketch presents a more polished, authoritative-seeming, finished effect, and her citations include an audit trail, notations of where data were obtained. Donna's sketch is written in present tense, and Kim's sketch is written in past tense.

> Cara P_____ is slightly heavy, very outgoing, confident, and literate. She's taking preparatory math and ENC 1101 this summer. That she smokes surprises me. She seems somewhat of a leader, particularly socially. Lauren seems to follow her. She's a bit trendy I think; her clothes range from artsy long skirts and T-shirts to the usual college student attire: shorts and T-shirts. She doesn't wear a lot of makeup, and her hair is usually parted down the middle and tucked behind her ears. She wears two silver rings and usually participates in class discussions. She seems almost eager to meet with me and discuss her writings, often offering to read something.
>
> Cara consciously strives for the role of writer, writing in her spare time, sharing her writings with me, comparing her poetry to Morrison's, etc. She has five poetry books and says she writes poetry often.

In high school she wrote for the newspaper and the literary magazine. She started a story in fifth grade that grew to thirty pages. Apparently, teachers have praised Cara's writing ability and steered her toward writing contests and writing conventions.

Her first encounter with writing in college wasn't as successful. Her first essay in Thom's class received a B—, which surprised Cara, even though she admitted her essay wasn't that good. However, she's used to whipping stuff out and being praised for it. She wrote her paper about a friend's suicide. Basically, she used a two-draft process with minimal changes between drafts.

—Donna Sewell

Joel Lalog
This is the first time I have ever talked to an English teacher. I mean I have talked to English teachers but not about myself. (Joel Lalog, Conference 1)

Joel was a Filipino-American, male student in his freshman year. He was a music major and had been studying music since he was six years old. In his questionnaire, he said, "Seeing myself as a writer is something that I cannot envision." He felt that to be a "writer" you have to be able to communicate your thoughts and appeal to "different people." He also felt that good writing "requires correct grammar, good writing tools, big words that must be looked up and have some type of purpose." He said, "When I write I think of doing things correctly first and then I think about what I am writing." Although his past experiences in writing classes are not great, he seemed eager to participate in a writing class that involved his own ideas:

> My previous experiences in other writing classes have been dull and boring. I am tired of writing boring, informative reports. I would like to maybe write a journal about my own experiences. This is something that I would enjoy very much (CNF 1).

—Haimes-Korn 1996, 42

Both sketches show a researcher looking toward the end of a project. Donna is using her sketch to decide whether she will use this student as a case-study informant. Kim wrote her sketches early and modified them regularly through the drafting process, eventually including them in order to set the scene of her study and to help the reader understand subsequent discussions. Harry Wolcott (1990) suggests using the past tense, even if it sounds odd to your ear at first, arguing that by the time you finish writing about your project, events will have taken place some time earlier. Choosing past tense keeps you from a lot of fussing over tense (but exact quotes, of course, as in literary texts, remain in the "spoken" present tense).

You may choose a different starting place than the character sketch. I characterized the class I observed as a whole, sketching the room, the curriculum, the teacher's goals (see Appendix B for the way Pat Hendricks also does this). I examined the teacher's instruction and the students' responses. I summarized my field notes day by day and commented on patterns that occurred each day, looking for any notable progression of educational events (because I was looking at the subject of change). I did not begin to make character sketches until I started to reduce the data for each of the five case-study teachers.

As Devan Cook drafted her dissertation, she composed a series of personal essays that were triggered by her interviews with working students. She had come to her project because of her interest in it as a working-class student herself. And, as a creative writer turning ethnographer, she was inclined to compose nonfiction in response to what she was learning. In a way, this writing served as a secondary set of field notes. Some of these narratives loomed large in her initial full-length draft but later were removed and saved and submitted to literary journals. Those she retained in the final report functioned as illustrative counterpoints to the students' narratives and as meditative critiques of the overall project.

In a similar manner, different methods of coding can lead to leads. Themes can be found by actively reducing data by the methods reviewed in Chapter Four. They can also be looked for by reading and rereading, by annotating the project texts, by conducting a close reading of data, or by turning data into more literary approximations that allow you to analyze them with the tools of the literature trade—theme, symbol, recurrent image, and pattern. To do this, Bonnie Sunstein suggests using ethnopoetic notation, which "offers a way to analyze what's important: the pauses and emphases, the combinations, selections, and repetitions of their [informants'] words (1996, 197). She offers this example (with the warning that presenting such examples in research reports requires an alarming-to-publishers amount of white space, making the already long ethnographic report that much longer:

> To analyze the transcript of my interview with Susan, I experimented
> with ethnopoetic notation, a procedure for analysis of oral speech,
> developed by folklorist Dennis Tedlock for the purpose of studying
> Native American verbal art, and adapted by sociolinguist Deborah
> Tannen for studying mainstream American conversation. Spaces and

line breaks suggest repetitions and pauses, often highlighting important segments of thought. Susan's oral descriptions offered me an interpretive frame when I noted them poetically:

I'm understanding
   that to read is to write is to listen;
   they're all the same thing.
But what is this?
   There's more to this.
   I almost felt as though I was in a little bit of a cult
   I got an uncomfortable feeling after a while
      because I thought,
   "These people are teaching us
   More than this stuff!!" (1996, 196)

For most of us, informal writings function as an exploratory tool.
This includes initial discussions of our charts and matrix tables, for we
can use these data displays as writing prompts. Just as the term paper
reporter is warned away from inserting quotes without connecting
them to the ongoing narrative, the ethnographer uses reduced data to
inform: A chart is included and discussed. Our first job is to understand
the data ourselves, and our second is to help our readers understand
what we have come to understand. Laurel Richardson notes that we
have to work to encourage our readers to read our texts, "the evidence,
the quotations, and biographical details. Because readers tend to skip
over indented passages, particularly those in fine print and those that
seem to go on and on and on, it is preferable for quotations to be type-
set like the text, and important that your interpretive work—the lead-
ins and lead-outs around the quotations—entice" (1990, 40). Reduce
and then describe what it is you are seeing and you are likely to produce a potential lead-in or lead-out, that is, a start or finish of a discussion section or chapter.

You work the text, and the text works for you. You prewrite, write,
and rewrite because "Ethnography is a thoroughly textual practice"
(Herndl 1991, 320). You can plan all you want, but you must finally
begin. Inevitably, you simply have to launch yourself into the draft.
Prewriting, preplanning, and preorganizing become problematic if they
allow you to delay overly long. Writers know that cleaning the house
and searching for one last book or article may be profitable procrasti-
nation procedures. Or they can stop you too often and for too long. The
key is to prewrite, write, and rewrite without fear of doing it wrong.
There is no *wrong*. There are only better or different interpretive texts
to be made of your previous interpretive texts. And having no text leads
you nowhere.

Just as you cannot begin too early, you benefit from regular recon-
siderations and recalibrations of your report organization, so long as

this pausing doesn't lead to blocking or endless stopping, and fussing and teasing out of possible forms that you neglect to fill with actual content. As you begin to draft, you may find that case-study reporting needs to give way to a discussion of themes and trends in the data. You may have assumed that you would use a linear chronology or a classic research report plan—methods, data, discussion—until you actually begin and find that a collage, a sketch, a story, a dialogue and meta-reflection upon that conversation, or other less orthodox strategies, are required to present a satisfactory report.

This suggests that the entire time you are writing—which is the entire time you are researching—you are reading. At the least, you need to be reading research to discover the shape, scope, and possibilities of reporting conventions (which is also the subject of Chapter Six). For the purposes of this book, reading and writing are unnaturally unlinked, and any writing research ethnographer must learn to read rhetorically (in the field and for the field), to study those reports that appear effective to her or that have received acclaim and broad professional dissemination for an understanding of the textual strategies that are available.

Obviously, the novice researcher will write to the profession from the more conventional edge of the style spectrum as she works to show her committee, colleagues, and eventual public readers that she is conversant with, understands, and generally accepts the assumptions of the disciplinary community she is joining. Even so, if she is like the rest of us, she'll be keeping her eye on the far edge of the style spectrum, looking, if not in this report then for revisions or future projects, toward the experimental, the unexpected, the strategy that is more accurate for or appropriate to her project or more in concert with her writing aesthetics and abilities. In this field, there are exciting possibilities for narrating and theorizing, but none of us can entertain them all at the first attempt. Paul Atkinson points out, "The successful construction of an ethnographic monograph is a considerable literary achievement" (1992, 5). By reading and writing ethnography, the researcher learns how others make texts out of their contexts and then does the same for her project.

Texts are authored, that is, constructed. Traditions of scientific style require author-evacuated prose, third-person reporting, passive-voice constructions, rhetorically cool writing. Currently, ethnographers compose far more author-saturated texts, those that acknowledge their own constructedness and invoke authority through overtly rhetorical and persuasive techniques. These texts are rich in I-witnessing and examinations of authorial personas. These authors believe that through such examinations and practices there is a better chance for engaging a reader in our sometimes confusing and always modest cultural journey. In this view, ethnographic reports become places where we learn "what it is to open (a bit) the consciousness of one group of people to (something of) the life-form of another, and in that way to (something of) their own" (Geertz 1988, 143). John Van Maanen believes that literary standards apply well to our written products:

> Literary standards are different, but they are not shabby or second-rate. When taken seriously they may require even more from an ethnographer than those formulated by the profession. Fidelity, coherence, generosity, wisdom, imagination, honesty, respect, and verisimilitude are standards of a high order. Moreover, they are not exclusionary ones, since those who read ethnography for pleasure and general knowledge are as able to judge whether they are achieved as those who read for professional development. (1988, 33)

To criteria from earlier chapters that ethnographic writing research is

1. work undertaken with an ethnographic intent, and

2. work that demands data to be collected and written down in a manner that optimizes our chances of being judged trustworthy as researchers, we can now add, and

3. work that is written up into reports that provide a satisfactory account, one that aims for fidelity, coherence, generosity, wisdom, imagination, honesty, respect, and (at least a certain type of) verisimilitude.

In attempting to meet these criteria, particularly the third one, the writing research ethnographer draws on abilities that are similar to those of the novelist. "Lederman (1990), for instance, writes of how the [field] note mediates Here and There: 'Produced and still smelling of There—musty, smoky, spicy evocations of people and places' (p. 73). The reading and re-reading of notes can thus be a sort of Proustian experience of remembrance" (Atkinson 1990, 17). Our ethnographic monograph functions as a Proustian Madeleine tea biscuit that we ask our readers to consume. With our words, we hope to transport them at least partially from their *now* to our *there*, the site we once studied.

Looking in Both Directions:
Patterns, Themes, Metaphors, Analytic Lenses

Here are some of the metaphors used in the research reports we'll look at in Chapter Six: academic dance; community of scholars; anatomy of a discourse community; collaborating with the enemy; what's a nice girl like you doing in a place like this, or why does Freud keep showing up in my research?; something old, something new; taking it personally; border talk; a divided front; filling in the blanks; through teachers' eyes; getting restless. Because we look to metaphors to help us make meaning out of our experiences, you may have already noted in the act of reading these that several of these writers borrow analogies of war (collaborating, enemy, border, divided front). In doing this, you've reduced the data set of metaphors and found a theme to investigate: You could study studies to see why this set of metaphors seems to prevail.

Some of these metaphors are used as book titles, and the rest are from chapter headings or chapter subtitles in tables of content pages, and they help readers (and authors) understand and better conceptualize the text to come. Some of the metaphors are reversals. Instead of a "united front," we read about a "divided front." Some pun, play on, or double meanings. Most help us make the familiar strange by saying the well known in a new way or by importing it into a new context in the effort to provide new understandings. Some metaphors point; some sustain a discussion. Some provide a way of extending insight; some are a result of—a summary of—the insight itself.

Ethnography is a language-based, textual process: "[T]he activity of interpretation is not simply a methodological option open to the social scientist, but rather the very condition of human inquiry itself . . ." (Schwandt 1994, 119–20). Because cultural analysis is part of normal human perceptive inquiry, it is no wonder that cultural research, like ethnography, relies to a tremendous degree (as all research depends to some degree) on rhetoric and tropes, on employing narration and metaphor, on depending on analogy and synecdoche. In her overview of literary devices used in social science writing, Laurel Richardson points to these techniques: "Synecdoche is a rhetorical technique through which a part comes to stand for the whole, such as an individual for a class. . . . DNA is a synecdoche for life, the test tube for experiment" (1990,17). "Metaphor," she explains, "is the backbone of social science writing, and like a true spine, it bears weight, permits movement, links parts together into a functional coherent whole—and is not immediately visible" (1990, 18). She breaks down narrative into several types—the more familiar forms of autobiography and biography and the social scientist's forms; she distinguishes here between cultural story and collective story. The cultural story tells members of a culture how to behave in their world—by providing the scripts of tradition—and the collective story "gives voice to those who are silenced or marginalized in the cultural narrative. . . . The collective story displays an individual's story by narrativizing the experiences of the social category to which the individual belongs, rather than by telling the particular individual's story or by simply retelling the cultural story . . ." (1990, 20–25).

In educational ethnography, metaphors will help you identify patterns. When I found teachers "naming" students in certain ways, I could start to think about those names, group them, and consider the way those groups spoke to teachers' beliefs about or labeling of students. When a student is termed "a weasel" or a teacher feels the student is trying to "lead her by the nose," we are learning about beliefs and biases and assumptions. We are not learning everything, just some things. These instances function at first as flags or pointers. And the rest of your data can be examined to see if there is merit in discussing it this way, at this time, for this project. You can look for other instances that support the pattern or further investigate this tendency. Then you must ask if that pattern lends insight or explains some of your original research questions. If it turns out that you don't have enough data, then the thematic metaphor doesn't warrant further study. That is, metaphors—like any initial categories or patterns—may prove misleading rather than revealing, so you (re)search the data for a better unit upon which to build a case, a portrait, or an analytic description. You build and renovate, you try this material and that material, you construct and reconstruct interpretations. Initial hopeful Lego palaces of insight are eventually rebuilt into sturdier, more serviceable row houses.

> When I designed this study, I was not looking specifically *for* teachers' metaphors but, as I analyzed data from learning logs, interview transcripts, and video tapes, I could not help but note how often teachers used metaphors and comparisons to describe themselves as learners (one teacher used conversion metaphors, quest metaphors, science fiction—Dr. Spock—metaphors, cooking metaphors, and so on). They also used metaphors to describe their writing students. (Bishop 1990b, 6)

When I found teachers using conversion metaphors in their class learning logs, this alerted me to the way the teacher–educator for the class I observed was also using these metaphors: for example, when he mentioned "preaching to the choir." And later, as I looked to understand such metaphors, I found that conversion theory offered a major lens for examining teachers' pedagogical change processes. The metaphor, as we say, had power. It was not the only metaphor I might have used, but it seemed the right one at the time, based on the project; based on my participation, my observation, and my review of the data; and based on the theoretical discussions available to me at that time.

Ethnography is practice and process and product. Game and art. The play of the researcher's imagination across the fabric of an observable portion of our world. "If there is any way to counter the conception of ethnography as an iniquitous act or an unplayable game, it would seem to involve owning up to the fact that, like quantum mechanics or the Italian opera, it is a work of the imagination, less extravagant than the first, less methodical than the second (Geertz 1988, 40). The call of stories, the lure of narrative, the art of imagination, all energize the ethnographic report, for—along with finding metaphors that help us understand our data—we also look for story frames that can help us convey our tales. Like metaphor, narratives generate understanding and can provide organizational frames. (For a critique of ethnographic uses of these cultural frames, see Newkirk 1992.) Although narrative frames (the hero's story, the dramatic reversal of fortune, the happy ending) can overdetermine our reporting if not deployed as a direct result of data cues, we cannot have ethnographic reports without narrative. It is intrinsic to human understanding: "Narrative displays the goals and intentions of human actors; makes individuals, cultures, societies, and historical epochs comprehensible as wholes; humanizes time; allows us to contemplate the effects of our actions and to alter the directions of our lives" (Richardson 1990, 20). The practice of learning how to produce trustworthy and satisfying stories in ethnographic reports takes us into the arenas of creating convincing cases, composed of careful analytic detail and reported—traditionally—through the use of thick description.

Turning and Returning to Triangulation as Process: Thick Description and Case-Study Reporting

The crucial elements of narrative in case-study reporting are sequence and consequence. Through an aggregation of details (achieved from layerings of confirming, triangulating detail in descriptive layers), we produce a sense of verisimilitude, lifelikeness, trustworthiness. A satisfactory account. Although case reporting is not the only way to shape narrative into ethnographic reports, it is one of the most common methods, and decisions made in this form may be applied to narrative decisions made throughout your report.

We can see thick description more clearly as a trope when we remember Harry Wolcott's observation that we're trying to "can" all the data possible, for thick description gives us the satisfying illusion of a can crammed full. When attempting this, narratives are probably our most powerful reporting technique. Thomas Newkirk reminds us that "Narratives are embedded in all academic discourse—even the most austere; each has conventions for telling that indicate to the writer what should be attended to and what should be ignored" (1992, 132).

It's the breadth of our gaze—creating a culture or a cultural moment—that causes ethnographers so many writing-it-up-and-sharing-it-widely difficulties: Thick description literally is thick, resulting, as I mentioned earlier, in research reports of unwieldy proportions. "Faced with the dilemma of having more to pack than a suitcase can possibly hold," suggests Harry Wolcott, "the novice traveler has three possibilities: rearrange so as to get more in, remove nonessentials, or find a larger suitcase. Qualitative researchers have comparable [writing] options" (1987, 62). In essence, the "cool" rhetorical model of science offers only a straitjacket for our warmer ethnographic fullness. Additionally, who we are affects what we write. Our reports are full of ourselves and others. Jennifer Hunt claims, "There is also little doubt that the sociological narrative is partly autobiographical, reflecting something about the researcher's personality as well as those of the subjects who enter the ethnographic dialogue." From this perspective, fieldwork, she believes, is, in part, "the discovery of the self through the detour of the other" (1989, 41–42).

This is how it was, you will be claiming as you compose a case: This is who this self saw. Necessarily, you try to portray both yourself and your informants in a sensible, accessible way. This is such a difficult rhetorical feat that many contemporary ethnographers are advocating and/or exploring co-authoring with their informants (Sullivan 1996; Chiseri-Strater 1996; Reason 1994, among others). Co-authoring, of course, has its own particular problems of authority, ethics, intentions, motivations, and time.

Cases are, however, constructions, and you'll wonder more simply how to choose a case and how to infuse the report with a sense of a life lived. It is reasonable to let your readers know how you made your choices (often this is done in the methods section), and postmodern ethnographers of the phenomenological school often add metacommentaries, dialogues with informants, and cautions for readers. You may build up a representation and then critique it as well.

> The ethnography embeds and comments on the stories told by informants. . . . It includes the ethnographer's own accounts of incidents, "cases," and the like. They too are transformed and enhanced by their recontextualization in the ethnography itself. These narrative instances are collected and juxtaposed in the text so that their meaning (sociological or anthropological significance) is implied by the ethnographer and reconstructed by the reader. (Atkinson 1990, 13)

The narrative of a case study usually highlights the voice(s) of the informant(s):

> One of the primary ways to meet both literary and science writing criteria is through variety in format and voice. You can use one-line quotations, sometimes standing by themselves, sometimes in droves; mid-length quotations (5–10 lines) by themselves or mixed with one-liners; short phrases quoted within the body of the narrative; long(er) quotations broken into paragraphs, deployed when the reader cares about the character or the topic; and episodes, ministories embedded within the larger narrative. Similarly, including quotes with a variety

of language patterns, images, slang, and regionalisms makes texts both more alive and more credible. (Richardson 1990, 39–40)

Because of this need to quote to create character, I cautioned you earlier to keep an audit trail for tracking down the appropriate quote and to take care in interviewing and transcribing so that the quote is preserved in the first place. In some areas, my advice disagrees with that of Laurel Richardson. While I agree that you have to entice any reader into a text, I also cautioned you earlier to take care with regionalisms so that they represent the informant in a dignified and appropriate-to-your-project manner—the manner that he or she would choose for such representations.

But who do you choose and why, and how do you construct cases? For most of us, the intrinsic case, as defined by Robert Stake, is the preferable form: "In what we may call intrinsic case study, study is undertaken because one wants better understanding of this particular case" (1994, 237); he opposes these to instrumental cases, which are developed to help build theories. If you refer back to the historical discussion in Chapter One, you'll see that the intrinsic case would naturally inform the anthropologically derived project, while the instrumental case would be more useful for the sociological project, because sociologists are generally trying to build models of human systems. The intrinsic case is "undertaken because the case represents other cases or because it illustrates a particular trait or problem, but because, in all its particularity and ordinariness, this case itself is of interest" (Stake 1994, 237). Stake believes we cannot avoid generalizations in these cases but rather that we perform this generalizing to help others understand what we ourselves have seen in the data, given the limited reporting space we always have at our command "to encapsulate complex meanings into a finite report but to describe the case in sufficient descriptive narrative so that readers can vicariously experience these happenings, and draw their own conclusions" (Stake 1994, 243).

At this point, it seems useful to hear three other researchers' justifications for their case-study reporting choices. In her thesis, Angel Barbee explains how she made case choices from eleven students in a class she entered as researcher:

> I reviewed my four original [case-study] choices—two of whom, Margaret and Laurie, had stayed with the project; I felt that my initial instincts were right on these two, and I decided both would be distinct and valuable case studies. The other two students, Taneshia and Fred, for reasons I'll discuss in the first two interchapters [of the thesis], stopped participating. Several other students who had initially told me they would cooperate also drifted as the semester wore on, and my decision for the final two informants came down to a pool of five. I chose

one of them because he was the only male (Jarrett) who had remained a participant, and I felt his voice needed to be heard; the other
(Shantel) had quite a dramatic story to tell, one that I knew must be
included. I do regret that I cannot devote time to all of those who met
with me so faithfully, but I think that it would be too much for a study
of this size. I did include a third interchapter to address an interesting
exception to the typical pre-1101 [pre-first-year] student which I felt
merited attention, though not that of an entire chapter. Also, after
writing the four case studies, one of them (Laurie's) did not contribute
the depth I had anticipated to my study, so I have converted her case
study to the last interchapter. I have decided that more insight would
be gained by getting an in-depth look at the three students I have ultimately chosen—Shantel, Jarrett and Margaret (who chose to be
called by their real names rather than pseudonyms for my study).
Each one of these students is unique in his or her own right, each with
a story that needs to be shared. (Barbee 1997, 20–21)

In her discussion, Angel addresses several points that other case-
study researchers will want to consider. She had initial ideas about
which student she might report on, but those ideas were modified by
reality. Some students provided less and less information as her study
progressed, so she could not construct cases based on their experiences. One student was chosen because he was the sole representative
of his gender. One case was useful for the way the student did not fit
the general pattern that she felt she was seeing. One of the cases she
drafted later seemed less useful for her report and she reduced it in
length in the thesis to allow more space to discuss the three most pertinent cases.

Angel Barbee's case-study students chose to be designated by their
real names, confounding the social science–based convention that
participants should be reported upon anonymously. "While most researchers disguise participants' names and associations to protect them
from potential embarrassment or harm, this strategy also prevents participants from receiving recognition. In fact, as researchers paper over
participants' identities, they eliminate any opportunity for public ac-
knowledgment or praise" (Williams 1996, 40). Angel's students may
have decided to opt for the small glory of her public acknowledg-
ment of their help, and their decision may also indicate the comfort
they felt working with this researcher. Angel's statement that she
would have liked to have written case studies for all of the students at-
tests to the writing-it-up challenges an ethnographer faces; what is fascinating to you, you have to admit at some point in your process, may
not be as fascinating to your intended reader. You will have to make decisions. And you will also want to report the basis of those decisions, as
Angel did.

In the next excerpt, we hear Kim Haimes-Korn announcing a two-fold organization plan. She tells us how and why she constructed her case study of one student, Romeo, but she also reminds readers that the case in this chapter is recounted chronologically to let us see how the class in which Romeo was a student—Kim's own class—was organized and experienced. Other case studies in her dissertation are not limited by this temporal organization, showing that cases do not have to be reported in a similar manner in each instance. Same case-reporting patterns (like those in my 1990 monograph) harken back to ethnography's sociological roots, where the author is presenting cases for comparison and contrast. While reporting the same data in the same manner can prove functional by making differences apparent, a decision to organize this way tends to pour individuals into a same-seeming mold, constructing them as more similar than they may feel themselves to be or comparing them on only one major identity aspect (in the case of my study, more as teachers than as fully drawn individuals). Kim explains her choices:

> There are many possible ways that I might describe Romeo's story, including multiple ways of seeing him as person, as a student, and as a writer. However, in this chapter my goal is to recreate key scenes in Romeo's progression throughout the course to show how he named his experiences in writing. In some sections I draw heavily on our conference talk, others I show more specifically his writing choices and speculate on his writing processes. Although I concentrate primarily on my one-to-one conferences with Romeo about his writing, I also draw on several key class meetings and written student responses that focus specifically on his writing choices. . . . Part One [of this case-study chapter] generally describes Romeo as a person with his own lived experiences, Part Two begins to draw on the responses of others [in class] and Romeo's reactions to them, and Part Three looks more closely at the specific development of his texts. I intend the chapter to create a portrait of the class structure and assignments as well as a picture of one students' individual response to the class. (Haimes-Korn 1996, 51–52)

Kim's discussion highlights the constructedness of her case chapter. At the same time, she makes her rhetorical bid for trustworthiness because she points to her triangulation procedures (building her discussion from conferences, interviews, class notes, and Romeo's class writings—print artifacts; all the major data sources at her disposal). She also outlines the sequencing of her reports, which highlights the fact that she could have presented this data in another format. She provides us with a sense of her primary and secondary goals for this chapter.

In her dissertation, Devan was constantly reviewing her decision-making process; she did much more theorizing, ethical problem posing and general metacommentary, and she was doing so because she felt her population of students was unique and liable to misrepresentation:

> I was looking for connections and for stories as well as for how connections reveal stories and stories make connections. As Thomas Newkirk writes, "narrative pattern is part of the cultural equipment we use to make sense of human behavior" (139). [My choosing] Ethnographically-oriented case study meant that this was research in which stories constitute meaningful research results. (Cook 1996, 24)
>
> Data from the interview transcripts can be read in many ways, and I have struggled to find an approach that remains faithful to the lives and language of working writing students. Classifying, categorizing, generalizing, abstracting, interpreting, and the like are all risky moves. Many times I suspected the best move would be to simply publish the transcripts; the sorting-out of narratives upon which this section is organized is far from the whole story. (Cook 1996, 89–90)

In her dissertation chapters, Devan eschewed the more traditional case-study reporting methods and allowed the seams to show as she interwove transcripts, metacommentaries, and analysis, asking the reader to be an active co-creator of the text to a greater degree than did Kim and Angel. Devan's concerns were certainly also the concerns of Angel and of Kim, but they dealt with those concerns differently in their final reports.

They will also become your concerns as you consider where you stand in relation to the community you studied and try to embody that stance in your written report. At this point in your writing, you will ask yourself to look even more closely than before at roles, relationships, and representations, and to look yet again at your data and your reporting of site, scene, field, and fieldworker.

Looking Twice as Hard as We Thought We Could: Ethical Representation and Reporting

> [M]essy texts are messy because they insist on an open-endedness, an incompleteness, and an uncertainty about how to draw a text/analysis to a close. Such open-endedness often marks a concern with an ethics of dialogue and partial knowledge that a work is incomplete without critical, and differently positioned, response to it by its (one hopes) varied readers.
>
> —George E. Marcus 1994, 573

The theories and practices of ethnographic text building can contribute to the postmodern discussions now current in English Departments. When you compose messy, open-ended, and/or critically positioned research reports, you are composing in contemporary textual territories that ask you (and your readers) to consider for whom you are speaking, for what purposes, and with what results. You will want to consider the influences of gender, race, and class on your positions and on your representations. "As we write our research texts, we need to consider the voice that is heard and the voice that is not heard" (Clandinin & Connelly 1994, 424). You must continue to ask (and answer) questions as basic as, "So that's what you study/saw/said; what *didn't* you study/ see/say *and why*?" "While it is easy to narrate instances in which we connect with our informants, it is more difficult to describe moments when we do not. But, in some ways, this information is just as important to understand" (Montford 1996, 219).

In the past, positivistic research had the chance of alienating humanities-trained compositionists because of its confining style palette. Today, ethnography may be moving composition researchers closer to their English studies colleagues—in literature and in creative writing. Often the writing research ethnographer's textual practices and evolving theories about texts have more in common with those who use critical theory to re-envision the role of reading and writing, subjective and objective stances, aesthetics and literacy in the humanities, than they do with those building theoretical models in the natural and social sciences.

Nonetheless, writing research ethnographers, continue to borrow heavily from the developing discussions in sociology and anthropology. In those fields, postmodern examinations are in full swing and in some cases have paralleled or preceded the discussions in literary critical theory (see Trinh Min-ha [1988] for an example of the merging of both areas). And compositionists are now joining the conversation. For instance, feminist and postmodern theories suggest new, ethics-oriented ways to evaluate the qualities of ethnographic texts. Bonnie Sunstein provides an excellent list of questions you might ask about your own research report (and these questions can be applied to the reports you read as well):

1. Whose views of reality are these? Mine, my informants', someone else's inside my informants' culture?

2. How do I know what I know? Who constructs this knowledge/my informant, my informant-as-persona?

3. Do I organize data my informants' way, my way, or some way they or I see it because of someone else's theoretical construct?

4. Am I representing a character, creating, or re-creating a person? What histories, contexts, frames, or screens constitute that person?

5. What is the sense of place I am building? What details of setting do I use to organize and locate what I see?

6. What is my evidence? What values and assumptions do I already bring to my interpretation of it? How did I collect this evidence? Where? Under what conditions?

7. What does my evidence show? About me? About my informants? About the others around them? What other ways might I represent this evidence?

8. What is the foreground? Who describes it? I, or the people I portray? What other foregrounds are there? What backgrounds might there be? Described in whose voices?

9. Might I shift point of view and tell a similar story? (1996, 198)

Sunstein's questions can help you improve your own project because they take you immediately to the heart of ethical issues regarding the construction(s) of texts. She is not asking that you desist or deconstruct (in the humorous sense of exploding) but rather that you carefully consider your writing-it-up decisions and share those decisions with your readers. It is possible that educational ethnographers have a heightened sense of how situated and potentially self-interested their reports are because they often visit the sites of cultures that are already familiar.

The truth of a text cannot be established by its verisimilitude. Verisimilitude can always be challenged. Hence a text can be believed to be true even as it lacks verisimilitude. (The opposite case holds as well.) Challenges to verisimilitude in qualitative research rest on the simple observation that a text is always a site of political struggle over the real and its meanings. Truth is political, and verisimilitude is textual.
—Norman K. Denzin & Yvonna S. Lincoln 1994, 580

Throughout your research you can expect to encounter places where you will need to pause, reflect, and (re)consider the decisions you make. It will be hard to find quick or simple answers to your questions. You can read about ethical decision making whenever you can. You can record your decision process—options, choices, results of choices to the degree that you can apprehend those results—and then you will have to continue on. Usually you discover what you learned about ethics after the fact: during the writing-it-up phase, during the next project, as you attempt to teach others to go into the territories you have only just begun to explore. Brenda Brueggemann was able to identify four time periods in her research that resulted in conflicts, that raised ethical considerations. She notes,

> (1) the conflicts between my preestablished participant–observer roles and those particular participant and/or observer roles that were constructed in the process after the study began; (2) the conflicts of interpretation, unclear messages, and representation that occurred as I first tried to write the study for my dissertation; (3) further conflicts that occurred as I began trying to present and publish my results in various literate and oral settings; and (4) the ongoing conflicts, throughout the entire study and the years since, arising from my attempts to involve the subjects to let their own voices become a part of my representations of them. (Brueggemann 1996, 21)

These issues arise regularly in ethnographic writing research: Who speaks for whom, how, why? Similar issues also arise in writing classrooms today as teachers and students share their cultures on an every-class-meeting basis. The work of Mary Louise Pratt has engendered regular discussions in this area for compositionists, who feel their work takes place in the contact zones Pratt has described. To the degree that is true, our ethnographic writing reports inhabit the same territories: "Autoethnography, transculturation, critique, collaboration, bilingualism, mediation, parody, denunciation, imaginary dialogue, vernacular expression—these are some of the literate arts of the contact zone. Miscomprehension, incomprehension, dead letters, unread masterpieces, absolute heterogeneity of meaning—these are some of the perils of writing in the contact zone" (1991, 37).

Once again, I'd suggest that while these issues need to be considered on a regular basis by the novice researcher—in fact, he won't be able to avoid them, for they are part and parcel of ethnographic inquiry approaches—he also has set them aside at times in order to write at all. To rephrase E.M. Forster: You won't know what you say until you say it; you won't know the particular issues of ethical representation you are grappling with and need to address until you encounter them in the field and write them down in drafts. Sometimes you will only notice them after the fact as you let the data "talk to you." But you have to speak—draft—to understand: An unwritten masterpiece is an unread masterpiece as surely as a problematically written one will be.

In fact, at this point, many of your problems are still more immediately those of your own identity. They arise from trying to figure out who the devil *you* are at the moment(s) of writing, of authoring your report(s).

Whose Voice Is It Anyway:
Educational Ethnographer as Author

> The question of signature, the establishment of an authorial presence
> within a text, has haunted ethnography from very early on, though for
> the most part it has done so in a disguised form. Disguised, because it
> has been generally cast not as a narratological issue, a matter of how
> best to get an honest story honestly told, but as an epistemological one,
> a matter of how to prevent subjective views from coloring objec-
> tive facts. The clash between the expository conventions of author-
> saturated texts and those of author-evacuated ones that grows out of
> the particular nature of the ethnographic enterprise is imagined to be
> a clash between seeing things as one would have them and seeing
> them as they really are.
>
> —Clifford Geertz 1988, 9

We now realize there is no such thing as "things as they really are,"
but we used to think they could be so reported—as factual, fixed, and
true. Ethnographers today worry less about trying to see things as they
are and more on explaining how their enterprise grew from a careful
reading and is presented in a certain way. This represents, in part, a
movement from a focus on methods to a focus on voice and reporting
style.

Clifford Geertz claims that "the writing of ethnography [which]
involves telling stories, making pictures, concocting symbolisms, and
deploying tropes is commonly resisted, often fiercely, because of a confusion, endemic in the West since Plato at least, of the imagined with
the imaginary, the fictional with the false, making things out with making them up" (1988, 140). Positivistic methods do not appear to tell,
concoct, or deploy. And so, ethnographic methods are suspect to the
degree to which they question this prevailing tradition. Yet positivism
is a position, and a very firmly entrenched one. As William Firestone
explains,

> Scientific writing is a stripped-down, cool style that avoids ornamen-
> tation, often stating conclusions as propositions or formulae. Forms of
> data presentation are supposed to be interchangeable. . . . This absence
> of style turns out to actually be a rhetorical device in its own right
> (Frye 1957). The use of propositions, for instance, is a means to empty
> language of emotion and convince the reader of the writer's disen-
> gagement from the analysis. If one of the threats to the validity of a
> conclusion comes from the writer's own biases, as is considered to be

the case in science, then any technique that projects a lack of emotion has considerable persuasive power. (1987, 17)

Cool style relies on the appeal to reason. The requirement for cool reasoning, for instance, is laid out for all novices in the *Publication Manual of the American Psychological Association,* which instructs,

> The scientific journal is the repository of the accumulated knowledge of a field. . . . Familiarity with the literature allows an individual investigator to avoid needlessly repeating work that has been done before to build on existing work, and in turn to contribute something new. A literature built of meticulously prepared, carefully reviewed contributions thus fosters the growth of a field. (1983, 17)

As I read this "cool" description of the field of science, I note the absence of a first-person author (indeed, the APA manual itself assumes the author-less authority of divine creed) and the implied logic of *previously proven* scientific truths. Examining the passage, I see easily that "The style of science is social in its entirety, a well-policed communal property" (Gros 1991, 934). In this example, the policing vehicle is the APA manual, which tells initiates not what to say—that is, it doesn't help them choose and design their research projects—but how to say, in a rhetorically appropriate manner.

Just as scientific writing gains power from the use of cool style, the writing of ethnographic stories has often been viewed as lacking in rigor and validity when writers indulge in what I call its "warm(er)" styles— vivid subjective narratives that are, inevitably, meditative and interpretive. These narratives, of course, rely greatly upon the ethos of the author: The work of Clifford Geertz, for instance, is read widely because we enjoy reading Geertz, the author, as much as we enjoy reading his study results. And Geertz is well aware of his rhetorical powers: "I've always argued that in part I'm represented in my texts by my style, that at least people won't think my books were written by anybody else, that there's a kind of signature in them" (Olson 1991, 262).

Understanding cool and warm styles may help you better understand you own initial struggles with writing it down ethnographically. Those who come to this method from the positivist position may also have confused the imagined with the imaginary, the fictional with the false, making things out—people, situations, patterns, understandings—with making them up. And they have to learn that data are displayed to help us construct our imagined, fictional, and made-out understandings, but data can never "prove" them.

Sometimes writing it up proves to be more problematic than writing it down, because writing up an ethnographic narrative includes creating a believable, interesting, and authoritative authorial identity.

Readers look for a trustworthy and convincingly constructed guide. Geertz claims (somewhat humorously) that

> "Being There" authorially, palpably on the page, is in any case as diffi-
> cult a trick to bring off as "being there" personally, which after all
> demands at the minimum hardly more than a travel booking and per-
> mission to land; a willingness to endure a certain amount of loneli-
> ness, invasion of privacy, and physical discomfort, a relaxed way with
> odd growths and unexplained fevers; a capacity to stand still for artis-
> tic insults, and the sort of patience that can support an endless search
> for invisible needles in infinite haystacks. And the authorial sort of be-
> ing there is getting more difficult all the time. (1988, 23–24)

Being there authorially becomes increasingly difficult in the postmodern world, and, I would argue, in the world of writing research, in which
the line between our own and the studied culture may be a fine one—
someone else's classroom but a classroom like those we have known.
Often little but our methodological claims separate us from the teachers we study. That is, we claim more expertise than they, more than
their long-term residence in the culture may afford them, through our
"objectivity" and "methods." It can also be hard to claim such authority in the special genre we call "dissertation."

Conventions and Your Community: Research Reports as (Im)Pure Products of the Certification Process

Writing for credentialing is more like taking a trip than taking a journey,
is more fraught with the frustrations of being with a tourguide when
you would really rather be heading the expedition (and some times suspect you could do so better than the current guide). "Through trial and
error of this guessing game, Mara learned that although there is no
'right' way to write an ethnographic dissertation, there certainly seemed
to be many 'wrong' ways" (Casey et al. 1997, 125). Generally, the individuals who are allowed to experiment in their textual productions
are those who have already gained prestige in the field. Novice ethnographers have not—for many reasons—had the freedom to take the
risks and explore the writing-it-up avenues available to composition
studies' most well-known writers.

The novice ethnographer may be encouraged to start modestly, and
with projects of the dimensions we've considered here (which, if not
designed carefully, can quickly become immodest in proportions). This
is not necessarily an unreasonable request. The novice studies writers,

writing classrooms, or writing teachers, or other literacy sites with the aid of dissertation committees, members of which may have completed no ethnographies and read few themselves. The novice studies methods textbooks and does ethnography; she tries to be there. She must write to new audiences, assert her authority and methodology, and produce thick descriptions and convincing narratives. She learns that she is "telling stories" and "structuring narratives," and she also learns that these narratives appear radical or unreliable to those in more traditional research strands.

She does it anyway. The lure of ethnography is powerful and real and appeals, I believe, to our profession for several reasons. Ethnography challenges the dominant positivist view of making knowledge. It demands attention to human subjectivity and allows for author-saturated reconstructions and examinations of a world. Equally, it is generative and creative because writing research ethnographies are overtly rhetorical; they are producing informed stories and arguments about the world. In fact, Linda Brodkey suggests that we should write active, critical ethnographies intended to change institutions. She eschews the smoothly constructed story in which the narrator seems an "instrument rather than the agent of the narrative" (1987a, 72) and suggests instead that "a narrative voice is made most audible by interrupting the flow of the story and calling attention to the fact of narration" (1987a, 73). Narrative can be effectively self-conscious. And it may be most ethical to choose to be so.

Ethnographic arguments are built by means different than those used in quantitative research (arguments there, we need to remember, are also rhetorical but less transparently so). Such arguments challenge conventions of scientific reporting: "To place the reach of your sensibility . . . at the center of your ethnography, is to pose for yourself a distinctive sort of textbuilding problem: rendering your account credible through rendering your person so. . . . To be a convincing 'I-witness,' one must, so it seems, first become a convincing 'I'" (Geertz 1988, 78–79). To become a convincing "I" is a primary task of all writing research ethnographers, yet the "I" of the dissertation is rarely convincing (more on this in the next chapter). The writing research dissertation too often must still be author-evacuated because, generally, it must convince through an uneasy alliance—interpretive narratives garnishing a pseudopositivistic banquet. Mary Louise Pratt describes the results of the author-evacuated voice:

> For the lay person, such as myself, the main evidence of a problem is the simple fact that ethnographic writing tends to be surprisingly boring. How, one asks constantly, could such interesting people doing such interesting things produce such dull books? (1986, 33)

The benefit of jettisoning the cumbersome data exhibits of the pseudopositivistic proof, of moving from the position of "outside knower" to "I-witnessing" writer, includes finding a more powerful way to speak. The mix-and-match writing research dissertation ethnography may encourage bad habits; it can become confusing, cumbersome, and often downright boring, like most writing that provides merely an initiation into the academy. And certainly the ethnographic writing researcher is no longer the lone wolf of the current crop of program researchers. The increase of attention to this methodology presumes that new researchers will eventually need to spend less time defending methodology and therefore have more time for producing well-written research reports.

Despite the growth in our field of this method for credentialing, those undertaking fieldwork will continue to encounter challenges to their progress on all levels. But forewarned is, to a degree, forearmed.

> I was asked, for example, as I wrote up my concluding chapter, to be sure to include a section about the "representatives" of these two subjects. I was concerned both theoretically and practically about the possibilities for successfully doing this. I felt, for one, that such a request stemmed form an attempt to place phenomenological research in a positivistic frame—to somehow attempt to universalize and validate results that were indeed relative. But of course I did it as best I could, wanting the dissertation done more than I wanted to quibble over this point. (Brueggemann 1996, 27)

Ethnography changes the ethnographer. Conducting a first ethnography changes our relationship to the field, to research methods, to our own authority, and, often, to our research subject(s). We're no longer the complete novice, and, as Donna Sewell explains, we're somewhat seasoned and certainly sobered:

> I had thought . . . that the process of becoming authoritative was much quicker than this. But then again, I was forgetting the lessons of process pedagogy. Just as I learned about the process of doing research and could now design a better ethnographic project, I am also learning about the process of writing it up. At least, [after completing my ethnographic dissertation] I will be somewhat more prepared with the stamina and determination required for a lengthy project next time. While I fully realize the main function of dissertations is to credential scholars, at times I managed to forget my probationary status, just as I did when I completed studying for preliminary examinations. During those times I felt most like a researcher and less like a novice. After the first two disorienting weeks in the "field," I could see the project coming together even as I struggled frantically to keep interview appointments and collect documents. Especially during that first summer, I was a researcher.

Within the academic year, though, my roles became multi-layered again, as I was called upon to teach, mentor, serve on committees and do research; the next summer moved me back into a researcher role, but the role of researcher as writer, a new and scary one. And now, of course, in another academic year [as a new assistant professor], I am balancing mostly researcher and teacher [roles] again. (Sewell 1995, 233–34)

Chapter Six

Reading Ethnographic Writing Research

> As components of studies are evaluated . . . the primary referent should be the intent of the investigators and the research questions they claim to address, rather than what the reviewer thinks should have been done.
>
> —Judith Goetz & Margaret LeCompte 1984, 233

Responding to and Evaluating Ethnographic Writing Research

The more carefully you read the reports of others, the more skillful you'll become at choosing appropriate and effective reporting strategies for your own work. Reading ethnographic writing research and composing satisfactory ethnographic reports are reciprocal activities. The questions you ask about the research you read are the questions you will soon be asking about your own work. Equally, to be a strong reader of any type of text, it is useful to have written one. Having been there textually, you can respond to the genre from the inside out—be more authoritative in your analysis—and having been there also tends to make you a more understanding reader overall. When it comes to reading ethnographic writing research reports, it is worth remembering that

> We do not have perfect theoretical and epistemological foundations; we do not have perfect methods for data collection; we do not

have perfect or transparent modes of representation. We work in the knowledge of our limited resources. But we do not have to abandon the attempt to produce disciplined accounts of the world that are coherent, methodological and sensible. (Atkinson 1992, 52)

In a sense, you achieve self-discipline and enter your disciplinary community by reading a research report with the sensitivity that Paul Atkinson advocates. You understand that the researchers you read and the researcher you strive to be can never achieve perfection. At the same time, satisfaction inheres in aiming for the high standards Atkinson advocates: that your work be as coherent, methodologically sound, and sensible as you can make it.

In reading research reports, readers are participating in an interpretation; in a sense, they evoke, and work to complete through their understanding, the interpretation that the researcher began. To do this, they must choose from a range of possible interpretive or evaluative criteria. It is as impossible to evoke all the available criteria simultaneously as it is to be both exploratory composer and fine-tuning editor of a text. When writing, we shuttle between global and local concerns, finding it impossible to pay attention to both at once. Reading theorist Louise Rosenblatt (1978) asserts that the same holds true for readers; readers cannot fully inhabit practical and artistic—efferent and aesthetic—stances at the same time but must shuttle between these positions.

Readers of ethnographic writing research can choose to evaluate the research question and methodological choices the author makes; can choose to evaluate the narrative effectiveness with which the report is shared; can choose to evaluate the writer's voice, stance, degree of self-reflexivity and self-interest; can choose to work to reach beyond the writer to understand the community described and relate it to similar communities. While it is impossible to achieve all of these "readings" simultaneously, interested readers can certainly complete them—or some of them—sequentially.

If the phenomenologically oriented reader admits to the constructed nature of texts and reports about cultures, that reader must also try to understand the project on the basis of the researcher(s) reported aims and goals. Certainly you can still judge the project to have fallen short of those goals, but there is little use trying to compare the ethnographic writing report with a Platonically "ideal" report. Rather, read for what is there and what isn't there; what might have been included and why it seems not to have been; what choices have been made and the appropriateness of those choices. Borrowing from Peter Elbow (1986), I encourage readers of research to play both the doubting *and* the believing games. And it is actually more difficult to believe than it is to find a dissonant item and use it to dismiss a project. You would do well to believe as much or more than you doubt, for you, too, may soon be in the sobering situation of "being read" by those you study—your informants—and those with and for whom you study (in the case of co-researchers and dissertation writers). You would not want your work ignored due to a first-timer's momentary lack of clarity. Read others, then, as you would have them read you.

Also, it's wise to remember the degree to which your writing and your reading processes are inevitably a result of your beliefs and values:

> The urgency to fix hard standards of reliability, validity, and general-izability has given way to a provocative range of questions about power and representation that are manifest in the field and on the page. Many scholars now assume that interpretation is central to all research, that researchers' values permeate and shape research questions, observa-tions, and conclusions, and that there can be no value-neutral re-search methodology. (Kirsch & Mortensen 1996, xxi)

With these recommendations and claims in mind, I've ordered this chapter to highlight the questions that other researchers have posed about ethnographic writing research, some of which I'll apply briefly to literacy research that I have found valuable and provocative. By chap-ter's end, you will have an assortment of strategies and stances from which to choose. Not every question-set is useful or even appropriate for every piece of research; most research theorists recommend that you begin where the researcher began and evaluate the project on the project's own stated goals and terms. Also, I encourage you to try your hand at reading in these ways by using some of these criteria to respond to the three mini-ethnographies in Appendix B. Here again, remember that these are student projects; they are all first attempts. In that sense, they are perfect vehicles for reading practice, and they also require that you take an empathetic stance—play the believing game—and under-stand the limitations that were placed on these researchers (just as you will soon hope others understand your research contexts and con-straints). Also, you will certainly want to read fully the full texts of the research projects I can only point to in this chapter.

Basically, the questions researchers have asked over time about ethnographic writing research have paralleled the profession's move from the sociologically influenced literacy research to research that reflects the current influence of anthropologists and literary theorists. The movement is away from a concern with method and toward a con-cern for research conditions and ethics, and also toward methods for reporting and writing up texts: voice, story, self-reflexivity. This chapter follows, roughly, a similar path, looking at questions about method-ological design and definition, then moving toward questions of writ-ing personas and narrative styles, and ending with sections on experimental writing styles and the dissertation as a special reading case. In looking at these reading question-sets, you'll want to note the year the criteria were published to gain a sense of how the questions we ask about ethnographic writing research have evolved over time, just as our theories and practices have evolved.

Reading for Completeness and Creditability

Even though postmodern ethnographers often discuss authoring and representation of scene and subject, methods still matter. In fact, they filled the first three chapters of this book, as I distinguished between the traditional scientific research report format and the more particular requirements of ethnographic reports. Here, in summary, is the scientific report formula:

> Usually, though, research reports have five parts:
>
> 1. an abstract that provides a brief summary of the report,
> 2. an introduction that identifies the questions to be addressed in the report and provides a brief review of the most relevant literature,
> 3. a methods section that describes the participants, the materials, and the procedures for collecting data,
> 4. a results section that reports what was observed together with statistical analyses of the observations, and finally,
> 5. a discussion section that presents the author's claims about the meaning of the results. (Hayes et al. 1992, 11–12)

In this type of research, data are reported in an approved format and discussions cover expected territory; any report that fails to do so will be judged lacking and/or have to make a strong case for deviation from the expected norms. This format has everything in common with the traditional research dissertation, which still requires that an entire report be summarized in the space of a five hundred–word abstract and (generally) be reported in subtitled sections, as do current ethnographic reports that are published in educational journals such as *Research in the Teaching of English* and *Written Communication*.

The requirements of ethnographic writing research complicate the format for reporting and formulas for assessing the completeness and credibility of such reports. The following criteria represent the sociological perspective:

> A complete report of an ethnographic investigation should identify and discuss
>
> 1. the goals of the effort and the questions it addressed,
> 2. the conceptual and theoretical frameworks that informed the research activity,

3. the overall design or variant that characterized the endeavor,

4. the group that provided the data,

5. the experiences and roles of the investigators,

6. the data collection methods used,

7. the analysis strategies developed, and

8. the conclusions, interpretations, and applications generated.

(Goetz & LeCompte 1984, 233)

Judith Goetz and Margaret LeCompte's word choices (for example, *variant, endeavor,* and *applications*) point to their sociological orientation, as does the regular use of passive voice. For contrast, Stephen North is more influenced by the anthropological tradition (again, for me, this influence is indicated by North's word choices, such as *entering, inscription,* and *interpretation*), and even the small portion of "voice" found here is more informal (for example, *then* and *this*):

In outline form, then, Ethnographic inquiry follows a pattern like this:

1. Identifying Problems: Finding a Setting

2. Entering the Setting

3. Collecting Data; Inscription

4. Interpretation: Identifying Themes

5. Verification

6. Dissemination (North 1987, 284)

Book-length reports that aim for methodological completeness and credibility include Barbara Walvoord and Lucille McCarthy's 1990 *Thinking and Writing in College: A Naturalistic Study of Students in Four Disciplines* (abbreviated as *TWC*) and Marilyn Sternglass' 1997 *Time to Know Them: A Longitudinal Study of Writing and Learning at the College Level* (*TKT*). Following is a brief discussion of how each text can be examined by using Goetz and LeComptes' criteria.

How do the authors identify and discuss the goals of the effort and the questions it addressed?

TWC: In a sixteen-page "Preview of the Book," Walvoord and McCarthy identified their project goal as "a writing specialist pairs with a teacher from another discipline to study the students in that teacher's classroom" (1) to create a six-member team. Walvoord worked with the four disciplinary instructors, and Walvoord and McCarthy together analyzed data and wrote "we"-authored reports. Research questions were in service of finding similarities across the four classrooms in the areas of teachers' expectations for good writing and difficulties that arise as students worked to meet those expectations. Walvoord and McCarthy justified the study by citing numerous instances of other researchers' calling for more information on how students think and write in college and in different academic settings; this study looked at 100+ students in four disciplines, at three institutions.

TKT: Sternglass followed fifty-three volunteering students from three of her 1989 first-year writing courses "through their college years." She believed "Both writing development and the relationship between writing and learning can be best understood through longitudinal studies that consider all facets of students' experiences during their college lives" (xi). Her goal was to "examine the ways in which the development of complex reasoning strategies was fostered by writing, to determine the role that writing plays in learning, and to understand how the multifaceted social factors in students' lives affected their academic progress" (xiv).

How do the authors identify and discuss the conceptual and theoretical frameworks that informed the research activity?

TWC: Walvoord and McCarthy noted several conceptual–theoretical issues: How to search for common elements in four different classrooms at three institutions and how to state commonalties that cover all classrooms without becoming so general as to weaken the overall usefulness of the results. Inquiry framework: naturalistic, assuming "research questions, methods, and findings are socially constructed by particular researchers in particular settings for particular ends" (20). Classroom assumptions: "When students enter a classroom, they are entering a discourse community in which they must master the ways of thinking and writing considered appropriate in the setting and by their teacher" (21). And "Our definition of successful writing relies on no absolute or standard criteria, but, rather, upon teachers' judgments" (36). Analysis framework: Postdata analysis led to a focus on students' "roles," particularly that of "professional-in-training."

TKT: Sternglass believed that longitudinal study was the best way to examine writing development as based on arguments by other researchers, as noted in the research literature. Ethnographic intent is not claimed but several ethnographic strategies are employed—longitudinal data collection, regular interviewing, artifact analysis; participant observation is not discussed until Chapter 6, when the author provides a chart of "Seventy-four classroom observations in 20 disciplines [that] were made over the 6 years of the study" (163), and in Appendix A, readers learn that this observation was completed by research assistants. A major conceptual issue was "how *learning* should be defined" (19), and the researchers considered students' movement from unconscious to conscious uses of writing, writing to help remember facts, to help analyze concepts, and to construct knowledge new to the learner. Sternglass used examples of the nine case-study students in her report to illuminate "the usefulness of writing as a means of developing complex reasoning strategies for use in new learning environments" (20).

How do the authors identify and discuss the overall design or variant that characterized the endeavor?

TWC: Walvoord and McCarthy "chose the naturalistic inquiry paradigm" (19). "Our aim was to investigate the entire classroom community, but within that community to focus on a single 'salient event'—the writing assignment—the outcome of which was crucial to the life of the community" (22).

TKT: Sternglass' goal was to complete a longitudinal study with a multicultural urban population and investigate the relationship between writing and learning by examining the papers those students wrote across academic disciplines.

How do the authors identify and discuss the group that provided the data?

TWC: The four teachers chosen by Walvoord and McCarthy were Writing Across the Curriculum (WAC) workshop participants, had published on WAC, were experienced teachers with excellent evaluations, held doctorate degrees, were in their 40s, had been in positions at least five years, and were tenured. Walvoord asked these four teachers to collaborate because she judged them to be interested in their students, open to new ideas, and sufficiently self-confident to feel comfortable with her visits to their classes. Most were white and middle class or of working-class background. Students were chosen due to their enrollment in these teachers' classes.

TKT: Fifty-three students in Sternglass' three first-year writing classes agreed to participate in her project. "Of the 53 students in the classes . . . 21 identified themselves as African American, 26 Latino, 4 Asian, and 2 White. Thirty were males and 23 were females. Twenty-five were born outside the continental US, including 3 born in Puerto Rico." Case-study biographical sketches were prepared—using pseudonyms—for the nine students for whom "the most complete data in this study exists" (xvi).

How do the authors identify and discuss their own experiences and roles as investigators?

TWC: Walvoord and McCarthy mentioned that they are "writing specialists" (1). Walvoord began collecting data between 1982 and 1989. McCarthy joined in 1985 and "helped to shape and guide the data analysis, and critiqued the emerging chapter drafts written by the [researcher–teacher] pairs" (1). With Walvoord, she also coauthored the introductory and concluding chapters. Walvoord and McCarthy's experiences are not referenced directly in the case-study chapters.

TKT: After reading an essay by Patricia Bizzell, calling for study of multicultural writing students, Sternglass "wrote a note to myself in the margin: 'This is the long range study I want to do.' Having joined the faculty at The City College of City University of New York the year before, I realized that the student population there, comprised of students from a wide range of racial, ethnic, and social backgrounds, would constitute a meaningful study population" (xi). Her data are regularly compared to the research and/or calls for research of others in the field; author's experiences are not directly narrated until the final chapter (8—"Implications for Instruction and Research"): "I have not emphasized my own role in the interactions with the students because I thought it was important to let them speak with their own voices" (295).

How do the authors identify and discuss their data-collection methods?

TWC: "Because our initial research questions were broad, we collected a wide range of data about students' thinking and writing and about the classroom context" (22). Walvoord and McCarthy's project data included logs; plans or drafts; final papers with teacher comments; interviews by Walvoord; peer response and peer interviews; taped interaction with others outside of class; from one class, students' paragraphs describing self as writer; think-aloud tapes; and from two classes, students' class evaluations. Data are detailed in a comparative chart with discussion following.

TKT: Sternglass addressed data collection in Appendix A: Study Methodology and Questionnaires. The first semester, students were invited to participate, and those who agreed came to author's office for interviews during following semesters and to deliver papers and exams. They were interviewed at the beginning and end of each term, using structured, sequenced interview questions. At the beginning of the second year of the study, Sternglass' researcher assistants visited and observed the classes of willing students. Questionnaires are provided.

How do the authors identify and discuss the analysis strategies they developed?

TWC: Each student in each class had a drop file (11 × 15 envelope) of ten to 549 pages of data. Using this material, Walvoord and McCarthy conducted a three-stage data analysis: interpreting students' writing-process stories; constructing primary trait scales for students' papers; and conducting detailed analyses of specific aspects of students' writing. Further analysis looked at students' revision practices and structures in students' texts.

TKT: There was not a particular discussion of Sternglass' data analysis methods. More often, analysis was raised as it concerned the chapter topic, as in Chapter 7, "Case Studies": "The attempt here is to examine the students' entire experiences chronologically, bringing together interview data, student writing, instructional experiences, and testing requirements to construct a full picture of the students' development over their college years. It should be clearly understood that these will be academic portraits . . ." (197).

How do the authors identify and discuss the conclusions, interpretations, and applications their research generated?

TWC: "Because knowledge in this collaborative study was constructed by multiple researchers with varying perspectives and varying relationships to the classrooms under study, we have been careful to define these perspectives and to have all team members tell at least parts of their stories in their own voices" (20). Walvoord and McCarthy claimed that the study is local but may prove useful in helping to "inform theories and generalizations about writing in academia and about how students learn to think and write there" (49). They concluded by summarizing answers to original research questions, as seen in each of four classrooms; discussing the four teachers' methods; and deriving eight principles for effective teaching.

TKT: Sternglass began her report by explaining her desire to illuminate and respond to calls for more study on this student population. The final chapter provided recommendations for instruction: "The most significant central finding of this study is that students with poor academic preparation have the potential to develop the critical reasoning processes that they must bring to bear in academic writing if they are given the time" (296).

Once you have read a research report—and perhaps used questions like these to help you begin to interpret the text or to help you assess it's overall completeness—Judith Goetz and Margaret LeCompte suggest that such a report

> can be assessed for appropriateness, clarity, comprehensiveness, credibility, and significance to evaluate an individual study for internal integrity and to compare multiple studies for differential merit. These five criteria can be conceptualized as forming five scales:
>
> | | | |
> |---|---|---|
> | **1.** | Appropriate | Inappropriate |
> | **2.** | Clear | Opaque |
> | **3.** | Comprehensive | Narrow |
> | **4.** | Credible | Incredible |
> | **5.** | Significant | Trivial |
>
> (Goetz & LeCompte 1984, 233)

I'll leave you to apply these scales to the books I've just described in an admittedly telegraphic and oversimplified manner. Still, my reading of these reports did allow me to understand the two projects overall in a way that differed from general front-to-back reading. And even this brief analysis taught me two significant things about the studies. First, the Walvoord and McCarthy report is arranged more predictably in the format of the traditional research report, making it easier to assess the completeness of this text. Sternglass appears to have collected as much data, with as much care, but it takes more work on the reader's part to come to this conclusion. Second, it was less easy not only to assess completeness, but also to assess the research paradigm that informed *Time to Know Them*. Sternglass was less explicit about her research affiliations yet much more explicit than Walvoord and McCarthy about where she placed her work in disciplinary conversations, particularly those in composition concerning basic writers. Her work clearly grew out of and was a response to the discussions she details through extensive reviews of current literature.

Neither of these observations are value judgments at this point. Rather they are descriptions of my reading experience using these criteria, and they tell me that the second report might be better read using some of the approaches that are discussed next.

Reading for Methodological Intent

Chapter Two of this book presents a sample of reading for methodological orientation. In it, I examine the degree of ethnographic intent in the research of four (at that time) graduate student projects. The process I used there would be suitable for evaluating texts you read when authors to some degree label their work *ethnographic.* These criteria are the following:

- Ethnographic writing research is ethnographic in *intent.*
- Ethnographic writing research is participant–observer-based inquiry.
- Ethnographic writing research studies a culture from that culture's point of view.
- Ethnographic writing research uses one or more ethnographic data-gathering techniques.
- Ethnographic writing research gains power to the degree that the researcher:
  1. spends time in the field
  2. collects multiple sources of data
  3. lets the context and participants help guide research questions
  4. conducts analysis as a reiterative process

In addition, you could respond to a research report using the following criteria, developed by Norman Denzin (1994, 500–15), to assess a project's *completeness* as an ethnography:

> In order to satisfy the basic elements of the ethnographic ethic, the following "generic" topics should be included in ethnographic reports:
>
> - The contexts: history, physical setting, and environment
> - Number of participants, key individuals
> - Activities
> - Schedules, temporal order
> - Division of labor, hierarchies
> - Routines and variations

- Significant events and their origins and consequences
- Members' perspectives and meanings
- Social rules and basic patterns of order

These dimensions provide a template for the investigator as well as framework in which a prospective reader of the report can understand what contributes to *the definition of the situation*, its nature, character, origin, and consequences. (1994, 491)

These criteria help me to explain why I found Sondra Perl and Nancy Wilson's *Through Teachers' Eyes: Portraits of Writing Teachers at Work* (1986; 1998) a strong guide to ethnographic writing research methods, as well as enjoyable to read, when I began my own research. In fact, this project still seems usefully informing (though, like me, you may not be able to live up to the longitudinal strengths of their work). Certainly the population they studied was of great interest to me: teachers of writing. But even more, Perl and Wilson provided a strong introduction to a barely discussed (at that time) method of study.

Their book is firmly ethnographic in intent. When proposing in 1981 to study the writing instruction of teachers who had participated in a Writing Project summer institute in Shoreham–Wading River Central School District, Perl "argued that ethnography, the research method pioneered by anthropologists, was best suited to the type of classroom research she wanted to undertake . . . to study the teaching of writing from the perspectives of teachers" (9). Perl invited two teachers from the New York City Writing Project to collaborate and invited seventy teachers to participate. Ten accepted.

Perl and Wilson describe the Shoreham–Wading River Writing Project, its history and development. They describe the writing project classroom and writing participants' response in the project; eventually, they describe the district, school, region, and the classrooms they researched. For each of five case-study teachers, classroom settings and environments are detailed at length.

In their report, Perl and Wilson present the results of a four-year study (one year of participant observation in 1981 and three years of follow-up interviews, analysis, and writing). Sondra Perl and Richard Sterling worked with district teachers in the summer writing projects of 1979 to 1981; Nancy Wilson and James Carter joined Sondra Perl to study teachers' classrooms in 1981: Carter worked in elementary, Perl in middle, and Wilson in high school classrooms. Researchers spent four days a week in the town, sometimes staying in teachers' houses (of the ten teachers, two were couples), observing their classes daily for a full school year. The researchers and teachers formed a study group that met on Tuesdays for three years. Participants also included all of the students in the six teachers' classrooms during 1981 and various administrators.

Perl and Wilson and Carter visited classes, interviewed teachers, worked with the study group to review data, and continued to visit teachers classes in years two and three of the study (twice a month and once a month, respectively). Researcher Carter and three case-study teachers had to drop out of the project in subsequent years, leaving Perl and Wilson to compose the six case portraits, from their own observations in some instances and from the observations of others at other times. The book was co-authored, and teachers were asked to read materials and respond throughout.

Because so much data was collected by several researchers and over a significant period of time for a school setting, reports on teachers' classrooms were rich, varied, and extensive; researchers were able to describe the particular class culture and to look at it from the teacher's viewpoint, meeting the project's initial design goals. Perl and Wilson provided descriptions of how teachers taught, instances of teacher's experiencing classroom conflicts, successes, tensions, and resolutions. Because they worked to describe the classroom culture from the teachers' point of view, each chapter required different narrative strategies and case structuring:

> The chapters on Audre and Diane are longest, but while the chapter on Audre deals with a number of different aspects of Audre's teaching, the chapter on Diane explores one single issue in depth. In the chapter on Reba, we look closely at two first graders; in the chapter on Len, at four twelfth graders in a single writing group. The chapter on Ross follows a sequence of events; the chapter on Bill is organized around a theme (1986; 1998, xix).

You can see from this last description why I consider this book to offer novice researchers a primer of sorts, because Perl and Wilson's case-reporting strategies are methodologically sound and carefully reported, yet also varied and readable. According to the Denzin criteria, Perl and Wilson have created complete and satisfactory accounts.

While I have used most of Denzin's categories to guide me through my discussion of *Through Teachers' Eyes*, I might as usefully have chosen the questions provided by Michael Kamil, Judith Langer, and Timothy Shanahan in *Understanding Reading and Writing Research:*

> The following questions can serve as a checklist for understanding and evaluating ethnographic research reports and as a guide for researchers in communicating important information to their readers.
>
> 1. Has the goal of the ethnography been clearly stated? (What is it?)
> 2. Have the parameters of the context been clearly stated? (State them.)
> 3. Have data been obtained from varying frameworks within the context? (State them.)

4. Have one or more ethnographic methods been used? (Identify them.)

5. Have the recurrent patterns (for example, group membership) been described? (Relate them.)

6. Have the goals of the interactions been described from one or more points of view? (Which?)

7. Has the developing model been described? (What is it?)

8. Have the descriptions been regrounded? (How?)

9. What relevance does this study have for you? (1985, 49)

You might find it useful to read the book yourself, using these reading questions and comparing the notes you make to my notes.

In addition, several other reports of teachers' learning could be reviewed to see how different researchers used ethnographic techniques to different effect. My own study, *Something Old, Something New: College Writing Teachers and Classroom Change* (1990a) owes much to my study of Perl and Wilson's study. You'll note that I had fewer resources (one researcher), spent less time on the project (an unfunded dissertation), and limited my study to college teachers. In *Composing a Culture: Inside a Summer Writing Program with High School Teachers* (1994), Bonnie Sunstein studies the experiences of high school writing teachers enrolled in a three-week summer writing program. Perl and Wilson also reported on the results of teachers in their study who enrolled in a summer writing program, but their book focuses on these teachers after their writing-project experiences. Sunstein's book does the reverse: It offers an in-depth study of three weeks in the lives of teachers enrolled in the New Hampshire Writing Program, as detailed in three case studies.

Three other studies, although less ethnographic by research design, are worth considering in this bouquet of research on teachers' experiences. In *Eating on the Street: Teaching Literacy in a Multicultural Society* (1993), David Schaafsma investigates the stories teachers tell and the ways they interpret an event. He looks at the conflict that arose in "The Dewey Center Community Writing Project, a collaboratively designed summer writing program in Detroit's inner city" (xv) as teachers responded in dramatically different ways to a story which raised a major issue: "Should teachers confront poor black children about eating on the street, a conflict related to broader issues of authority and cultural difference?" (xviii). Schaafsma's story about telling stories is told in a variety of story formats, journals, discussions, interviews, and so on; he is not focusing on classrooms, but on teaching issues. Next, in *Seeing Yourself as a Teacher: Conversations with Five New Teachers in a University Writing Program* (1994), Elizabeth Rankin holds interview discussions with five new writing teachers and uses her analysis of these conversations to reflect on the research process as well as on these teachers' learning. Finally, in *Border Talk: Writing and Knowing in the Two-Year College* (1997), Howard B. Tinberg's study is again, like Rankin's study but unlike Perl and Wilsons' and Sunstein's studies, limited to college writing teachers, but this time considers teaching at the two-year-college level. Tinberg reports on discussions held by writing peer tutors and college teachers who "came together in the summer of 1994 to talk about writing, reading, and knowing" (ix). His report has something in common with Schaafsma's, in its use of journals, remembered and taped conversations, and so on.

If you read these five works, using the criteria for ethnographic intent that I presented in this section, you'll find that these criteria become increasingly less useful as researchers' stated goals and research designs move from the overtly ethnographic to the generally naturalistic to the narratively experimental. The more contemporary reports are as much about conversation, narrative investigation, and researcher self-analysis as they are about investigating the learning of others. For considering such reports, new reading criteria are necessary.

Reading Contemporary Research Reports: Self-reflexivity, Point(s) of View, and Narrative Perspectives

> Not only is our narrative presence inscribed in the stories we tell, but our assumptions about writing and discourse are refracted in the very forms with which we tell our stories. In short, the literacy events of others—the purported subject(s) of our inquiry—are inevitably framed in our own literacies, and that composition we call an ethnography takes on the shadings and hues of our own palette.
> —Patricia Sullivan 1996, 97

You've seen an illustration of Patricia Sullivan's assertion in the way I composed this book. In writing it, I was highly influenced by the studies I studied. As a teacher, I'm influenced by the study I completed. In doing this work, I affiliated with a certain developing tradition and I continue to teach from that tradition. For instance, I've pointed out how my own research was influenced by Perl and Wilson's project, and certainly my first dissertation student, Donna Sewell, was influenced by my research. Her research design grew from our discussions that I illustrated with anecdotes from my own work, which she had also read. As she designed her own project, she started from that discussion base and we worked to help her develop her own project, one that certainly improved on mine in that it took place over a longer time period and one that was greatly influenced as well by her reading of Elizabeth Chiseri-Strater's 1991 study.

In this way, my teaching about research draws its shades and hues from my professional palette, and Donna's ongoing research will continue to draw from the studies that shaded hers. Contemporary researchers are aware of the way their research is informed by their own literacy, and their projects often include an investigation of relationships—between members of a culture and between the ethnographic writing researcher and his subject(s).

If research is about interactions, then so is the reading of research. In *Academic Literacies*, Elizabeth Chiseri-Strater explored these interactions: "The research for this book takes place within overlapping and interrelated contexts that blur the boundaries between the history of the university and the life stories of the students, between public and private discourse, between learning and literacy, between researching then and writing now" (1991, xxiii). Chiseri-Strater's book presents a stylistically complicated narrative that investigates these interrelated contexts and boundaries as she studies two students—Anna and Nick—as they progress as writers through their first year of college. Writing about such research five years later, Chiseri-Strater notes some of the challenges of such reporting as a series of questions we might ask about her text and others like it:

> [H]ow much of our selv(es) is needed to guide the reader through the narrative about the other(s)? What do readers need to know and understand about the situatedness of the researcher and influences that affect her or his perspective that are relevant to an understanding of the informants in the culture under investigation? How much self-reflexivity is valuable to readers as a way of understanding the ethics and methodology of the research context? How are choices about self-disclosure made both on and off the page? Such questions about positionality haunt the ethnographer throughout the research process since, as Clifford Geertz has explained, positioning oneself during the field experience is subsequently connected to positioning oneself in the written ethnography: "Finding somewhere to stand in a text that is supposed to be at one and the same time an intimate view and a cool assessment is almost as much of a challenge as gaining the view and making the assessment in the first place" (10). (Chiseri-Strater 1996, 119)

Norman Denzin suggests that we can read research from an interactionist position; validity is assessed by exploring the process the writer used to make sense of his data, a procedure he terms VARA:

> *Validity-as-a-reflexive-accounting* (VARA) is an alternative perspective. . . . It places the researcher, the topic, and the sense-making process in interaction. . . . In keeping with the position that the social world is an interpreted world, not a literal world, always under symbolic construction (even deconstruction!), the basic idea is that the focus is on the process of the ethnographic work . . . :

1. the relationship between what is observed (behaviors, rituals, meanings) and the larger cultural, historical, and organizational contexts within which the observations are made (the substance);

2. the relationships naming the observer, the observed, and the setting (the observer);

3. the issue of perspective (or point of view), whether the observer's or the members', used to render the interpretation of the ethnographic data (the interpretation);

4. the role of the reader in the final product (the audience); and

5. the issue of representational, rhetorical, or authorial style used by the author(s) to render the description and/or interpretation (the style). (1994, 491)

Two other reflective researchers, Bonnie Sunstein and Brenda Brueggemann, offer criteria that can help us assess a writer's relationship to her report and how we present these relationships.

[I]t is useful to ask such key focusing questions as:

1. Where is the culture?

2. What is the researcher–writer's position in relationship to this culture?

3. Where is the history? Whose is it? Where does the researcher–writer find it?

4. What theory drives the researcher–writer's informants? What theory drives the researcher–writer?

5. What are the researcher–writer's sources of data?

6. What is the researcher–writer's position in relationship to the data and the text?

These questions offer a heuristic by which we can confront ethnography's tension and address our own positions as readers, writers, and researchers—between cultures, histories, artifacts, and theories. (Sunstein 1996, 181)

While Sunstein's questions continue to ground our reading of ethnographic methodology, Brueggemann's move is toward issues of narrative representation in qualitative research in general:

[Here are] questions that might guide us concerning representation in our qualitative research:

- What representations do we enter our research with? From the outset, how do we represent ourselves as participant–observer? As researcher–subject? As self–other?

- What representations inform and grow out of our ongoing interpretations of our data? Where and how do they conflict with those we entered with?

- What representations inform and grow out of our writing up the data?

- What representations are required or influenced by our various audiences?

- Which of our representations intersect, parallel, conflict with those of the subjects we are representing? Which give them voices, make them silent?

- Which of our representations give us voice, make us silent?

- And finally, is there yet another way we might ask these questions? Is there yet another way to represent? (Brueggemann 1996, 34)

There are several books that lend themselves well to analysis using questions about reflexivity, positionality, and representation. I've grouped these together because each addresses students' experiences as a primary research concern. First, Chiseri-Strater's 1991 book is written from an announced feminist viewpoint (she cites the work of Annas, Belenky, Bateson, Caywood and Overing, Gilligan, Grumet, Noddings, Rich, Showalter, and Woolf). Robert Brooke's 1991 *Writing and Sense of Self: Identity Negotiation in Writing Workshops* investigates the ways students negotiate their identities as writers and class members using psychological theory (Erikson, Goffman, Piaget), critical theory (Foucault), and literacy theory (Freire, Giroux, Vygotsky). Nancy Welch's 1997 *Getting Restless: Rethinking Revision in Writing Instruction* also relies on critical–psychological theory (Bakhtin, Freud, Lacan, Kristeva) and feminist theory (Anzaldua, de Beauvoir, de Lauretis, Frey, Gallop, hooks, Lourde, Rich, Trinh, and others). Given these researchers' influences, it is no surprise that the research reports constructed by these authors meditate on representation and interpretation more than they do on research methodology and data collection and analysis.

Works such as these have led ethnographic writing researchers from the halls of social sciences and anthropology departments to the parlors of literary studies. We trade in metaphor and storytelling and become aware that there are methods near at hand for analyzing our work for narrative strengths and strategies. Donald Polkinghorne suggests that we can look at plot:

> Plot is the narrative structure through which people understand and describe the relationship among the events and choices of their lives. Plots function to compose or configure events into a story by:
>
> 1. Delimiting a temporal range which marks the beginning and end of the story,
>
> 2. Providing criteria for the selection of event to be included in the story,

3. Temporally ordering events into an unfolding movement culminating in a conclusion, and

4. Clarifying or making explicit the meaning events have as contributors to the story as a unified whole. (1997, 13–14)

In his essay "The Narrative Roots of Case Study," Thomas Newkirk (1992) examines the way "The case-study researcher usually tells transformative narratives, ones in which the individual experiences some sort of conflict and undergoes a qualitative change in the resolution of that conflict" (134). Newkirk is not suggesting that we stop doing this, but that we understand that we are and examine the manner in which we do it. He continues in his essay to analyze several case-study representations, including one of his own, to show how researchers apply familiar narrative patterns to their interpretations. We couch our interpretations within classic narrative structures. For analyzing the way this has been done by all the case-study reports in the books I've cited in this chapter, you may find Joe Kincheloe's list useful:

[T]here are fictive elements in all representations and narratives. . . . One way to view these patterns (formulas) may involve emplotment strategies such as:

1. *Romance*—fables and epics, the animation of insensate things with sense and passion. Here knowledge is identified with the appreciation and celebration of the uniqueness and particularity of all things. A romantic analyst's work is completed when she or he finishes describing the phenomena in question.

2. *Tragedy*—classical Marxism, positivism, behavioral psychology, and reductionist cause–effect explanations. Here there is little real resemblance between the objects of the world. The process of change is best explained by the development of laws and/or mechanistic explanations of causality.

3. *Satire*—critical theory, psychoanalysis, existentialism, phenomenology, and other analytical forms that question previously established tropological/rhetorical explanations of the social world. Here existing structures are explained contextually and often ironically. Satirical analysis is innately critical of all forms of metaphorical identification or reductionism.

4. *Comedy*—Parsonian functionalism and the development of equilibrated cultural systems. Here attributes of ordered essences are established and particulars are generalized into stabilized universal truths (White, 1979).

5. *Absurdism*—nihilistic postmodernism, the post-ironic Baudrillardian breakdown of the relationship between signified and signifier. Here the possibility of meaning itself is brought into question. A return to prelinguistic perception and the loss of Enlightenment rationality in the return to myth is sought.

Obviously, these points are ideals and presented for heuristic purposes. In reality different formulas may bleed over their boundaries in
particular narrative forms. (1997, 65–66)

So far, I've been discussing how you can relate reading criteria and
question-sets to monograph and book-length studies. The short report,
the experimental report, and the dissertation or grant report all raise
particular reading issues, and I end this chapter by briefly considering
these types of texts.

Reading the Article, Essay, or Book Chapter

> Academic language poses at least two problems for reporting natural-
> istic studies. First, the single-voiced, monologic style of academic dis-
> course makes it a difficult form in which to present the multivoiced
> situations the naturalistic investigator seeks to represent . . . [and sec-
> ond] its avoidance of letter and confessional styles makes it an equally
> difficult medium in which to represent the evolving quality of natu-
> ralistic methods.
> —Lucille McCarthy & Steven Fishman 1996, 156–57

Book- and monograph-length ethnographic research reports suffer
from the constraints of academic conventions, as pointed out by Mc-
Carthy and Fishman; when authors choose not to abide by the conventions, they risk losing an academic audience, but they also risk boring them. Three hundred pages of author-evacuated prose can cause
any reader to begin to skim. It is no surprise, then, that the contemporary author is breaking these conventions, particularly by using both
letter and confessional styles, and some authors, as will be discussed,
are pushing the boundaries of literary style.

However, to the general constraints of academic conventions, ethnographers must add the constraints of size and space. Ethnographers
almost always feel they are trying to present too much data in too little
space. They chafe at the confines of a book chapter in an edited collection of essays. The academic journal presents them with an authorial
straitjacket in the form of a research article (one adhering more to the
conventions of scientific writing) or an academic essay (more discursive
but equally short—fifteen to thirty manuscript pages).

When reading any shorter research report, I'd direct you to any of
the previously suggested question-sets that seem most appropriate to
the researcher's goals, but I'd precede all these question-sets with the
qualifier, "Given the limited reporting space, how does the author meet

your reading criteria?" Or, to return to Harry Wolcott's quip that I reported in Chapter Five, "How well did this writer can the data? How well did she fit a few crucial clothes into her small suitcase?"

To learn how others have read shorter works, you might want to read the following "readings" of readings and then read the cited essays and articles yourself, using some of the question-sets in this chapter. In *The Making of Knowledge in Composition* (1987), Stephen North reads a *Research in the Teaching of English* article by Susan Florio and Christopher Clark, as do Janice Lauer and William Asher in their book *Composition Research: Empirical Designs* (1988). Lauer and Asher also look at a second study, by Alan Lemke and Lillian Bridwell, that appeared as an *English Education* essay. Michael Kamil, Judith Langer, and Timothy Shanahan (1985) apply their reading questions to a research chapter by Shirley Brice Heath. In his book chapter "Ethnography or Psychography? The Evolution and Ethics of a New Genre in Composition," Keith Rhodes (1997) reads an article by Carrie Leverenz that first appeared in an issue of *Journal of Advanced Composition*. These readings of research show you how other readers apply evaluative criteria to ethnographic writing research that has been shaped to meet the demands of chapter, article, and essay-writing conventions in our field.

Reading Experimental Texts

Contemporary researchers who are interested in writing don't always strive to meet the conventional expectations for research reports. John Van Maanen's *Tales of the Field: On Writing Ethnography* (1988) and Clifford Geertz's *Works and Lives: The Anthropologist as Author* (1988) explore the anthropological turn toward postmodern theories of research and representations of the research project. Van Maanen, in particular, charts the movement from authors' composing realist tales to a developing concern with confessional and impressionist tales of many types. For instance, he cites an ethnography that was composed in the manner of a murder mystery, after the chief in the community was murdered the day the researcher arrived "in the field." Van Maanen also cites other innovative and experimental anthropological works. Clifford Geertz discusses issues of authoring and creating an authorial persona, and examines the authoring process and writing tropes used by four classic anthropologists: Claude Levi-Strauss, Sir Edward Evan Evans-Pritchard, Bronislaw Malinowski, and Ruth Benedict.

Contemporary researchers are concerned with authorial voice and I-witnessing—with producing author-saturated texts (or with the impossibility of doing anything but this when writing from an I-witnessing stance). They also are interested in multiple-voicing, co-authoring, collaborating, creating collaged and fragmentary and open-ended texts, in producing texts that more accurately, to their mind(s), (re)present the contact zone evoked by Mary Louise Pratt (1991). It seems logical that the researcher who is concerned with the ethics of representation will become the writer who cannot but help be concerned with the ethics of representation; these concerns lead many current researchers to advocate more interactive texts—texts that in turn require more from their readers:

> Polyvocality in an ethnography creates a different kind of textual validity than one mediated by the univocal narrative. Since the reader— not just the researcher—has access to the textual data (at least part of it) that help inform theories and conclusions, he or she thereby assumes responsibility along with the researcher for figuring out how theories are being drawn. (Chiseri-Strater 1996, 129)

Because I have been interested in understanding experimental writing in my writing classrooms, I have been encouraging my students to investigate these styles in their essays. Their experiments have challenged me as a reader of experimental texts. In response, I've developed reading questions to help me read such texts. You might apply these questions to the intentionally experimental report, "Pico College," by Greg Tanaka (1997), which is printed in two columns, one labeled "story" and the other labeled "sidenotes."

1. Can I describe why this writing requires this style/format? (For instance, can I assume, as a reader, that these were intentional choices, not simply an easy way out or the results of a self-indulgent rhetorical display?)

2. Are there places in the writing where I sense that the researcher hid, patched, or ignored problems she was having in understanding her own writing goals or aims? (Did it seem as if she couldn't pull her two metaphors and/or interpretive lenses together, so she simply left white space or added a new subheading, assuming no one would notice discontinuity?)

3. If the author recast this as a more traditionally styled research report, what would he lose and what would he gain; what insights would the reader lose and what would the reader gain? (Does this seem, perhaps, a report that was more engaging for the writer than for the reader? Does the writer seem to be avoiding the hard work of analysis and asking the reader to work too hard to create an interpretation? Would this report in this experimental format be better considered an exploratory self-memo, and would the culture or material or reader be better served with a more traditional pre-

sentation, or, conversely, would casting it in the expected five-part formula of research reports poorly serve the design of this study, and why?)

4. In the published draft, did the writer pay enough attention to the reader? Has she done enough to "teach" her reader how to enter and make meaning from the experimental work? Does she convincingly share her reasons for her choices for this presentational format? If not, does the written report have enough power to make this argument implicitly? (For instance, sometimes it's okay to just come out and label a piece as exploratory, experimental, collaged, and so on, at the beginning and help the reader set her reading expectations; *alternate* and/or *experimental* doesn't mean "anything goes"; it means intentional in a different manner—does the writer usefully signal such intentions?)

I believe ethnographic research will continue to challenge researchers to be both conventional and experimental in the same project. They learn from reporting their research in expected ways and then push the boundaries of those conventions to see what can be learned by presenting data in new forms and formats. Then, they have to hope that their readers apply the appropriate evaluative criteria to take them at their experimental words.

Reading the Ethnographic Dissertation or Grant-Funded Report

> It seems, then, that qualitative dissertations look like they do for reasons that may or may not be integrally connected to the type of research undertaken. Institutional expectations, pleasing the dissertation committee, timelines, and hopes for professional publication may mitigate against an emergent, nontraditional format.
> —Judith M. Meloy 1994, 6

As you read other dissertations on the way to completing your own, remember: The researcher may not have always wanted to make the writing-it-up decisions he chose. In fact, you can assume he probably wanted to write a somewhat different report. You can see these differences when you compare dissertations to dissertations that are turned into books. To do this, look up the dissertations written by Chiseri-Strater, Sunstein, Welch, and me, and you'll see how different products grew from the same data. And there are different but equal constraints on those who write reports to funding agencies; these agencies will require that certain questions be answered in a certain order; there is rarely room in these reports for narrative or I-voiced work.

Often when you read a dissertation, you'll see the seams and notice the influence of committee, department, university, and/or field expectations on the shape of the final product. These writers may have been asked to have a summary abstract for an open-ended exploration, to format in a certain restrictive way, to fit narrative into a scientific report architecture, to adhere to a certain number of fixed or expected chapters rather than a more innovative model of chapters and interchapters, or data and commentary, and so on. To read a dissertation well, then, you will probably want to read it from several perspectives: at a minimum, from the perspective of the credentialing committee, as well as from the position of the researcher or qualifying candidate.

In Judith Meloy's study of dissertation writers, the writers in a reading group developed questions they would ask of a naturalistic research dissertation. You may find these useful not only for the dissertations you read, but also, as always, for the dissertation or funded report you are working to produce:

> Yet another product of the Study Group [of naturalistic dissertation writers] is a set of questions they generated around the issue of quality in qualitative research.
>
> **Verite:** Does the work ring true? Is it consistent with accepted knowledge in the field? Or if it departs, does it address why? Does it fit within the context of the literature? Is it intellectually honest and authentic?
>
> **Integrity** (as in architecture): Is the work structurally sound? Does it hang together? In a piece of research, is the design or research rationale logical, appropriate, and identifiable within a paradigm?
>
> **Rigor:** Is there sufficient depth of intellect, rather than superficial or simplistic reasoning?
>
> **Utility:** Usefulness, professionally relevant. Does it make a contribution to the field? Does the piece have a clearly recognizable professional audience?
>
> **Vitality:** Is it important, meaningful, nontrivial? Does it have a sense of vibrancy, intensity, excitement of discovery? Is the proper personae (or voice) used for the researcher author? Do metaphors, images, or visuals communicate powerfully?
>
> **Aesthetics:** Is it enriching, pleasing to anticipate and experience? Does it give me insight into some universal part of my educational self? Does it touch my spirit in some way? (Meloy 1994, 44–45)

I like the way these criteria humanize the dissertation process, allow it to be in service of the researcher, even while acknowledging the authority of the research community the researcher is working to join. I hope this book helps you understand your research project as a journey that leads to personal enrichment and educational insight. With that in mind, I'll leave you to develop your own best reading criteria from the criteria and values shared by the researchers I have quoted in this chapter.

Afterword

Taking It Back (Home) and on to the Next Project

> I call ethnography a meditative vehicle because we come to it neither as to a map of knowledge nor as a guide to action, nor even for enlightenment. We come to it as the start of a different kind of journey.
> —Stephen Tyler 1986, 140

Now it's time for my big claims: Ethnographic writing research can improve your teaching, deepen your understanding of writers, and encourage you to "read" educational settings more critically and more carefully. Like David Bleich, I believe that "ethnographic work changes the classroom by changing the social relations of teaching and learning" (1993, 192). I believe it not only changes, but also improves those relations. I believe an apprenticeship to this method of inquiry will do the same for you.

While you may be required in your job to conduct research, you will probably benefit personally as a teacher by studying the issues that seem most crucial to you. And, quite simply, to offer a good reading of data, you must find that data compelling, because you are required to return to it again and again. If, in returning, you're not engaged, or if, because of poor research design, your return is tedious, inefficient, or ineffectual, you will not fare well. Therefore, to even attempt the ethnographic practice of creating an ongoing "thick description" of a culture, you must be engaged at all levels of meaning making.

To paraphrase Stephen Tyler (1986), your final product is actually the result of a particular type of meditative journey. Because of the special nature of this journey, you'll find the culture and the construction making most compelling when you have both private and professional commitments to making meaning out of the events you're co-creating through your ethnographic attention.

For humanist—rather than social scientific—researchers; for writing program administrators wanting to know more about programs; for teachers eager to understand classrooms; for writers determined to learn more about writing—this inquiry method is both profitable and pleasurable, frustrating and deeply engaging. It represents voluntary (and I believe) necessary travel into sites of literacy learning that we may have thought we knew but benefit from seeing anew in order to affect and understand them. If the world, as James Clifford claims, is getting cartographically more and more unified, we still sometimes have yet to truly map the neighborhood—the classroom we inhabit and the classroom next door.

> I prefer sharply focused pictures, composed in ways that show the frame or lens. Ethnography, a hybrid activity, thus appears as writing, as collecting, as modernist collage, as imperial power, as subversive critique. Viewed most broadly, perhaps, my topic is a mode of travel, a way of understanding and getting around in a diverse world that, since the sixteenth century, has become cartographically unified. (Clifford 1988, 13)

Lest I sound too evangelical at this point, I'd like to say that the changes I expect you to undergo as an ethnographic writing researcher are not mystical or spiritual (though they could be, because any change-oriented enterprise could be). They are intellectual and practical and engaging changes because the researcher discovers how to read and write and think better, to sharpen her latent skills of perceptions, and to humanize sites of literacy.

The overly busy individual who steps to one side within or just outside of his normal work routine, who self-assigns research or accepts a research assignment, finds he has scheduled in potentially transformative social inquiry. He will view himself and his worksite differently when he returns to it, for social inquiry encourages him to raise ethical questions more often and to be more alert to opportunities for civic action:

> Writing for others takes place in the research text. In a fortuitous twist of fortune, the expressions of meaning contained in research texts are often profound for the self. Just as serving the self serves the research community, so too serving the community in research texts also serves

the self. . . . Personal experience research is a form of public inquiry
that has the potential for transcending the specialties of research in
particular subject experience. . . . (Clandinin & Connelly 1994, 425)

Additionally, ethnographic writing research as an ongoing enterprise and reflective inquiry as practice predispose you to ask questions
about literacy that matter. As you undertake your next research project,
you will feel more authoritative than you did during the first project.
Now you may be able to worry less about closeness to a culture (as when
a graduate student studies a peer's classroom and has to determine the
degree that prior friendship and assumptions about the teacher and
classroom will influence the scene of research) and more about guar-
anteeing your engagement and committing your time. This is probably
best done by setting up intrinsic goals that are as strong or stronger
than your extrinsic goals.

To stay engaged with your data and your writing commitments,
you'll need to do as poet William Stafford suggests and "lower your
standards" in order to begin at all. Instead of waiting for a future sab-
batical or an unharried year of teaching, or being awarded a grant in a
competitive grant environment, accept what you can get done, study
your classes, look to community literacy projects, encourage program-
matic self-study, and work at the micro- and mini-ethnography level if
you can't work at the macro and long-term, multiparticipant level (and
not all of us want to do the latter, anyway). By seeing yourself as a researcher, you encourage continued research.

You also learn a great deal about writing by the act of writing research, whether your work sees the light of public print or not. There
are important lessons to learn from the ethnographic writing research
composing process—even when you need to let the data go or even
when your final reports take an unexpected turn. This is a lesson I have
had to relearn with each project, large and small, and it's a lesson I see
my students learning, and relearning. And, because you can't return to
the field (the academic literacy site is no longer convened), as classic
anthropologists sometimes were able to do, it stands to reason that you'll
focus on and want to learn all you can from the inquiry process itself.
Process writings, whether they show up in a final product in a manner
now being undertaken by some postmodern ethnographers or in the
form of intermediary texts that are later edited out of the final product,
can provide insight. Stephen North suggests that you should expect to
do this juggling of realities and genres, given that ethnographers, as he
sees it, are "Serving as a kind of alternate reality brokers, they [ethnog-
raphers] deliberately juxtapose one imaginative universe with another,
struggling, in the effort, to make both more intelligible—to themselves,
to us, to the inhabitants of those alternate universes" (North 1987, 279).

Your second entry to the field may represent the first time you truly feel like a professional. It becomes time to claim your membership in our research discourse community—particularly if you are transforming a dissertation into journal articles or a research monograph—and to evaluate the direction of your continuing research. Completing the first ethnography and then going on, as a learning, fallible, yet engaged researcher, helps you realize that living (and enjoying) the ethnographic life overall is what you've really been learning; and, if the life, fits, I'd say, wear it.

For me, it has been a fine fit. There are few things so pleasurable as participating in the imaginative and systematic thinking that an ethnographic stance requires. The drafting of texts, also, activates many writerly qualities and valuable challenges: "[T]his issue, negotiating the passage from what one has been through 'out there' to what one says 'back here,' is not psychological in character. It is literary. It arises for anyone who adopts what one may call, in a serious pun, the I-witnessing approach to the construction of cultural descriptions . . ." (Geertz 1988, 78).

There is something very satisfying about working to become a convincing "I," although that "I" changes regularly. The "I" of your first ethnography will give way to the "I" of future projects. Each witnessing is constructed; each journey teaches you and encourages you to travel on. Having been there and back again, I hope that you'll allow yourself to learn from both failure and success, to be both idealistic and pragmatic as you embark on your research travels once again.

A Prospectus
Writing Sequence
by Donna N. Sewell

Prewriting and Planning

Rough Notes: Student Literacies

My dissertation focuses on the writings of first-year college students and hopes to begin to answer some of the following questions: How do students use writing in their lives? How do they define writing? by function? by involvement? What types of writing do they do? How do their uses of writing relate to literacy?

I am doing ethnographic inquiry into one summer session of ENC 1101, maybe a Summer Enrichment class, and the other classes the students take. In addition to studying this one class, I am following the students from this class for the rest of the academic school year.

Sources

Sources to consider include Robert Brooke's *Writing and Sense of Self* and Walvoord and McCarthy's *Thinking and Writing in College*. I should read primary sources on ethnography (Geertz and Van Maanen). Also, research into literacy should be considered, such as Elizabeth Chiseri-Strater's *Academic Literacies,* as well as student perceptions and attitudes embodied in such works as Jennie Nelson's "This Was an Easy Assignment."

The ERIC database should also be researched by the following keywords: ethnography, naturalistic-research, context-based research, classroom-based research, classroom research, writing research, fresh-man-composition, student-role, college-English, college-freshman writing instruction, student-attitudes and identity negotiation.

Research Methods

- Field notes from participant-observation in a summer ENC 1101 class
- An initial open-ended survey that asks students to spell out the types and purposes of writing for them
- A journal kept by the students in which they write down daily the types of writing they've done that day, their feelings about the writing, and the amount of time spent on it
- Interviews with all students (13?) within the first three weeks
- A refined, more detailed survey (Likert scale) for students to complete toward the end of the semester
- Interviews with six students (again toward the end of the semester)
- Group meetings every three weeks with students (split students into three groups so that I'm meeting with one group a week); these meetings should be on campus somewhere convenient for all
- Photocopies of all the text artifacts produced by teacher and students
- Interviews with teacher (three times: before semester, midsemester, and after semester)
- Background information on students (?): SAT scores, grades
- Research journal detailing the process of understanding the community
- Photocopy of all students' writing assignments from all classes

Questions

What type of class to enter? Summer Enrichment classes offer a more cohesive community, as these students enter smaller classes that encourage more student-teacher interaction and they often take classes together. Thus, the data collection procedures may be easier if half the students are all taking a history class together too. Also, a six-week semester does not allow much time for community building, so the extra cohesion of students being in a program together may be helpful. The students in Summer Enrichment programs generally all live together in one dorm. (Last year, it was DeGraff.) If I do enter such a class, however, I need to find as much background into the Summer Enrichment program and into Horizons as possible before summer. Most of the

Summer Enrichment students feed directly into Horizons and Multi-Cultural Support Services, I think.

How much should I ask of the teacher? And who should be the teacher? How much should the teacher be told of the project? The real question for me is whether or not I should ask the teacher to sponsor the type of journal I'm looking for. I want access to all the students' texts, but I don't know that I want the students to keep the writing journal I'm talking about as a class requirement. What does that do to students' attitudes toward my project?

Sources

Sources about ethnographic research include the following:

Bogdan, R. and S. Bicklen. *Qualitative Research for Education: An Introduction to Theory and Method.* Boston: Allyn & Bacon, 1982.

Brodky, Linda. "Writing Ethnographic Narratives." *Written Communication* 4 (Jan. 1987): 25–50.

Diesing, P. "Ethnography." *The English Record* (1984): 2–6.

Doehny-Farina, Stephen and Lee Odell. "Ethnographic Research on Writing: Assumptions and Methodology." Lee Odell and Dixie Goswami, eds. *Writing in Non-Academic Settings.* New York: Guilford, 1985. 503–15.

Erickson, F. "What Makes School Ethnography 'Ethnographic'?" *Anthropology and Education Quarterly* 4 (1973): 10–19.

Florio, S. and C. M. Clark. "The Functions of Writing in an Elementary Classroom." *Research in the Teaching of English* 16 (1982): 115–30.

Geertz, C. *The Interpretation of Cultures.* New York: Basic Books, 1973.

Glaser, B. and A. Strauss. *The Discovery of Grounded Theory: Strategies for Qualitative Research.* New York: Aldine, 1967.

Goetz, J. P. and M. D. LeCompte. *Ethnography and Qualitative Design in Educational Research.* New York: Academic Press. 1984.

Heath, S. *Ways with Words: Language, Life, and Work in Communities and Classrooms.* New York: Cambridge UP, 1983.

Kantor, Kenneth. "Classroom Contexts and the Development of Writing Intuitions: An Ethnographic Case Study." R. Beach and L. S. Bridwell, eds. *New Directions in Composition Research.* New York: Guilford Press, 1983. 72–94.

LeCompte, M. D. and J. F. Goetz. "Problems of Reliability and Validity in Ethnographic Research." *Review of Educational Research* 52 (1982): 31–60.

McCall, G. L. and J. I. Simmons, eds. *Issues in Participant Observation: A Text and Reader.* Reading, MA: Addison Wesley, 1969.

Mosenthal, P., L. Tamor, and S. Walmsley, eds. *Research on Writing: Principles and Methods.* New York: Longman, 1983.

Shatzman, L. and A. Strauss. *Field Research.* Englewood Cliffs, NJ: Prentice-Hall, 1973.

Wilson, S. "The Use of Ethnographic Techniques in Education." *Review of Educational Research* 47 (1977): 2452–65.

Sources about literacy include the following:

Bleich, David. "Reconceiving Literacy: Language Use and Social Relations." Chris M. Anson, ed. *Writing and Response: Theory, Practice, and Research.* Urbana, IL: NCTE, 1989.

Chiseri-Strater, Elizabeth. *Academic Literacies: The Public and Private Discourse of University Students.* Portsmouth. NH: Boynton/Cook, 1991.

Tannen, D. "Oral and Literate Strategies in Spoken and Written Discourse." R. Bailey and R. Fosheim, eds. *Literacy for Life.* New York: NILA, 1983. 79–96.

ERIC Searches

Using "literacy and (college writing)," I brought up 14 citations, including the following:

Rose, Shirley K. "Autobiography as Representative Anecdote: A Burkean Paradigm for Research on Literacy Cultures." Paper presented at CCCC (38th, Atlanta, GA, Mar. 19–21, 1987). [ED 286189]

Welch, Kathleen E. "Autobiography and Advanced College Writing." Paper presented at CCCC (38th, Atlanta, GA, Mar. 19–21. 1987). [ED 281229]

Using "Writing-instruction and role and (college English)," I brought up 38 searches, including the following:

Brooke, Robert. "Lacan, Transference, and Writing Instruction." *College English* 49 (Oct. 1987): 679–91.

Gregory, Marshall W. "Writing, Literacy, and Liberal Arts." *ADE Bulletin* 82 (Win. 1985): 27–32. [420.5 A849]

Metzger, Elizabeth. "Do as I say and (Not?) as I Do or How Teachers of Writing Write." Paper presented at the CCCC (33rd, San Francisco, CA, Mar. 18–20, 1982).

Mueller, Roseanna M. "Teaching Writing through Literature: Toward the Acquisition of a Knowledge Base." Paper presented at the Mid-West Regional Conference on English in the Two-Year College (21st, St. Louis, MO, Feb. 13–15, 1986). [ED 273963]

Using "Freshman-composition and writing-research and student-role," I brought up the following citation:

Worth, Anderson, and others. "Cross-Curricular Underlife: A Collaborative Report on Ways with Academic Words." *CCC* 41 (Feb. 1990): 11–36. [805 C697]

Using "Literacy and Writing-Instruction and Ethnography," I brought up nine citations, including the following:

Morris, Richard W. and Conan N. Louis. "A Writing of Our Own." Improving the Functional Writing of Urban Secondary Students. Final Report. University City Science Center, Philadelphia, PA. [ED 241668]

Nardini, Gloria. "Towards an Ethnographic Understanding of Adolescent Literacy." *Writing Instructor* 9 (Fall–Win. 1990); 45–56. [805 W9561]

Using "student-attitudes and (college writing)," I brought up 21 citations, including the following:

Anson, Chris M. "Composition and Communicative Intention: Exploring the Dimensions of Purpose in College Writing." 1984. [ED 257076]

Brent, Rebecca and Richard M. Felder. "Writing Assignments—Pathways to Connections, Clarity, Creativity." College Teaching 41 (Spr. 1992): 43–47. [370.5 I34]

Lofty, John. "Bridging High School and College Writing." *Freshman English News* 18 (Fall 1989): 26–27, 30–31. [420.5 F885]

CIJE Searches: Feb. 1993 Volume

Search Term: Literacy

DeStefano, Johanna S. and others. "Open to Suggestion." *Journal of Reading* 36 (Oct. 1992): 132–35.

Pugh, Sharon L. "New Perspectives on Reading and Writing or 'There's No Place Like Home': Keynote Address to IRA College Reading Improvement Special Interest Groups, May 1991. *Forum for Reading* 23 (1-991–92): 7–14.

Search Term: Writing (Composition)

Larsen, Elizabeth. "The Progress of Literacy: Edward Tyrell Channing and the Separation of the Student Writer from the World." *Rhetoric Review* 11 (Fall 1992): 159–71.

Penrose, Ann M. "To Write or Not to Write: Effects of Task and Task Interpretation on Learning through Writing." *Written Communication* 9 (Oct. 1992): 465–500.

Search Term: Teacher Role

Brann, Eva T. H. "St. John's Educational Policy for a 'Living Community.'" *Change* 24 (Sept.–Oct. 1992): 36–43.

The Dissertation Prospectus

Writing for the Academy and for the Self:
The Literacies of First-Year Students

How do students use writing in their lives? How do they understand and meet the demands of the academy? Do they write outside of school? If so, what for? Understanding student literacies is vital to composition research. How literate are students? How multiple are their literacies? One basic question remains: For what purposes and how often do students write?

As a college-level composition teacher, I present writing as tool for understanding ourselves and our worlds. I also, however, want students to produce better writings, to gain control of some of the conventions of writing. Although I believe these two goals are connected, they do not always mesh, thus pulling me in different directions.

As a teacher, I sometimes mistakenly assume that students write only under academic demands and, even then, only to the assignment's specifications. However, Mike Rose reminds me that students are highly literate: "Reading and writing, as any ethnographic study would show, are woven throughout our students' lives" (354). Rose's words challenge me to understand student literacies, to back away from teaching writing until I understand students' uses of writing.

Before trying to help students write, I feel compelled to understand writing on their terms. Several recent articles and book-length studies work toward such understandings: Elizabeth Chiseri-Strater's *Academic Literacies,* Jennie Nelson's "This Was an Easy Assignment," and Lucille McCarthy's "A Stranger in Strange Lands." Appropriately, all of these studies depend upon ethnographic methodology. Janice Lauer and William Asher summarize ethnographic research:

> Ethnography engages researchers, sometimes as participant–observers, in a study of writing in context. . . . Using a variety of methods, they collect a rich array of data, taking field notes, interviewing, collecting writing samples and whatever other information is available. They analyze and code the data, identifying, defining, and relating what seem to be important variables, and finally report their study in the form of thick descriptions. (48)

Ethnography highlights context, refusing to remove writing from its environment. While experimental, clinical, and formal studies, to borrow Stephen North's research categories, all inform our knowledge of writing, ethnographic inquiry seems the most appropriate way of understanding students' uses of writing.

Ethnographic inquiry does not operate under the rubric of the scientific method, following a linear model of hypothesis testing. Instead, as an Ethnographer, I adapt my study to the community as North insists:

> Ethnographers cannot identify their investigative problems until they see them. And even then, formulated problems—questions and answers about what happens in that community, and what it means— must be regarded as tentative, subject to partial or total revision either as the investigator's understanding of them grows clearer, or as things in the community change. (286)

Thus, my initial questions may change as I enter the culture and gain access to the participants. My main responsibility as a researcher lies in accounting for the community and its ways of making meaning rather than in sticking to preconceptions. While Lucy McCormick Calkins dismisses a linear model of research as an oversimplification (126), ethnography is, of course, less structured than other methodologies. John Dean, Robert Eichhorn, and Lois Dean emphasize ethnography's more responsive nature: In fact it aims to make a virtue of non-standardization by frequently redirecting the inquiry on the basis of data coming in from the field to ever more fruitful areas of investigation" (20).

Field work in composition, however, poses unique problems, as Howard S. Becker and Blanche Geer point out: "In interviewing members of groups other than our own . . . we often do not understand that we do not understand and are thus likely to make errors in interpreting what is said to us" (324). As a researcher, I carefully explore terminology with students and teachers rather than assume our words mean the same things. My interpretations are tested against student as well as teacher perceptions. Such triangulation protects the integrity of the research.

To begin to understand how students use writing personally and academically, I follow four students through three semesters of college, beginning the summer term preceding their freshman year. In addition to observing the environment of a first-semester writing course, I also study the students' uses of writing in other disciplines and in their personal lives. While guided by other theorists' and researchers' terminology of the functions of writing (see Florio and Clark and Britton), I heed North's advice not to accept such models without testing them in the new environment (281).

Literature Review

Qualitative research covers a wide range of methodologies and topics. Calkins develops categories to distinguish between types of naturalistic inquiry: descriptive case studies, ethnographically oriented case studies, and teaching case studies (130–31). My research falls under the second category. Calkins describes this type, in which

> researchers become participant observers in a natural setting, spending at least a semester (and often a year or two) as live-in observers. Data are gathered through a range of methods, with overlapping information coming from field-based observations, formal and informal interviews, questionnaires, and analyses of written products. (130–31)

These methods comprise most of those in my research project: observing and participating in freshman writing classes, interviewing students and teachers, studying students and their writings for a year, and analyzing student writings.

This research begins with an ethnographic study of one first-year composition class, in which I function as a participant–observer. Becker and Geer describe the role of a participant–observer as one "in which the observer participates in the daily life of the people under study . . . observing things that happen, listening to what is said, and questioning people over some length of time" (322). Participating in this composition class allows me access to students in transition, negotiating their identities as they move into the intellectually demanding but more socially free environment of college. How do students handle this transition?

Participant observation places me in the environment as an interested observer without the authority of the teacher. This lack of teacherly authority works to my advantage by putting students on a more equal plane with me. To reinforce this equality, during the summer my only role is that of a researcher; I am not teaching. From previous research projects, I know that while students may initially be self-conscious around a researcher, they soon become accustomed to my presence, sometimes to the point of disrupting class.

Ethnographic inquiry has been put to a variety of research uses, including studying the use of writing in other disciplines. Walvoord and McCarthy's *Thinking and Writing in College* exemplifies such usage. Lee Odell, Dixie Goswami, and Doris Quick focus on the heart of questions about academic literacies:

> What must one know or be able to do in order to write well in, say, biology or sociology? What analytic skills will one need in order to write a well-thought-out case study or laboratory report? What qualities of style and organization are important for a given discipline? Do different disciplines vary in the demands they make of writers? Do lab reports entail conceptual, stylistic, or organizational skills that differ from those skills required for a case study? (175)

How is writing used in academic disciplines? How do students understand these writings? Moving beyond the writing classroom allows me access to student encounters with such writings.

The study of discipline-specific academic discourse has gained status at many universities. Writing across the curriculum programs attempt to incorporate writing in academic disciplines other than English. Definitions flourish for writing across the curriculum, often becoming entangled with theories and pedagogy about writing to learn. However,

Anne Ruggles Gere claims a distinction between writing across the curriculum and writing to learn: "Writing across the curriculum aims to improve the quality of writing, while writing to learn focuses on better thinking and learning" (6). A more accurate distinction might be between a focus on discourse analysis and a focus on writing-to-learn strategies.

The push for discourse analysis aims to make students more rhetorically flexible, more aware of the contextual nature of writing. Worth Anderson et al. deal with the differences between the freshman writing courses and courses within other disciplines: "The 'discourse community' defined in composition was rarely reproduced later because students and teachers in other introductory-level classes operated in two very separate and often conflicting rhetorical worlds" (11). Such conflicting worlds evaluate writing by other criteria and use writing for other purposes, as Elaine Maimon emphasizes, "The forms of writing within a particular intellectual community manifest modes of thinking within that community" (111). Anne Herrington urges that writing be used to help students learn the language and thought patterns of particular disciplines: "The writing assignments should be used as opportunities to learn to use the particular patterns of inquiry of a discipline, whether they be processes of observation and generalization or a problem-solving process of applying a general principle to specific situations" (381).

Because conventions are community-sanctioned, they are fluid. Geoffrey Chase emphasizes the messiness of learning: "But discourse communities and the conventions that characterize them are not monolithic and, further, the ways in which students learn or do not learn those conventions are varied and complex" (14). Thus, when we speak of academic discourse, we encourage a monolithic view of academic literacy that may not hold true; academic literacies may be a more appropriate term.

Operating between proponents of discourse analysis and writing to learn are C. H. Knoblauch and Lil Brannon. In "Writing as Learning Through the Curriculum," Knoblauch and Brannon work to change the notion of writing across the curriculum from one that works to teach the forms inherent in a discipline (correct writing) to one that works to use writing to engage students in intellectual discipline-specific dialogue. Thus, they argue for using writing-to-learn strategies to immerse students in discipline-specific writings.

The focus on writing to learn primarily develops from Janet Emig: "Writing represents a unique mode of learning, not merely valuable, not merely special, but unique" (122). Writing-to-learn pedagogies often depend on students developing personal relationships with the subjects (Moffett's I/it). Emig also discusses the need for personal connection: "Successful learning is also engaged, committed, personal learning" (126).

Not much research exists on students' personal uses of writing, except by expressivists who see personal writing as a way to break away from dry academic prose. However, Chiseri-Strater uncovers how two students (Nick and Anna) write for themselves.

Methodology

This research is shaped by one over-arching question: How do first-year writers use writing to make sense of the demands placed upon them by the undergraduate curriculum and to make sense of their personal lives? Other research questions include the following:

- What functions do academic and personal writings serve for first-year writers?
- What are students' perceptions of academic discourse?
- How do students categorize their writings?
- How do first-year students perceive the required writing course as an introduction to college writing?
- For what does the writing course prepare them?
- How do students compare/contrast the writing required of them in varied disciplines?
- How often do students write?
- What attitudes do they hold toward writing?
- What types of writings are encouraged in the undergraduate courses?
- To what degree do students understand and adopt the terminology of their teachers?
- What prompts self-sponsored writing?

To begin answering these and other questions, I follow four students through three semesters of college beginning in the summer session. For a quick glance at data collection, see the chart in the appendix.

My research methodology develops from the work of several other researchers, such as McCarthy, Nelson, and Chiseri-Strater. McCarthy follows a student through three consecutive semesters as well, though she starts with a second-semester freshman. McCarthy states her goal precisely, "The ultimate aim of this study is to contribute to our understanding of how students learn to write in school" (236). This is my goal, too, but I am also interested in how students use writing in their personal lives.

This study begins with an ethnographic inquiry into a first-year writing class to study the culture of this class in which students first encounter writing in the university. The first-semester writing course meets every day for seventy-five minutes. The instructor is an experienced teaching assistant within the first-year writing program. I function as a participant–observer within this class, attending and audiotaping class daily while taking field notes. I also interview the teacher twice and the eight key informants weekly.

The students I work with in this project came to college six weeks early. They attended the "IC" session of our university schedule during the summer. I choose to begin my research at this point because we require students to take two writing courses their first year. By starting in the summer, I can observe what happens when students are no longer required to take writing courses during their spring semester. What are their attitudes toward writing? Do they choose or avoid writing-intensive classes? Do they write outside of class?

To ensure that four students will remain available at the end of the academic year, I begin my research with eight subjects from this composition class. And my research is not limited to this one class. I also follow each student into one other academic class each semester to help understand the writing required of them in that particular discipline. Although I am interested in observing students' use of writing in all their classes, my resources limit me to one additional class per student per semester. The students and I negotiate which other classes I observe. To understand the writing in these varied disciplines, I meet with and interview the instructors and observe the classes on the day(s) that writing is discussed. In our interviews, students and I discuss the ways in which they use writing in all these classes as well as in their personal lives. Their writing logs also provide opportunities for us to record students' personal and academic uses of writing.

Fall semester, I continue to meet with students regularly for interviews, though we drop back to a bi-weekly schedule. In addition, the number of students drop from eight to six at this point. Of course, the number may drop because of student attrition, but if not, I will force the decrease so that I may observe fewer students in greater depth. I have no intention of focusing on eight students, because I risk losing depth of inquiry with such a large number. I observe the students' writing classes (ENC 1102: Writing about Literature or an appropriate substitute) once a week and interview their teachers once during the semester. Also, the students and I negotiate another class for us to try and make sense of. As before, I meet with and interview the instructor about the ways in which they use writing in this class, and I observe any days in which writing is discussed.

Spring semester, we follow this same schedule, except that I only keep track of one class for each student because they will no longer be in required writing classes. The students and I decide which class to focus on, giving preference to writing-intensive classes or classes in their major. Also, the number of students drops from six to four. We still meet bi-weekly for hour-long interviews, and I still interview teachers.

Data Collection

Data collection methods include my field notes, interviews with research students on a weekly basis, interviews with the teacher, students' writing logs (see appendix), and student writing samples.

Field notes. During the summer, I attend the composition class daily and audiotape the class as well as keep extensive field notes to help me understand the community being formed. My notes focus more on student and teacher reactions and interactions, while the tapes catch the verbal exchanges. I transcribe the tapes daily for complete records of classes. I also participate in in-class writing activities and group activities but don't work on out-of-class activities and projects. The non-composition classes I attend only when the teacher plans to discuss writing. I tape those class sessions and keep field notes of them as well. During the fall semester, I attend each student's composition class at least once every two weeks. My notes allow me an opportunity to observe students' initial encounters with writing in the academy.

Interviews with students. During the summer session, I meet with the eight key informants on a weekly basis for roughly an hour. These interviews are audiotaped and transcribed. To help keep the interviews roughly parallel, we focus each interview around certain areas (writing background, interpretations of writing assignments, successful writing, personal writing, student life, academic writing), but we also let the conversation flow to pick up student concerns that I may not have noticed. Each student is interviewed separately. These interviews, along with students' writing logs, provide most of the data about their personal writings.

Interviews with teachers. I meet with the composition teachers (summer and fall) at least twice (during the first week of classes and after the semester ends) to help me understand their goals and backgrounds. I also interview the teachers in other disciplines to discuss how they use writing in their classes and to ask permission to observe those days that writing is discussed. These interviews allow me a new perspective on writing against which to test the developing interpretations of the students and my own. We will discuss assignments, the uses of writing, discipline-specific writing, etc. These interviews not only provide needed triangulation, but they also help me make sense of classroom activities.

Students' writing logs. Students keep track of the ways in which they use writing and the amounts of time spent on these uses. These forms consist of checklists previously constructed and tested on myself. Students write the amount of time in minutes spent on each activity. During interviews, I quickly total the time spent on writing so that we may discuss and analyze any trends for that week. Each student produces a quick freewrite during the interview in response to the completed form. Forms are updated according to student needs. This form provides the major data source on time spent writing.

Writing Log

Name: _____

	Mon	Tues	Wed	Thurs	Fri	Sat	Sun
Letter writing							
Essay writing							
Revising							
Note taking							
Doing homework							
Brain storming							
Doodling							
Listing							
Journal writing							
Writing poetry							
Writing songs							
Miscellaneous							

Note: Please indicate the time in minutes.

Writing samples and assignments. Students submit one sample of each type of academic writing they produce for each class during this year-long research project. Also, I collect copies of all the writing assignments they receive in the focus classes. These assignments, along with teacher interviews, help me understand academic writing demands. In addition to samples of academic writing, the students submit a sample of each type of personal writing: letters, lists, poetry, etc. Too often, we think of students only in terms of their academic performance. I want to see more of the whole person. Academic literacy cannot be separated from personal literacy.

Research Log

In addition to field notes, I keep a research log in which I puzzle through situations, committing myself to short writings after each addition to my data collection: participant-observation of classes, interviews with students, etc. These writings allow me to focus in on problematic aspects of data collection, interesting trends, emerging patterns.

Data Analysis Procedures

Data collection is an overwhelming process. To keep from being overwhelmed by the amount of data coming in, I continually condense data. Every week I read my accounts of the class based on field notes and transcripts and make notes of the salient features. I memo myself in regard to such salient features, including interesting excerpts from the classes, interviews, or writing samples. Thus, data reduction is an ongoing process.

Writing logs are precoded so that they may be quickly added and analyzed.

Works Cited

[Works cited are included in the Bibliography at the end of this book.]

Data Collection

Summer 1993

- Observe one first-year writing class daily.
- Interview teacher of composition class during week one and after semester ends.
- Interview eight students weekly.
- Collect writing logs from students weekly.

- Collect writing samples of each type of writing (personal and academic) students produce during semester.
- Identify one additional focus class for each of the eight students and interview these teachers.
- Observe focus classes on days writing is discussed. Collect class handouts (policy sheets, writing assignments, etc.) from composition class and focus classes. Collect class notes from students on days writing is discussed in focus classes.

Fall 1993
- Observe second-semester writing classes for six students biweekly.
- Interview teachers of composition class during week one and after semester ends.
- Interview six students bi-weekly.
- Collect writing logs from students bi-weekly.
- Collect writing samples of each type of writing (personal and academic) students produce during semester.
- Identify one additional focus class for each of the six students and interview these teachers.
- Observe focus classes on days writing is discussed.
- Collect class handouts (policy sheets, writing assignments, etc.) from composition class and focus classes.
- Collect class notes from students on days writing is discussed in focus classes.

Spring 1994
- Observe second-semester writing classes for six students bi-weekly.
- Interview teachers of composition class during week one and after semester ends.
- Interview six students bi-weekly.
- Collect writing logs from students bi-weekly.
- Collect writing samples of each type of writing (personal and academic) students produce during semester.
- Identify one additional focus class for each of the six students and interview these teachers.
- Observe focus classes on days writing is discussed. Collect class handouts (policy sheets, writing assignments, etc.) from composition class and focus classes. Collect class notes from students on days writing is discussed in focus classes.

Permission Form

Permission

As part of my dissertation, I will be studying the uses of writing by first-year students. I will not use your name or identify you in any manner. A pseudonym will be provided to discuss your work. I function in this class only as a researcher and in no way does your work with me affect your performance in your courses. By signing the form below, you grant me access to your work and provide permission for me to use your work.

Signature _____

Printed name _____ Date _____

Mini-Ethnographies

Devan Cook: Considering Feminism, Pedagogy, and Underlife

[T]he *phenomenological* Ethnographer's chief investigative tool must be his or her own consciousness.

—Stephen North 1987, 303

The field is not merely reported in the texts of fieldwork: it is constituted by our writing and reading.

—Paul Atkinson 1992, 9

Frame

Field Notes from the first day observing Group 5, a peer-response group in Sandra's first-year writing class: .

> 9-14-93 [A writer from another group, April, has just read a 500 word exploration on abortion.] Josh asks about something in the paper,

the choice of aborting a defective fetus. "You mean you'd rather kill your baby yourself?" Sherae offers her opinion that it's easier for the mother to abort, though she doesn't say what's easier about it. No one questions her on this. Josh says he sees what's being said, "Well, it's your choice." Then he stretches: "Abortion. It's a shame."

Immediately Bryan chimes in with a question about the Wild Pizza. Then there's a fraternity discussion. Michelle and Sherae watch silently while Bryan and Josh talk. Josh is planning a road trip to someplace where the weather is better or cooler. The next reader, a guy with a shaved head, reads. Josh responds to his writing: "Cool." Then the men are on to intramural football. The women are silent, silent.

9-16 [A full-class discussion about racial issues that quickly moves into a general discussion of stereotyping.] None of the black students talk. People sort of can't decide who the bad guys are, except skinheads. Sherae finally speaks up and argues. She doesn't sound angry, just firm.

[later] After typing all these notes up, what really stands out to me is the silence of the women in Group 5.

My research partner, Ron DePeter, and I began our mini-ethnography with ideas about methodology: we would observe the classroom, take field notes, interview members of the class, distribute a survey, and interview the teacher, Sandra Teichmann, twice. Our goal at first was to see what there was to see; something, we felt sure, would suggest itself to us as a topic for further exploration, and we could test-drive what we had learned, that ethnography is hypothesis-generating. On our first day in Sandra's class, during the week I had told myself was a "see what's going on and get my feet wet" week, I sat in on Group 5 because there was an empty seat beside them when I came in right before class began. In Group 5 were Josh, a tall student with a flushed face and two rings on his right hand—silver arrangements of tiny skulls—who (almost always, I discovered) balanced in his tipped-back chair next to the window, who kidded around a lot and to whom everyone else in the group seemed to defer; Bryan, with red hair shaved at the sides, who sat next to Josh, also in a tipped-back chair, and talked mostly to him; Mike, who sat at the other side of the table from Josh and Bryan and made more comments directed to the readings and fewer about intramural football; Michelle, a white woman with a long brown ponytail who sat next to Mike and listened, laughing often but rarely saying a word; and Sherae, a black woman who sat at the head of the table and stared out the window or into a space above the center of the classroom. The silence of the women, in marked contrast to Josh and Bryan's almost constant talk (I want to say chatter here) about football, fraternities, or whether or not they got a letter from home struck me: it wasn't so much that they talked less as it seemed unusual or significant to me if they said anything: I noticed the sound of their voices.

I suspect that Sherae's position with regard to the group relates to race as well as, and perhaps more than, gender issues.[1] At first I had planned to focus on her and her writing, but when I asked her how she felt about this, she said she'd have to think about it and didn't respond, ever. She even missed the next class day, and when the class format changed, I decided that pressuring her was foolish and that the study could and ought to be altered to accommodate the new situation better. If Ron and I observed a whole group of which she was a part, we could take advantage of both our and their numbers, we thought.

Sandra's 1101 classes run in a somewhat unusual way that requires some explanation. According to the course guide, students are responsible for completing 29 exploratory writings of 500 words each as well as 4 extended exploratory writings of 1500 words: this class used the newspaper as a text and all assignments, which Sandra put on the front table to be picked up before every class, were related to the subject of control. The class we observed, ENC 1101-70, met on Tuesdays and Thursdays for 75 minutes beginning at 2:00 p.m. in RBB 109. The class works on a small-group format, and each Tuesday, 5 previously designated students go around to each group and read their writing aloud to the members of that group, followed by a 10-minute discussion about the content, the ideas in the piece of writing. After 10 minutes, each reader goes on to the next group. Also on Tuesday, each student exchanges her writing with another student (response pairs are written on the board each Tuesday). For Thursday, each student must write 500 words in response to her partner's 500 words, first saying what he or she read—summarizing the ideas contained in the writing—and then offering her disagreements, questions, or confusions about it. On Thursday these are read in the same round-robin fashion: the last 15 minutes of class is saved for a full-class discussion, when one pair of response partners (also picked by Sandra) reads their writing to one another out loud, and the class members then join in what seemed to me to be a kind of forum or an FSU *polis* for the 1990's.

I am not sure I have explained this properly: the class mechanics continually confused me, though the students seemed to understand them well. One of the first things I noticed about the class was how smoothly it operated without the constant questioning, foot-dragging, whining, or other types of low-level resistance which make me dread my own classes at times: "Tell me the assignment again" when the student has an assignment sheet in hand, or "A thousand words? *No*, really." Sandra had told her students

> this is your class, it's student-centered, you're running the class, I'm here to show you how to do it. . . . I think I gave them that idea on the

first days that I talked to them, and then everything that is done . . . is their responsibility. . . . I reflect anything that comes to me back to them. (Interview of 9-29)

After Ron and I observed for two weeks, the class format changed in response to student feedback requesting less small-group work, more full-class discussion time, and a loosening of texts and subjects for writing. Sandra was presenting papers at conferences for the last week and a half of the five we observed, and she designated small groups to be in charge of the class during her absence—to do the lesson or class discussion, give the assignment, read the writings, take attendance, and so on. The first of these student-led classes took place before she left, as a kind of dry run.

With this change, my original idea—that I might observe one writer among the small groups' interactions—lost a little of its panache: with so many more variables operating in the mix, drawing out a conclusion or any kind of narrative line became less likely. At first I was fascinated by the workings of what I perceived to be a contradiction: a student-centered classroom in which the teacher maintains control of the apparatus of its functioning and requires an amount of work approximately double or triple that of most first-year writing teachers at this university, yet encounters less resistance than I, who ask for fewer words. Where did she find such authority? And more importantly, where could I get some? I was tired of students ignoring invitations to discussion, tired of loud and constant socializing (and sometimes little writing) followed by heartfelt confessions: "You know, I really need an A." Perhaps the answer lay in the classroom structure—something I could "borrow." Perhaps it was in Sandra's personality, which is not transferable or stealable: in that case, I had no hope and might want to consider reapplying to my former employer, the U.S. Postal Service. At this point in the semester, my students' resistance to reading ("This story is twenty pages long!") and to bringing working drafts to class ("It's in my dorm room on disk. Isn't it okay if we work on a computer?") combined with the sheer volume of their cross-talk to make me feel amazed and/or desperate. Sandra's students talked about their work, at least some of the time. More importantly, they arrived with drafts, ready to work, and if they didn't, I never heard them offer excuses. I was ready to be inspired, and I was jealous, though neither emotional stance was one I considered particularly ethnographic or even scholarly.

So I was confused about goals and anxious about the project when Elizabeth Chiseri-Strater's *Academic Literacies: The Public and Private Discourse of University Students* helped to clarify my initial research question: "We need to provide opportunities for students, male and female, in our classrooms to have experiences shaping ideas through collaborative talk, rather than monologic discourse" (1991, 148). I observed how male-dominated both the class as a whole and Group 5 seemed, how silent the women in it appeared. In a class with 14 men and 9 women and a small group with 3 men and 2 women, part of this apparent domination may be a natural result of numbers. But as I listened to talk about intramural football and fraternities while the women barely spoke for class period after class period, I wondered whether, in this student classroom community where the woman teacher had seemingly stepped aside, the male power structure in language was free to reconstruct itself in this environment, too, to the detriment and exclusion, the silencing, of the women students. I wanted the women students to be able to proceed with their own identity negotiations in this class—to work out who they were in the contexts of the classroom, to construct themselves as participants in the class's various discourses, both oral and written. Somehow, in some far-fetched sympathetic way, I believed that if women students could find voices for themselves in this classroom, outnumbered as they were, then I could find a voice for myself teaching my own classes and in the academy as well. In my classes, I felt silenced. And as a feminist, I felt both situations deserved investigation.

But in the foreground of my thoughts, ethnographic research became a process of self-examination: every day I reflected on the data and how it related to my classroom and *my* teaching, and the circuitous route my observations took through my brain, like trickles of water descending a slight and littered slope, depended on my identity negotiations as a woman teacher of a certain background, politics, and personality. I had not thought I was entering the setting without preconceived hypotheses, and to that end I tried not to bring my teacher-self to class with my student-self, who sat down in Sandra's class rushed and thirty seconds late, carrying book bag and perplexed look perhaps caused not only by my confusion as to what I might be doing in the class, but by the sometimes conflicting demands of various stances I was taking there. As a participant–observer, I wanted to be part of the class, one of the students, and I am a real graduate student (not a freshman) concerned with meeting the requirements of an ethnography class while casting my tangled skein of thoughts forward to begin obsessing about my dissertation research. At the same time, I could never forget that I was a teacher who felt inept, sitting in a class which seemed to work miraculously well—in essence, a student teacher. I had speculated that by observing women in small writing groups, I could clarify my thinking and find new issues and questions for my dissertation prospectus (a major concern for my student-self). But I also wanted to know more about Sandra's teaching methods. I had talked to her enough about how her classroom works to know that she shares some of my pedagogical goals:

she believes that students ought to write and read a lot, as I do, and when this semester began, she reported students willingly producing huge amounts of writing and involving themselves in classroom discussions about it. I felt I needed to learn more: my feelings about problems with discipline and authority in my classes have gradually changed from annoyance and incredulity to the suspicion that I may not survive as a teacher.

I agree with the Feminist Sophistics Pedagogy Group that "as feminist graduate students and faculty who teach composition we do not experience the same authority in the classroom as white male, middle-to-upper-class graduate students and faculty" (Eichhorn et al. 1992, 98). The teachers I know who are men don't seem to experience the same kinds of problems with authority issues that I do (neither do most of the women, a fact that I'm not at all sure how to interpret). I share Karen Powers-Stubbs's concerns: "As a new teacher, my authority in the classroom was one among the myriad of issues on my mind. . . . But as a new feminist, my questions and anxieties about teacherly authority differed from those generally articulated by my fellow graduate students" (Eichhorn et al. 1992, 311–12). In fact, I want to be respected in my classroom, but not to be an authority, and the line along which most of my problems seem to lie is the line between encouraging students to question, challenge, and think for themselves while encouraging them to involve themselves in the class's reading, writing, and talk. As a new teacher and as a woman teacher, I feel my authority challenged by tenured full professor-type (mostly male) teachers: I also feel it challenged by my students in the classroom. In neither situation do I always want to be an authority, but I would like to have the option, if and when I need or want to.

Again, because what I found in the course of this research might well be shaped by what I was looking for—if ethnography, as both North and Atkinson suggest (see the epigraphs), is a process that investigates not only the researched but the researcher—then I need to be clear that I was concurrently involved: examining myself and this classroom phenomenologically, weaving what proved to be a tangled web indeed. Ron saw the classroom differently, and for me this difference resonates, showing how signed and authored our texts are and how autobiographical ethnographic writing can be. I agree with Patricia Sullivan's opinion that "the concept of dispassionate, disinterested inquiry has itself arisen from patriarchal ideology" (1992, 55). When I write about the parallel I found between the small-group identity negotiations of Michelle, a woman in Sandra's classroom, and my own identity negotiations as a woman teacher, it is appropriate to question my metaphoric leaps.

Teaching raises questions to me about my position as a woman teacher and the positions of my women students in relation to that, questions which are deep, involved, and will not go away. In none of our class readings have people admitted doing ethnographic research to save themselves as people and professors, or at least they don't say so: no one claims to have used ethnography to improve the quality of her life, and I feel decidedly two-faced about admitting that my aims were not of the purest or most intellectual. Sandra positions herself clearly in a relationship to the academy; she knows she's here to participate in the intellectual community's discourses. Teasing out threads in the process of researching and writing this essay, I have at least recognized where I might also consider positioning myself: that, too, is a process of shaping, of reconstructing my selves as they continue to enter classrooms as feminist student and teacher.

Inside the Frame: Data

From Sandra's Course Information Sheet, Fall 1993:

Writing will be a tool you use for thinking and preparing yourselves for class discussion. Our classroom will be a meeting place for us as a community of readers, writers and thinkers, and we will use class time for discussion of ideas being investigated through the writing. In this classroom, each and every student's voice is important and worth being heard as we deal with timely subject matter and subjects that affect each of us in our everyday lives.

Field Notes:

9-21 Michelle reads first, an article on lottery tickets. I can barely hear her read. The men sit back, sprawled in their seats, backs to the wall. . . . Josh reads a bubble gum wrapper. Bryan drinks Coke, Mike jiggles his leg and talks about money in this society and the possibility, twenty years down the road, of paying for your groceries with a bar-code implanted in your arm, some sort of universal debit card. Michelle laughs. Mike nods and laughs. Josh talks about his projected major. Sherae stares out: she isn't focused on the group.

9-28 Pauses are now getting longer—students are encouraging their friends to read. "Aren't we done?" one asks.

Sandra says, "You don't want to read anymore? You don't have to—you can leave."

She doesn't take control; she leaves it to the community to decide what happens? This is interesting.

9-30 [sitting with Group 5]

Sherae is at a different table from anyone else, at right angles to the table where the others are sitting. Her behavior makes me wonder again if we are really tipping the balance here in this group: I feel quite uneasy.

10-5 [Dry run, a sort of practice for Sandra's absence during which each group in the class is scheduled to teach once. Today Group 1 (our group is Group 5) is in charge. Sandra is observing and present, available to answer questions or offer suggestions.]

Josh and Sherae start the attendance list—interesting. They take a leadership position even though they aren't the lead group today.

Suddenly, for no reason I can see, Josh shouts out, "Let's change this and talk about our favorite breakfast cereal." And that's that—the end of class, thirty minutes early—and Josh ended it.

10-12 [Group 5 in charge. This is also the day we distributed our survey with Group 5's approval, so class began late.]

Michelle's expression seems more open and relaxed, and I haven't noticed her giggling nervously with her hand in front of her face lately.

2:20—Josh stands up and starts to talk. Someone asks him whether "they're really going to make us do something in class?" He replies that "It could be fun, if you make it fun. It's all in how you see it." Josh is becoming a teacher! "We're going to take 20 minutes," he says, "and do a sketch to explore your mind on paper." "Draw," he says. "Everybody can draw. Anything you want. After 20 minutes, trade pictures with someone else in another group, take it home, and write about it. That's your assignment."

"Cool," Amy says.

Jamie comes in late and asks what we're doing today. Josh says, "Sign the attendance sheet and turn in your homework to him." He points to someone in Group 3. Josh sits and draws quietly. When people make noise, he looks up. This is freedrawing: is he going to suggest that the noisy students get back on task? It's interesting how the same issues come up. Ron looks at me and mouths the words—Is that really all there is to it? He looks pleased and amused: I know I am. Just tell people to try something you enjoy doing, then dive into it yourself. When we started this project, I thought Josh was awful—thoughtless, a boring freshman, maybe a big frat guy, insensitive to the women in the group. I've changed my mind, though I still don't think he's Sir Galahad. Today's performance was winning in its sincerity, simplicity, and thoughtfulness.

At 2:40, Josh encourages people to draw for 5 more minutes. After 5 minutes is over, he says, "Everybody who is done can go ahead and trade. If not, you can keep working." Someone asks who they should trade with, and he tells them to trade with someone from another group. Then he says "when you write about the other person's drawing, try to think about what he was thinking." Someone suggests that they gather and shuffle the drawings and then pass them out, and somebody else agrees. "I'm gonna keep all these—seriously. So I can, like, have ideas," Josh says, chewing gum, flipping through the stack as if he really can't wait to see what's there. He takes the one on top and passes the rest out.

On the way out the door, Josh comments to a friend, "I love taking charge of English classes."

Excerpts from our first interview with Sandra, 9-29-93:

Our lead question is "What's going on in your class?"

Sandra: I sort of have gone in there, okay, this is your class, it's student-centered, you're running the class, I'm here to show you how to do it, but I don't really care if you do it or not . . . then everything that is done is . . . their responsibility. . . . I reflect anything that comes to me back to them. . . .

They do get responses but they get them from their small group. But I'm just another voice in the crowd. . . . I've backed off, and so they almost have to take over because somebody has to do something, not gonna be me. Well, I facilitate, and I show them how to do it. . . . Things happen—not because of me, but because of them.

I firmly believe that there's no purpose in writing unless you're really writing it for your own purpose first, and then to share that with someone else, what you have to say. . . . I think we should be coming to the university with the purpose of thinking as individuals, and really developing that, and so that's what more I'm after. You could probably say that I'm teaching a class in thinking more than I'm teaching a class in writing. I'm using writing in a practical sense, I'm not using it as an end in itself, it is not a product in my class ever, it is a process, it is a real process, a process of thinking, and that, I don't see it as a writing process. That's what my goal was, to have this little community of people that was an intellectual community rather than a place where they had to come and sit. . . .

Well, you know what their thing is . . . to get a job. They don't see a university as an intellectual institution, and very few people do, and that really bothers me. I have a political thing I'm doing here, I guess, in a small way I'm blasted off on my own little thing. Maybe that's not the correct thing to do, but I think . . . that . . . what I'm expected in the English department is teach writing, and I think I'm teaching writing as well as giving them a taste of the world.

Devan interviews Josh:

Devan: What do you think about Sandra as a teacher?

Josh: I think she's doing like what I was doing with that art thing, she's taking it all in, and then thinking about it to herself, and so, then she'll come up with her own ideas, her own decisions about whatever we were talking about at the time, so, (pause) if that's how she wants to do it, that's fine with me.

Devan: What do you think she's up to in this class?

Josh: I think she's learning—from us, at the same she's teaching, I mean she's giving us ideas, but I'm, I'm sure she's taking a lot of our ideas and, and just like I said, rearranging them, or however she deals with them in her own way, so then she's exploring herself at the same time she's getting us to explore, and, I like it, I'm glad.

Devan: Any other comments about the class—to record for posterity?

Josh: *This* stuff is like stuff you grow on, you know, it's, it makes you think and it makes you look at things different, so you'll remember it, you know, it's like, it might not be like actual things you'll remember, but it's things that make you think about different things that make you feel different about stuff around you, so . . . guess that's all I got to say.

Devan interviews Sherae:

Devan: I guess that's another way of asking what you think the purpose of the class is. . . .

Sherae: I think she wants all of us, like even herself, to open our minds, and be willing to learn and think, and not be set in your own ways and think that, "Well, this is what I think and that's how it is and you can't change," but to allow yourself to learn. . . .

Ron interviews Michelle:

Ron: So, for this class you think it's helping you a lot too, cause they're fulfilling the assignments, but in other classes . . . cause they're gonna have different expectations, it would be harder—?

Michelle: Right now it doesn't matter. I can just sit down at the computer and write 500 words in a half an hour if I'm writing in the first person, it's so easy, but then if I had to write about one topic, I don't know, I don't think I'd be able to do it, it would take me a long time.

Ron: Did you feel that you had the chance with the writings to kind of write about whatever you felt . . . ?

Michelle: Yeah, because, well, she told us one day, don't be like into the situation where you know it all, this is a mindprint that I want to read. She's like, I want to know what's going on in your head, and I think that's neat, because that way she gets to know us, as individuals, not just as students.

Ron: About the day your group ran, taught the class, what was your impression of that?

Michelle: I thought it was kind of fun. Um . . . I don't know, Josh kind of took charge, he's like "Okay, I've got the quote, this is what we're doing," he was all excited about it, and . . . I mean, that was okay, cause I wouldn't, I'm not the kind of person that would want to get up in front of the class . . . I'm not like that. It was neat, though.

Michelle's Exploration 8, a group self-assignment, begins:

My group thought it would be neat to write about a video game. Well, I complained about it, but being the only girl in a group full of guys who try to act macho, it got me nowhere. How can I write a "detailed descriptive meditative exploration" on the video game "Virtual Racing"? First of all, this game is a lot like "Pole Position." . . . I watched Brian waste his money on it one time, but I had to leave because I felt like an erupting volcano. Needless to say, I *was* not very happy about the topic my group had chosen. I will, however, act mature and write about it without complaining anymore. This totally ties in with the theme of control that Sandra likes so well. . . .

Michelle's Exploration 16, a midterm self-evaluation:

10-25-93

I think my writing is valuable to the people reading it, also. They get to see how my mind works (I say that like it is a privilege). But really, I think it is. I'm not trying to be cocky, but I am basically a closed person, and I only tell my close friends my thoughts. I think this makes my writing in this style that much more valuable.

My contribution to the world with my writing is that I am learning more about myself now, so then when I am older and a leader, I will not have problems with insecurity, self-esteem, or anything like that because I will be very sure of myself and who I am. I will owe it all to Sandra and ENC 1101 at FSU. It is hard for me to know if anyone reading this can follow it. My thoughts are so clear in my head, but sometimes I do have trouble getting them on to the paper.

Reading Fragments Inside the Frame

This class's underlife, "behaviors which undercut the roles expected of participants in the situation" (Brooke, "Underlife" 141), is well-developed, and Sandra has stepped aside to let the underlife be a large part of the class's life, to a much greater extent than it might be in a lecture class. I've already discussed my concerns about whether student-centered came in this classroom to mean male-centered. But Sandra also teaches thinking or writing as a thinking process—her approach is not "writing-to-learn" exactly, but writing as exploration, as thought, so it might be appropriate to question whether Michelle and Sherae felt their thinking and explorations were excluded. Did Michelle and Sherae feel marginalized and excluded in the classroom discourse, or were they participating in the class's underlife—and their own identity negotiations—in a different mode from, but just as fully as, the men?[2]

And what roles might Sandra as a teacher have played, and be playing now? While Michelle had doubts about whether she could write for a more structured classroom, as she told Ron, she does seem proud of herself and her writing: she believes that people who read it have been granted the privilege of seeing how her mind works, and she says that she feels more sure of herself as a result of the class and of the class' writing: "When I am older and a leader, I will not have problems with insecurity, self-esteem, or anything like that because I will be very sure of myself and who I am." Granted, this comes from a self-evaluation, where a certain amount of hyperbole is to be expected, but the fact that Michelle specifically identifies areas having to do with identity negotiation (insecurity, self-esteem, and who she is) as what she has learned in ENC 1101 seems to indicate that Michelle is well satisfied with how the classroom has allowed her to carry out those negotiations. Such a statement might, according to recent writing about women and composition, be somewhat surprising. Five short weeks of observation by an ethnographic novice isn't nearly enough to answer these, but I believe I can point to some good starting points for further study.

In "Feminism and Methodology," Patricia Sullivan writes that women students enter an academic community in which men have largely determined what is important to know, how knowledge is organized, how knowledge is made, and, most importantly for composition scholars and teachers, how knowledge is expressed . . . feminist scholars take issue with the assumption that discourse is gender neutral, that the literate practices of male and female writers and readers bear no traces of their differential relationships to culture (1992, 40). Women students, although they can "master" academic discourse and, in Sullivan's memorable phrase, "cross-dress . . . in either adversarial or disinterested modes of discourse" (1992, 40), are rarely given the chance in the classroom to write in a way that is theirs. Other feminist composition researchers agree with Sullivan: in "Composing as a Woman," Elizabeth Flynn writes that "the fields of feminist studies and composition studies have not engaged each other in a serious or systematic way" (425). Her argument, built on Carol Gilligan's *In a Different Voice* and Belenky et al.'s *Women's Ways of Knowing*, in discussing stages by which women find voices,[3] mentions the same silence I found obvious and disturbing in Group 5: "Silent women have little awareness of their intellectual capacities. They live—selfless and voiceless—at the behest of those around them" (1988, 427). Elizabeth Chiseri-Strater, in referring to the same text and relating it to Anna's classroom experience, says that "The authors of *Women's Ways of Knowing* have identified the beginning stage of some women's thinking as 'silence'—a description that reflects the important metaphor of 'voice' in understanding women's growth as thinkers" (1991, 38). Elizabeth Flynn pushes a bit harder toward her conclusions than Chiseri-Strater when she writes, "We ought not assume that males and females use language in identical ways or represent the world in a similar fashion. And if their writing strategies and patterns of representation do differ, then ignoring those differences almost certainly means a suppression of women's separate ways of thinking and writing (1988, 432). And in "Transforming the Composition Classroom," Daumer and Runzo state that "language is characterized by the silence of women and that women's silence empowers men while it perpetuates the myth of male superiority" (1987, 51). Daumer and Runzo, as well as Flynn, then, would insist on a feminist pedagogy, perhaps one similar in aims to the one Laurie Finkel (1993) describes in "Knowledge as Bait: Feminism, Voice, and the Pedagogical Unconscious." Or perhaps not so similar—since Flynn's article, feminist teaching strategies have become more specific and at the same time, less clearly "right" or "wrong," and it is probably significant that Finkel doesn't cite Flynn's essay. In discussing the "finding" of a voice, Finkel states that the issue is not so much "discovering" a voice as "fashioning" one from a discourse. Feminist teaching strategies attempt to intervene in the construction process, with the goal of freeing and "empowering" a woman student "to participate in the transformation of her world" (14): the issue becomes less a fear of women students' silence than an effort to make silence the first stage in finding a "voice."[4]

I am uneasy with my worrying about Michelle's and Sherae's silence in the group because they didn't seem worried about it. If Michelle writes, as she did in her midterm evaluation, that *My* contribution to the world with my writing is that I am learning more about myself now, so then when I am older and a leader, I will not have problems with insecurity, self-esteem, or anything like that because I will be very sure of myself and who I am, then we ought to grant her the dignity of belief. I would like to suggest that though Michelle and Sherae talk little in class, they may not be in the "silence" stage of feminine empowerment in thinking, and to present an alternate reading of what's going on in Sandra's class based on the work of Robert Brooke (1987).

I have written that perhaps Sandra's class is student-centered in such a way that some of the male group members' underlife sufficiently dominates to become, in a sense, the whole classroom's life. Now I argue against this idea, for in a writing classroom, both students and teacher participate in institutional underlife. The writing classroom, which encourages collaborative thinking instead of received knowledge (workshops instead of lectures), is by its very nature a place different from much of the rest of the university, a place that, as Brooke writes, "necessarily involves standing outside the roles and beliefs offered by a social situation—it involves questioning them, searching for new connections, building ideas that may be in conflict with accepted ways of thinking and acting" (141). He even claims that "we seek to change our pedagogy to allow the possibility of the writer's identity" (151). It's been easy to see the male students' underlife in this classroom: the women students' underlife and what Brooke calls the teacher's "disruptive" stance toward the academy (148–49) are less loud, but they exist.

Silence can be read as student underlife: "those private activities whereby an individual divides her attention between the class activity and something else" (148). When Sherae stared out the window or at a spot hovering over the middle of the room, perhaps she was resisting the classroom interaction, saying there was much more to her than this workshop group and this assignment. When Michelle refused to be drawn into conversations with the men about fraternities and sports, perhaps she was enacting her independence from her group—not silence so much as resistance.

Jumping to conclusions about student behaviors is all too easy; I am more inclined to believe that for Sherae, silence might have had more to do with resistance than it did for Michelle, and that Michelle is more involved in the "process" of fashioning a "voice," since what we know of her indicates that she doesn't maintain the same position all the time in her writing and in the classroom. She's quiet; she thinks she's not learning what she needs to learn to write for other classes; she doesn't like the men's choice of assignment but goes ahead and does it anyway; she feels sure of herself and who she is in her writing and thinking, sure of her ability to contribute to the world. It is also quite possible, given the limited scope of this study, that factors other than the classroom affected both Michelle's thinking/writing and her feelings about her identity: she is a first-semester freshman. A new boyfriend or a slob roommate might well be more important than anything that happened in ENC 1101: students don't live in a vacuum any more than we do.

In terms of the university, Sandra is very involved in underlife, very disruptive. She has given her students a mechanism whereby they have become the center and focus of the class; in one way, she functions as another member of the audience, not as the authority. Students write and talk to each other, not to her exclusively. She sits back and to the side, rarely occupying the front-and-center position of a lecturer. In her course guide and in our interview with her, Sandra, in positing her idea of the university as an intellectual institution and arranging her classroom as a microcosm of that idea, resists, as she well knows, many of the university's other self-definitions.[5]

In her classroom, then, Sandra models a very different kind of teacher identity, and her students recognize it as such. In her interview, Michelle said, "She's like, I want to know what's going on in your head, and I think that's neat, because that way she gets to know us, as individuals, not just as students." Josh agreed: "I think she's learning—from us, at the same she's teaching, I mean she's giving us ideas . . . I'm sure she's taking a lot of our ideas . . . so then she's exploring herself at the same time she's getting us to explore. . . .

According to these students, Sandra sees them as people (with identities) and herself as a fellow learner rather than as a lecturer. But she is also the teacher and granter of grades: her position is as multi-faceted as Michelle's. No matter how student-centered this classroom may be in practice, finally a classroom is centered on more than one level, and at least one of those levels belongs to the teacher, who is "the leader of all the groups . . . because the purposes of group interaction had[ve] been established by him[her]" (Brooke et al. 1989, 71). As a leader, then, Sandra models the behaviors she would like her students to adopt in the class: she expects them to share in discourse, to partic-ipate in the intellectual community of her classroom. When Michelle writes of the value she places on writing and thinking and her clearer sense of self, she might be referring to Sandra as a model. After all, "Our own style of leadership . . . can directly affect the way students perceive their writing and their interaction" (Brooke et al. 1989, 84). During class, Sandra tends to talk very little: many classes go by with-out her making statements or giving directions to the class as a whole. Knowledge of class protocols and daily dittoed assignment sheets make such hands-on steering of class activities unnecessary, though she al-ways talks in an interested and friendly way with any student who ap-proaches her. Michelle may not feel outnumbered or resistant: instead, she may feel it more important to, like Sandra, be involved in her own thinking.

When I read Ruth Ray's "Composition from the Teacher–Researcher Point of View," I found much that paralleled my observation of Sandra as a teacher as well as her students' observations of her, particularly the idea that "learning and knowing are collaborative, and that teachers learn as much from their interaction with students as students learn from teachers" (1992, 177). Her teaching gives up "attempts to control students' learning" (178) and assumes, with Peter Elbow, that "Even though we are not wholly peer with our students, we can still be peer in [the] crucial sense of also being engaged in learning, seeking, and being incomplete" (qtd. in Ray 1992, 175). In collaborating in mean-ing-making with her students and in her insistence that what takes place in her classroom must be real, she indeed "assumes that differences among people are a resource, not something to be eliminated in the name of education, remediation, socialization" (Cooper quoted in Ray, 1992, 176). Differences are to be talked and written about, thought over, learned from, lived in.

Or so it seems right now. Though Ruth Ray's teacher–researcher model seems to work for Sandra (though I'm not suggesting that she has either read or adopted Ray's ideas), my conflicts about teaching, which students pick up on, will probably continue to cause my position in the classroom to be ambiguous. Sandra is a person who thinks her teaching through and then works out her thoughts in her classroom practice; I am likely to continue to be more indecisive, both afraid of my students and in love with them, constantly unsure of how to act. Like Michelle, I struggle more in the process of negotiating my position.

Or perhaps the teacher–researcher stance will be a good one for me to adopt in my continued positioning: through the processes of this ethnography I became increasingly aware that my own resistance, which impacts on my interwoven teacher-self, student-self, and feminist-self, is a major issue for me. At first I thought that since my major stance in living has been argument and rebellion or resistance of various kinds (it's a kind of habit, a personality quirk, and a choice), my students picked that up right away. But many of them seem not to know how to interpret it, or to realize that though I don't feel very committed to the power politics of the academy, I am committed to the discursive intellectual community it is possible to find here, a community valuable for its subversiveness. (The title of Julia Kristeva's doctoral dissertation, *Revolution and the Word*, has resonance for me.)

As a teacher and a feminist, I resist paternalistic norms and attitudes found in the university—learning received rather than constructed, socialization into the job market or the corporate culture rather than into discourses and explorations. Of course, not every aspect of this or any other university is universally stifling: I resist that sort of categorization as well. And as a student, subject to the same institutional pressures as my students, I resist—grades, parroting back the right information in class, starting salaries. What I want to do is learn, converse, identify to myself and to my students the complex position of participating in the university's discourse while resisting its power. In my classroom, my underlife has been the submerged iceberg, the shark whose fin surfaces menacingly to confuse everyone. The position of teacher–researcher allows me the freedom to model the teacher as student, to undercut the whole institutional question of authority, and to make meaning with students (as students) in a more real way. Learning and teaching in this way means collaboration, not being quiet, and certainly not being silenced.

Endnotes

1. The class had three black students, and from what I observed, their interactions with the white students in the class, as well as with each other, would have made a fascinating study. I would like to emphasize that I do not

necessarily consider Michelle and Sherae as two women who would ordinarily spend a lot of time talking to each other as friends or even as acquaintances— as Ron pointed out to me, people often don't join in conversations because they aren't interested in the topic under discussion. Sherae's distance from the group seemed more actual than Michelle's; she usually sat within hearing and speaking distance at another table adjoining theirs.

2. Ron, observing at other times, saw Michelle "chatter." What I wondered was whether, as the men seized control of discussion time after time and ended talk about the reading to broach other, more exclusively and personally male topics, they were, in a sense, enacting a belief that their interests are global interests (though I'm not suggesting this was intentional). Mike seemed, in his own way, as distanced from the group as the women—coming in late or being absent, missing the interview, saying little, and when he spoke, often questioning or resisting Josh's or Bryan's statements.

3. According to Belenky, "the quest for self and voice plays a central role in transformations of women's ways of knowing" (qtd. in Flynn, 427) and is thus a critically important event for women both as thinkers and as writers.

4. I'm not making claims here for an essential self.

5. Career education, grant-seeking and administration, management of professional athletes and entertainers, the purveying of money, power, and influence—my feelings about the university can be pretty negative.

Works Cited

[Works cited are included in the Bibliography at the end of this book.]

Ellen Schendel: Entering the Gray Area: Accepting Authority in a Pre-1101 Composition Class

I am planning to make you—each one of you—the center of this class, a class that is to be about you and your relationships to each other and to society, and to the university as a whole, and to myself too. But it focuses on each one of you. I'm interested in each one of you, what you think; I'm interested in you individually and in the ideas you are starting to develop as you enter this university, and I think we'll get to those things through writing. That's what I intend—to use writing as a tool for thinking and for working through issues (Sandra's introduction, September 8, 1993).

My name is Ellen Schendel, and I'm a first-year Master's student in English. I'm going to take this class for four or five weeks as part of a class project for one of my other classes . . . and we study student writing courses, is what we do. I'm new to Tallahassee and Florida State, and so far I like it. I've never been anywhere in Florida beside Tallahassee (My introduction, September 8, 1993).

Hello, class, this is my son, M.V. He will be joining—he will be joining this class. M.V. is from Pensacola, Florida. He is here to get a good education. I am sure he will have a very prosperous year (M.V.'s introduction, from his father's point of view, September 8, 1993).

This is my worst enemy, Chris. He is the one that lets me outside, but will never let me back in. He never checks my food bowl, and he's always kicking me off his bed or couch (her name's Chelsey—she's a Yorkshire terrier) (Chris' introduction, from his pet's point of view, September 8, 1993).

Sandra Teichmann's pre-1101 class meets once a week, on Wednesday's from 12:15 to 1:20 in the Florida State University Reading and Writing Center. Eight students are taking this course as a prerequisite for 1101, which they will take next semester. At the end of the semester, they will not receive a grade; they are taking this course satisfactory or unsatisfactory.

Sandra has taught writing courses for several years, and this is her third year as a composition graduate teaching assistant here at FSU. This is not her first time teaching a pre-1101 course.

Chris and M.V. are two students in the class. They, and their classmates, are first-year students. Besides attending the Wednesday classes, all eight students must meet each week with Sandra for a half-hour conference, where they discuss their journal entries and coursework.

Sandra's syllabus clearly states that to receive a grade of satisfactory, they must attend all classes, complete all assignments, keep up with their journals, and meet with her for their half-hour conferences each week.

By the time we left class that first day, we all knew why we were gathered around a long table, half-obscured by partitions in the Reading and Writing Center: Sandra, to "teach students . . . to use writing as a tool for thinking, for exploring some of the many possibilities here at the university and in life" (written response, November 10, 1993); the students, to fulfill a requirement in order to take 1101 next semester; and myself, to fulfill the requirements for my rhetoric and composition course. Over the din of tutorials and other classes being conducted and the occasional cackle from a group of tutors joking with each other behind the front desk, Sandra informally greeted each student as he or she cautiously approached the table, unsure at which table to find her. Sandra introduced herself to each student, and asked them their names so that she could check them off her list. I was already there, a few seats to the right of Sandra, unsure of what to do with my tape recorder; I held it right underneath the table until everyone seemed situated and Sandra picked up a stack of papers, signaling the start of class. Around 12:25—ten minutes after class was to begin—Sandra passed around her syllabi, and asked everyone to write down four introductions of themselves for the group, each in a different voice: as a parent, as a pet, as a funny friend, and as we wanted to introduce ourselves. By the end of the class period, only a few students (such as M.V.) had explicitly stated why they were in the classroom, as Sandra and I had. By the end of my six weeks of observation, it was obvious to me that while my goals and most students in the class were fulfilled (to complete requirements), Sandra's were probably not going to be realized.

It's hard to write this ethnography. It seems that many ethnographies, such as Elizabeth Chiseri-Strater's *Academic Literacies* and Robert E. Brooke's *Writing and Sense of Self*, deal with "conversion" narratives—those that end happily, or at least with some sort of revelation about student writing. I'm not so sure my data leads me to that sort of conclusion. In answering my interview questions, Sandra certainly does not see these eight students as asserting authority over their writing, writing about their opinions and feelings, as the course objectives section of her syllabus states:

> Through reading, exploratory writing in response to reading, and class discussion this class will work toward an expression of and development of ideas which relate to us as individuals to society. In this course and in your writing, I value *respect, self-involvement, curiosity, risk-taking* and *thinking*. Writing will be a tool you use for thinking and preparing yourselves for class discussion. Our classroom will be a meeting place for us as a community of readers, writers, and thinkers, and we will

use class time for discussion of ideas being investigated through writing. In this classroom, each and every student's voice is important and worth being heard as we deal with timely subject matter and subjects that affect each of us in our everyday lives (italics in the original).

It seems strange to begin this ethnography at the end, but perhaps that is the best way for me to tell this story. After I collected most of my data, I asked Sandra to respond in writing to several questions based on my observations. In answering whether she considers the students as writers, and thinks the students consider themselves to be writers—accepting the authority she is trying to shift from herself to them—she responded:

> Though I in no way express this judgement [to the students], I consider [them] as writers in only the very basic sense of using writing for purposes of minimal written communication. I treat these students with the same respect I extend to any student, and I expect each one of these students to take absolute responsibility for his or her own success, just as I do in any other class.

I think these students do not consider themselves writers, either. This is probably because of the uncomfortable situation they find themselves in: reluctantly attending a university where they have immediately been labeled as inferior to all other entering first-year students. Perhaps this feeling is only magnified as each one of these students is placed in a situation with others like themselves (November 19, 1993).

> 9/8   Had my first algebra quiz. Don't think I did too great!
> Went Enc. 1905 for first time.
> Shared how my dog would introduce me.
> Unusual b/c I don't like to speak in front of people (Chris' journal).

Like six other students in 1905, Chris and M.V. are first-year students. According to his journal, Chris' parents divorced when he was three, and he has lived with his father and step-mother since then. Almost every one of his journal entries makes mention of his parents and/or brother. The affects of the divorce seem to seep into his life often, especially during one weekend when he was supposed to be working on a paper for his Gordon Rule history course:

> 9/15   Today I'm trying to decide whether I should go home this weekend and try to do my paper or should I stay here and do it.

> 9/16   I decided not to go home, but I think my parents were really looking forward to me coming down. I think I can get my paper down faster if I work on it by myself instead of trying to visit and get it

done. I would rather go home on a weekend that I don't have to do anything.

Started looking at history paper. There's no easy way to do it. It is going to be the longest paper I've ever had to do. I wish I had another week to do it so I could go home. Next week my brother has a game on Thurs. night. So even if I went home I couldn't see him play.

At this point in the journal, Chris writes about how his paper progresses. His mother in Indiana calls him on Friday evening to see how his paper is going. The next day's entry reads:

9/18   Finished the rough draft. . . . My mom in Indiana called at 7:00 p.m. She was off Lade Bradford Rd. [in Tallahassee]. They figured my paper would be close to done so they would surprise me.

The next day's journal discuses a shopping trip with his mother, during which she bought him a word processor. He writes that he hopes that will make his paper "a little easier."

But the next few journal entries relay a not-so-happy incident with his father, in which he seems to get mad at Chris for spending time with his mother when he was supposed to be working on his paper. Chris writes:

9/20   My Dad thinks I knew she was coming. He's mad b/c he wonders how I did the paper w/her, but I couldn't go home and do it. I guess divorce parents get jealous of each other or something. When I get married I'm going to try and wait to have kids, so if things don't work out I don't have to put my kid in the middle of me and his/hr mom.

Chris' feelings about the relationship he has with his father, and his commentary on divorce continue throughout the journal. At one point, Chris mentions that his roommate's parents may be getting a divorce, and that his roommate (who is never named in the journal, always referred to as "my roommate," just as his brother is always referred to as "my brother") stayed up all night one night talking about what it is like when parents divorce.

Chris' journal did not start out so prolific. In their first conference together, Sandra told Chris that he should write more in his journal, which had, until that point, consisted mainly of brief sentences summarizing his day: "Need to clean up the house," "Going to 1st FSU vs. Clemson football game," "Went to first church service in Tallahassee. Guy was funny."

While Chris occasionally mentions in his journal that his father wants him to do well in school, it is the subject of grades that M.V. comments on most often in his journal. Almost all of his journal entries (especially at the start of the course) deal with how his classes are going.

Interestingly, while Chris wrote about the specific problems he has with his coursework (he can't go home, he can't type well, he's not interested in the topic), M.V. writes generally about his classes, but also seems to be pressuring himself into making good grades:

> Sept. 8   School was boring as usual. I met my English teacher or counselor and I found out what group I am in. English might be an okay class. I have to get ready for it. I have to adjust to doing a lot of reading and writing again. I hope this class will improve my skills. . . . I am looking forward to completing this class successfully and then moving on to the next class. This English class requires a lot of thinking and put down ideas that you have. . . . I am going to try and do my very best in this class. I plan on making my counselor (teacher) and my parents very proud of me. I plan on making much progress in my work.

This feeling of wanting to make his family and others proud of him is expressed frequently in M.V.'s journal.

As you can probably tell by the above journal selections, Chris seemed to be more open to telling Sandra about the people and events in his life than M.V. is. Besides his family and hobbies and friends, Chris writes about his other classes, his girlfriend, and a few assigned entries that Sandra requested of everyone in the class (defining "conversation," what the writing experience is like for each student). Chris' journal entries are frequent (almost every day), and, upon Sandra's request, vary from a half page to a full page.

Seemingly a man of few words, M.V.'s journal entries are sporadic, and almost every one is exactly a page long. Several of the entries become repetitious, as if he is trying very hard to fill up that page (Sandra suggested to her students that a page a day was sufficient in fulfilling the journal requirements for the course). After a few weeks of reading his depressed journal entries, Sandra scrawled at the top of one page a (hopefully more uplifting) journal topic: Happy Journal Entry. M.V.'s entries did tend to border on depressed:

> Sept. 9   My classes require a lot of time. I really am not in a studying mood yet. I know I have to make good grades and make my parents proud of me. . . . I can't be letting a whole lot of junk clog up my head.

Interestingly, Chris' entries do not have any comments written on them—except for a page on which Sandra suggested some books Chris might like to read, the result of a journal entry in which he admitted to not liking to read. M.V.'s journals, however, contain several comments by Sandra: Write in this journal!!! At the end of a single journal M.V. had written for the previous week, and a scrawl in the margin of one surface-level account of his class day. Sandra also circled some words as if to correct them—one, to clear up a reference problem, and a second to correct a confused homonym (their to there).

I found these corrections to be quite interesting, as Chris' journal entries are full of left out words, subject–verb agreement problems, and misspellings. He confronts this problem in one of his entries:

> 9/22   When I write I feel it slows me down. Because I think to far ahead of my writing. A lot of times I leave out words b/c I think bout it, but I forget to write it down.

Each Wednesday at 11:30 a.m. and 1:30 p.m. I observed Chris and M.V.'s conferences with Sandra. Sandra conducted the first few conferences in her office. She would sit in her desk chair, her back to her desk and windows, Chris or M.V. across from her, with me off to Sandra's right. Her office, like most TA offices, is cramped—four desks, several chairs, and many books lined on shelves around the walls, above the desks. During most of these conferences, another TA sat at her own desk, an occasional student dropping by to talk to her. Every once in a while, she would interrupt the conference between Sandra and Chris or M.V. to ask Sandra a question, or to comment on where she was about to go (to check on another student's file, to make sure that she had permission to park close to the building because she had to leave late at night). Occasionally, the phone on Sandra's desk would ring and she would have to answer it. Once, I inadvertently caused an interruption; the TA in whose chair I would often sit during these conferences came in to do some work at his desk. After shuffling some papers around and deciding out loud where he would go in lieu of sitting in on our conference, he left.

After the first few conferences in her office, Sandra decided to conduct them in the Writing Center. While we were not interrupted by other TA's and students, on occasion, the din in the Writing Center made it hard for us to hear each other.

Sandra used the students' journal entries as springboards for casual discussions. Sandra would read an entry, pausing to ask questions of the student, directed either to elaborate or explain what he had written. After the first couple of weeks, Chris seemed comfortable elaborating on his story, even sitting forward to interrupt Sandra's reading on occasion, updating her on how the event turned out, or even, on his own, elaborating on a story that the event seemed to touch on. After the first week, Chris seemed to be talking to both Sandra and me, even asking direct questions of me ("Were you at the Georgia Tech game?").

M.V., however, seemed content to let Sandra read. He answered her questions slumped in his chair, looking at the ground, his voice quiet and low. Very rarely did he even look at me during these conferences;

it seemed that as far as I was concerned, I, like my tape recorder, could take in the conference, but not really participate.

In class, no matter how much they talked to Sandra in their conferences, M.V. and even Chris were quiet. As I stated earlier, there are eight students in the class. There are four men, four women; five of the students are black (three women, two men), and three white (two men, one woman). There did not seem to be any major connections between any of the students; they all seemed to be acquainted with each other only through this course, with the exceptions of two students who, by the third week, realized that they were also both taking the same large lecture course.

Each week, the students sat in different places, not only among each other, but also within the Writing Center. The first week, we met Sandra at a long table behind partitions; the second week, at the same table, although half the group discussed their essays at a round table near the computers on the opposite side of the room where we had sat before. The next couple of weeks I was with the group, we met near the computers, although no one seemed to sit next to the same person from week to week. In fact, I noticed that upon entering class, the students seemed to pick seats around the table where no one else was sitting on either side of them—like one would in a situation with strangers.

The class assignment for the first week was to write an expository essay on a *Tallahassee Democrat* article (students drew from a specific section to narrow their search, such as fashion, food, editorial, etc.). The second week the class met, Sandra split the class into two groups and asked each student to read his or her essay aloud; the group was then to discuss the ideas in the exploratory essay.

I joined Chris, Lisa, Erik, and Sharnda's group. We spread out at a round table outside of the partition—which made it hard to talk and hear each other, as the Writing Center was loud, like the first week.

During the first half of the discussion time, while Sandra was with the other group, the students read their papers one after the other without discussing anything about what they had written. When Sandra came over to sit with us, she asked a series of questions of each student about their papers, but the students seemed resistant to both interacting with each other and elaborating on what they had written. The next two classes progressed the same way: the students would read their paper to the others, and, unless Sandra was there, they did not discuss their ideas.

Sandra was gone for two weeks to give papers at a conference. She asked that the class meet even though she was not there, to "just get together as a group of writers and talk." While she was gone, the students were expected to meet both weeks, discuss their papers, and, at some point over the two weeks, meet with another student in the class to conduct an interview which they would later use to write a paper about that person. This interview time, Sandra explained, would take the place of their regular conference with her.

Only five students showed up at each of those next two classes (a different three were absent each time), and only one student was prepared to read her paper at each class. The first class without Sandra was especially uncomfortable; besides not really being sure what to do, the class was unsure of where to even meet (a tutorial session was going on at the table the group had recently become accustomed to sitting at). This time away from Sandra, though, did make the students come together as a group more than they ever had before, albeit in mutual complaining:

Shii: I'm giving this 'til 12:30, and then I'm leaving.

Sharnda: What do we do, anyway?

Shii: I don't know. We shouldn't have to be here anyway.

(The rest of the students agree with her) (October 13, 1993).

Before leaving the Writing Center in a bit of a huff, another student, Kerry-Ann, said to me that she was mad because her interview partner didn't show up for class, and since she didn't have his phone number, she couldn't do her paper. Being an assignment behind due to someone else in the class made her rather upset.

When Sandra returned to class, she asked the students how their sessions alone had gone. The students responded with "fine," "ok," "all right." When I later asked Sandra how she thought the class performed in her absence, she replied:

> I don't know how the class performed when I was gone. When I asked questions, the one-word responses were fine, okay, and so on. Perhaps you know. You were present.

Apparently, none of the students chose to approach Sandra about feeling frustrated or confused during those two class periods.

As Sandra indicated in her introduction on the first day of class and on her syllabus, she wanted this class to focus on the students. She told the class before she left for her conferences that she did not think they needed her there to read and discuss their papers; the class was, after all, about their ideas.

Throughout my time with the class, it seemed as if Sandra really did try to get the students to accept the authority she offered to them. After listening to a student read his or her paper, she asked the group to voice their opinions about the student's topic and what he or she said about that topic. Very rarely did any of the students respond with their opinions. Sandra contends that

> [These students] seem to differ from those in two other classes I have taught in that, with the exception of one or two students, there seems to be little or no interest in learning for the sake of learning. Generally, these students seem to be reluctantly attending FSU. They are here because their parents expect them to be here or they are simply killing time until they can transfer to another school where a boyfriend or girlfriend attends, and so on. Besides being here reluctantly, they are in this supposedly "non-remedial" class while their peers are engaged in ENC 1101. No matter how much I or anyone else says or acts as if this is not remedial, the situation appears to all concerned as such, so the morale is NOT great. . . . Other classes I have taught are full of students who have interest and enthusiasm for the business of being at the university or at the community college, if not for the purpose of learning for learning's sake, then at least for the purpose of getting a degree in order to get a good job (November 10, 1993).

I think that the morale problem has its roots in several environmental factors. As the weeks wore on, the Writing Center environment became increasingly more quiet and conducive to discussions, but I wonder if the background noise during the first few weeks set a precedence that the students seemed to follow. Perhaps the students found it futile to discuss during the first few weeks, because they could not hear each other, and therefore got used to being quiet among themselves, depending on Sandra to assert herself over the group's silence just as she had over the Writing Center's noise. Sandra dealt with this problem by acknowledging how loud the Writing Center was, and encouraging students to speak loudly, often asking them to repeat themselves when other students complained of being unable to hear the conversation. Very rarely did she paraphrase or repeat a student's comment, leaving responsibility for the comment as well as its presentation in the student's hands.

As I mentioned earlier, the students never got into a routine of sitting in the same comfortable spot, or even next to the same person. Perhaps this lack of getting into a routine stems from the fact that they met at various tables throughout the Writing Center. I wonder if the lack of a "home," or familiar place to meet, made it difficult for the students and Sandra to feel like they were forming a culture, perhaps even intensifying the feeling that they were all thrown together into the "non-remedial" situation without really wanting to be there. I also think that being stuck in the Writing Center adds to the students' feelings that they are not in a "real" class. It meets once a week and in the Writing Center, while most of their peers are taking composition classes that meet two or three times a week in regular classrooms. The students do not receive a typical grade for 1905—a grade they can figure into their GPA, something that at least Chris and M.V. are very concerned about.

In an interview, Chris confirmed much of what I have concluded thus far.

Me: Is this what you expected, out of this class? When you thought about taking English in College?

Chris: Yeah, kinda, I guess. Well, I wasn't sure, because I couldn't get into . . . I barely missed getting into regular English, so I had no idea what this class was going to be.

Me: You feel like you would be ready for [regular] English?

C: Yeah, I feel like I should have been in regular English the first time. I shouldn't have been . . . there's no reason I'm in this class.

Me: Do you like keeping a journal?

C: (immediately) No. I always forget to write in it every day. And plus, I'm a believer in say what you want to say, and don't write it down, because if you write it down and somebody finds it or whatever, it can always be used against you. When I have a girlfriend, I never write down anything too serious or too . . . I just tell her.

Me: So, do you keep up with it? About how many times do you think you write in it?

C: Really, I usually don't write in it every day. Just the night before, I think back on the week, what I did each day, and then write it down when I do these things.

Me: What about taking the class pass/fail as opposed to . . . for a grade? Is that . . .

C: It kinda seems like a waste. You do all that work for a satisfactory. And basically, if it's pass or fail you can do all the way up to D work and still get a satisfactory, if it's pass or fail.

Me: Do you think you're working as hard in this class as you would, if you were getting a grade?

C: No. I mean, I'm doing all the work just so I can get a satisfactory, but, it's better if you get a grade. It helps your GPA out. It's not a hard class, and so if I had a grade, my GPA would be better. The way my classes are going, I need a better grade to help them.

Me: What about how quiet the class is sometimes? Do you think it's something Sandra can avoid more? Or do you think it's just the way the class is?

C: No, I just think it's how the class is. The way the people are. I don't say much in there either 'cause you don't [know] the people very well, and even if you do, you still . . .

Me: You don't know your classmates?

C: I know a couple of them. I say hi to them and stuff, but even if I did know them, I don't know if that would help us speak out. 'Cause we got people with all kinds of different opinions and different colors, so you don't want to say one thing and get them mad because there are only eight of you. You get a whole class mad, and then . . .

Me: Do you find that's how you feel about it when you write something? Because you're going to be reading it out loud?

C: Yeah, because there was one article I almost picked out when we had to pick out something out of the *Flambeau* [campus newspaper]. It was about black college students not getting enough money, or, you know, being cheated in the system. I mean, that irks me right there, but it wouldn't have been exploratory writing; it'd been very opinionated. And I would have upset half the class probably.

Me: So you find yourself censoring what you're doing?

C: Yeah. When I type stuff up, I watch what words I use. 'Cause I don't want to use, like big words that might impress the English teacher, but the kids would look at it like, "Well, what a nerd."

Me: What about in your journals? Do you censor yourself in your journals like you do in your exploratory writing?

C: Not really.

Me: You fee like [Sandra's] open to hearing whatever?

C: Yeah, she said to keep a journal and write what you wanted. Sometimes I put like "pissed off" in there and stuff, just to see what she'd say, she just reads right through it.

Me: So, what do you think about class when she wasn't there? Do you think it worked? Do you think it was a flop?

C: I think she shouldn't have had class. I don't think her . . . we were there, but nobody was saying anything, nobody wanted to read . . . actually, some people did read. But, still, I mean, the rest of the time . . . I think she should have just given us the day off.

Me: Why do you think she did that?

C: I don't know why she did it. I don't know if it was so we would maybe talk more to each other and get to know each other or what. I'm not sure.

Me: Is this class different than other classes that you're taking?

C: Yeah. Because I'm not getting a grade for it.

Me: Is your homework different?

C: Yeah, I don't understand all the way about the exploratory writing, how you look at something in different ways than you normally do. Because each person looks at something a certain way, and that's just how you look at it. If you look at it in a different way than you usually do, then you're not writing about yourself anymore.

Me: Is it hard to respond to someone else's writing?

C: Yeah, because if you really disagree with them you don't want to say it, you know what I mean? You don't want them to get mad or anything, you know. Start an argument with them or something. And why would you want to write about it if you disagree with them? That seems to keep a grudge going or something.

Me: You think people would hold grudges?

C: Well, yeah.

Me: Do you think that if you wrote something that offended someone in a paper it would be worse than just saying it? Or the same thing.

C: Same thing. But, if you speak it you can start to back out of it, but if you write it and they read it, then once they start reading . . . you can't cover it all up.

Maybe there is a happy ending to this ethnography, after all. Sandra's goal for the class was to have each student feel as if his or her opinion is significant, and to be able to express that opinion through writing. I think that this interview with Chris demonstrates that at least he (and I suspect others in the class) does, in fact, have a certain amount of respect for writing. Chris seems to see writing as permanent, significant, and to engage in writing as risk. Perhaps the lack of morale that Sandra perceives these students to have is due partially to the environmental factors that I discussed earlier, but also to a misinterpretation on the students' part as to what Sandra really expects from them.

Sandra often told the class not to be afraid to elaborate, to express their opinions. In class, she once even expressed dissatisfaction in their journals. A hand-out that she gave the class one day began with this statement:

> I'm somewhat disappointed in the journals. These are to be a place where you **THINK**.

In assigning exploratory writings, she encourages the students to "think about the topic in a way you've never thought about it before."

For a student such as Chris, who has quite a bit of respect for writing as a daunting, ominous, permanent medium, doing two seemingly contradictory things for the same teacher in the same class is, no doubt, confusing. He is being told to think, to explore how he feels about things in his journal, but then to suspend those feelings and approach his essay topics in a different way. For Chris, feelings and opinions cannot be suspended. They reflect how he thinks about a topic. To go beyond his first impressions is to take a great risk—of offending someone else in the class, of sounding pretentious—and may put him in an uncomfortable place, a place in which who he thinks he is (the Chris with opinions and feelings) is challenged. From Chris' point of view, Sandra wants him to feel and think in his journals, and then move beyond that somehow in his exploratory writing.

This gray area beyond first impressions and gut feelings is the area in which Sandra wants her students to gain authority: to state their views, but also to problematize them. Robert Brooke points out in discussing how students form identities in writing workshops that:

> The writing workshop approximates a microcosm of the pluralistic society in which students live. It is not a neutral environment. The writer's roles it makes available for students arise out of a very clear set of values. The workshop classroom values personal experience and self-reflections, tolerance and consideration for plural perspectives, dialogue, responsibility, and commitment to action. If students become apprentice writers in those roles, they are likely to leave the workshop better able to carry those roles into their lives a members of families and communities (1991, 139).

Sandra is attempting to form this kind of a culture in which students of various backgrounds and ideas can come together in mutual respect and openness to share their insights with one another. Chris, by expressing some fear of being too open in class, demonstrates that perhaps the class has not formed as this type of culture yet, perhaps because of the environmental conditions I mentioned earlier. Perhaps if the class were more like those that the students' peers are taking, they would be more willing to put themselves into the class, accept the authority Sandra is attempting to give them, and take risks—the very kinds of risks that Chris is unwilling to take.

I think this class has taken an important step towards becoming this kind of culture. Chris and M.V. both said (several times, in fact) in their interviews with me that Sandra encourages them to think and really cares about what they have to say. Both Chris and M.V. are more talkative in their one-on-one conferences with Sandra than they are in class. Perhaps they are more willing to take risks with Sandra alone because she has assured them that anything they say to her will be respected (Chris even tests her on this point by writing "pissed" in his journal). Both Chris and M.V. are aware of what Sandra wants from them—to think. In this way, Sandra has succeeded with her students; they know what she wants and expects from them. Now they just need to take risks to make the class work.

Chris: [In conferences], I like the part about telling [Sandra] my problems or whatever, but I don't like it when she says, "So you're saying that because of this . . ." You know what I mean? She tries to sometimes take things too far. They could be simple, but sometimes teachers take things farther than they actually are.

Me: What do you think she's trying to do?

C: She's trying to get you to think.

Me: Does it work?

C: Sometimes it does. I can't tell if she's trying to get me to think, or if she doesn't understand and needs me to explain it more or what. Almost all my English teachers are like that, though—my last two English teachers. I like it straight-forward, easy, open/close, just do it. English teachers like the gray, they live in the gray part, they don't like it black and white.

Patricia Hendricks: Poetic Technique: An Ethnographic Study

Selecting and Shaping the Study

John Van Maanen says that, "We rarely read of unsuccessful field projects where the research was presumably so personally disastrous to the fieldworker that the study was dropped or failed ever to find its way to publication" (1988, 79). If Van Maanen is correct, and I suspect he is, then this ethnography represents an exceptional case for it is, indeed, about failure. I believe it is about my own failure to embrace the ethnographer's role as participant–observer and the resulting consequences of that failure. Too, I believe this ethnography tells the story of a class that failed to develop into anything beyond a group of strangers who happen to have weekly contact. In both cases, however, failure doesn't necessarily mean worthlessness.

I wasn't terribly comfortable with the idea of an ethnographic study. In fact, the very methodology of ethnographic research—the inserting of oneself into already established groups, the pushing to get information from strangers, the assumption of an "I'm just like you" role—has proven to be very difficult for me in times past. After forty-four years of living and having had several experiences that required like skills, I felt I knew that ethnographic research would be difficult for me to attempt. However, as unlikely as eventual success might seem, I decided to make the most of the situation and at least study something I thought I might personally enjoy. And, not unimportantly, something that would fit my already busy schedule.

I found three classes that met my very general requirements for the study, those being a class where I could study a site that was writing intensive and a class that I could actually work into my schedule for two months. Two First-Year Writing classes (one ENC1101, one ENC1102) and one Poetic Technique class fit both requirements. Since I was teaching a First-Year Writing class of my own, ENC1101-11, I was advised by my peers to try the Poetic Technique class. The following is a description of a generic Poetic Technique class as listed in the *Florida State University, 1995–96 Undergraduate General Bulletin*:

CRW 3311. Poetic Technique (3). For aspiring poets and critics. Study of the elements of poetry, some practice in writing poetry.

Class chosen, I began to formulate questions, possible perspectives to investigate. I have to say, though, that uppermost in my mind was to approach the site without an agenda beyond the obvious fulfilling of my own course's requirement. The following extract illustrates my initial thoughts concerning just what I was about to do and why:

September 11. From *Mini-Ethnography: Project Proposal Draft*

I don't know what goes on in "creative" writing classes here at FSU in 1996. Why do students enroll in a Poetic Technique course? What do they expect? What do they want to accomplish in this type of class and what do they hope to gain from it? If they have goals for their own writing, do they reshape/recast assignments to meet their own needs? I will need to observe classes before I can even begin to form meaningful questions about this type of class.

I didn't know who the instructor was for the class I would be entering since it was listed as being taught by *staff* in the *Fall Directory of Classes*. However, I soon found out that the instructor for this class was none other than my Teaching Assistant mentor, Rex West. A poet, Rex is finishing his dissertation at FSU and is employed as an Instructor this year, a step above Teaching Assistant but a one-year-only appointment. I approached Rex in the graduate lounge and asked about conducting an ethnography study of his class. While interested, Rex said he would have to ask the class what they thought. Soon after this initial contact, Rex told me his class said yes, they would like to have me come into their class. In fact, according to Rex, the class was "excited" and expressed quite a bit of curiosity about my study, wondering if they would be able to read the final report.

I began to think that perhaps my misgivings were groundless and this ethnography thing would work out quite nicely. I also began to get excited about observing a class about poetry writing. I have no training in poetry other than a one-semester course taken in the early 1970's, but I have an interest in how poetry might be taught. I had recently (Fall, 1995) taken a course at FSU titled *Writing as Outreach* which, I came to find out, required me to work with and in *Runaway With Words*, a program that teaches poetry writing to at-risk youth in alternative learning sites. I became very interested in that program and have since become more involved with it. I think part of my interest in Rex's Poetic Technique course may have had a direct link to my work with *Runaway With Words*. But mostly, I was just excited that I had found a class to observe and so I began the work of preparing to enter the site.

Pre Site Entrance Communication: E-mail Correspondence

Me: Rex—Geez, if I only had an extra 24 hours per week I think I might get caught up within six months or so—I don't know if you will get this before your class Tuesday, 17 September, but I wanted to let you know that I will be there (bells may not be on). And while I had hoped to talk to you before my initial visit, I don't see it happening.

Your office hours just about mirror my graduate class times: I do want to get together so I can "interview" you for my project but mostly I want to know your feelings on a couple of subjects including: How I should enter the classroom. Should I just arrive and blend into the class landscape or should I announce my presence by briefing the students on the project's purpose?

Rex: Blending is good.

Me: What is your comfort level concerning audio-taping our initial interview and class meetings? (may be a non-factor but I want to know what you think)

Rex: Don't care much for taping: it makes me feel like Nixon.

Me: What do you expect of me concerning participation in class activities/assignments?

Rex: Nothing.

Me: What do you want to know about this project?

Rex: I'm just here to help you. Although realize that I'm busier this semester than I've been in my life—classes, mentoring, job search, dissertation—so I can't contribute much.

Me: We need to agree that everything (short of suicide comments or threatening language aimed at you) I record, either by audio-tape or notes, will be considered confidential information releasable only by the informant.

Rex: Notes are fine with me. Please, no tapes.

Me: By the way, I really do appreciate you letting me come into your class. Anything I can do to reciprocate, just let me know.

Rex: Glad I can help. Just help someone else out sometime. Karma and all. You know. See you this week, Cheers.

I also asked for and received a Course Information Sheet from Rex. I hoped to gain some sense of what I was walking into and perhaps discover possible points of friction between course requirements and students' willingness to meet those requirements. The following is an extract from the Course Information Sheet Rex's students received earlier in the semester. More specific requirements, such as attendance and late arrival policy, textbook information, and a weekly course schedule, were also included in the sheet.

From *CRW: 3311 Poetic Technique*— *Fall 1996 Course Information Sheet, Rex West, Instructor*

Is this the right course for you?

This IS the right course for you if you . . .

- enjoy reading and writing poetry and are willing to explore a variety of its forms.

- see the value of traditional, formal poetry yet want to explore contemporary styles as well.
- like class discussions, collaboration, and want to talk in depth about poetry.
- have the dedication to complete a poem every two weeks and are willing to take that poem through several revisions.
- have the writing skills (including a grasp of standard grammar and punctuation) to complete poems and short responses to what we read.
- plan on attending classes regularly, arriving prepared and on time, and getting involved in class activities.

I'm ready to go and on 17 September, I enter my chosen site. I invite you to enter with me.

The Class Lives Its Life

September 17. First Meeting: *I'm tired and less than enthused about all this. But to be fair, I don't think I could have asked for a nicer more supportive person to work with. Hmm—where the heck is he? it's close to start time—ah, here he is.* As I walk back into DIF 236 (after just spending 75 minutes here in another class) and cross the room to get to a seat way in the back, Rex says "This is Pat and she's our ethnographer." *Man this class is packed in here like sardines—it's way too small for the number of students.* Rex begins the class by commenting on the Warehouse readings and the requirement the students have to attend one (or an equivalent event) and do a review. Rex reminds them to keep up on their work. He then briefly mentions that he will be talking to them about their class book today—"how we're going to do it." Rex sits on the bolted-down-to-the-floor table in front of the class and talks from that position. He then asks the students to take out the poem they have to turn-in that day, reread it, and on a sheet of paper write down Self-Evaluation and address the following: What do you see as the strengths and weaknesses of your poem—explain; set a goal for the next poem based on your views on this one; ask one question you want me (Rex) to address. Rex begins to write on the board as the students write their self-evaluations. *Rat-tat-tat-tat on the chalkboard. rat-tat-tat-tat. rat-tat-tat-tat—rat-tat-tat-tat. These guys are prolific writers for the most part; they want more time to finish their papers. The room is so quiet as they write.* One person arrives late; quite late actually; by my watch seven minutes late. Rex brings him the attendance roster after the student sits down and tells him to get with a neighbor for details of what they are doing. Another student comes in, 9 minutes late.

Rex begins to gather-up the packages of writing. He does this personally and one-by-one. As he completes the process, Rex compliments
the entire class for their hard work on the poems. He then begins to talk
about the class book, referring to the items he has written on the chalkboard. He says, "This is the fun part, the best part" or something like
that. He talks about each job group in turn, describing what each job
might do. *Rex roams the room—he seems to have lots of energy.* Rex ends his
discussion saying, "I envision it being beautiful."

Rex re-introduces me and asks if I could say a few words about the
project. (He knows I will be passing out a brief questionnaire though he
has not seen it yet.) I introduce myself as a graduate student, someone
who has never been in a poetic technique class at FSU. I give the absolute
sketchiest information about what I'm doing here/why. I tell them I'm
going to hand out a survey/questionnaire, assuring them that they are
free to fill it out or not. I also mention that everything they might tell me
is confidential until the report is over and it will not have any impact
on their grade at all. I pass out the questionnaires and wait until the
students are done. *Students spend varied amounts of time on filling out the
questionnaire—they have already been told they are leaving early and I suspect
my questionnaire is about as important/welcome as a hangnail. Oh, well. I stay
behind and watch Rex negotiate with a student about an absence. LATER: I review my questionnaires, just reading them to see what I've got generally and if
I have a number of folks who will do a one-on-one interview. I am pleasantly
surprised that most are willing to get into this a bit more. Do I want to?*

Of the 25 students in this class, nineteen volunteer to participate in
this project beyond the first questionnaire. Though the other six certainly must have some impact on the dynamics of the class, I decide to
concentrate on the findings of these nineteen volunteers. I find I have
a fairly diverse group, the demographics of which are demonstrated in
Figure 4.

Figure 4

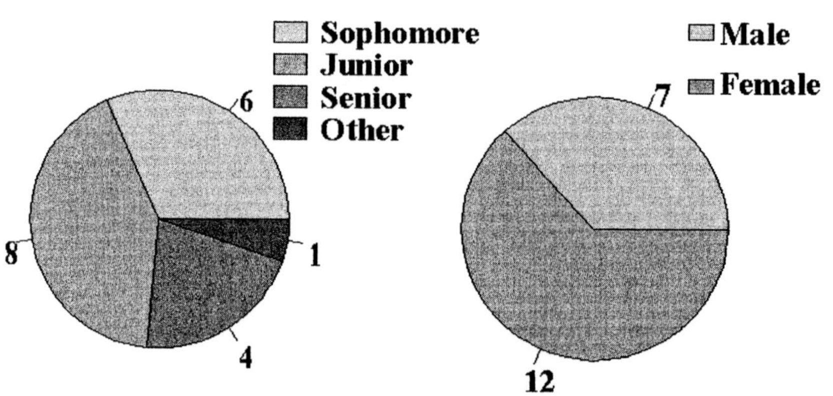

My initial questionnaire also posed some questions that might be considered as trawling—I hoped to find some issue, have some anomaly present itself early in my research. Unfortunately, this didn't happen but I believe a sampling of the responses of my nineteen volunteers does provide a good overview of what individuals bring to this class as well as some of their early attitudes. While I was not on-site during the first few weeks of school and so could not capture their initial reactions, this first questionnaire was completed in the fourth week and before that crucial first grade.

QUESTION	*SAMPLING OF RESPONSES*
1. When you registered for this course, what were your expectations?	to improve my writing skills; a schedule filler that might help my short story hobby; learning to write better poetry, also want to find out if I have any poetic talent; to fill a requirement as an English major; to take a personal love I have of poetry into a more polished skill and therefore better as a tool for expression; I had no expectations when I registered for this class—I only hoped that my writer's block would leave me after haunting me for about a year and a half; honestly I had low expectations of what a technique & peer-evaluation oriented class could offer me.
2. How would you define the purpose/goal of this class?	to learn the rules before you break 'em; to gain a deeper understanding of poems; since much is based on group interaction the goal . . . is limited to the level of thought of the students involved; to be able to express yourself without limitations and to openly evaluate your writings as well as the work of others; to learn more about contemporary poetry, become better readers and writers, and to appreciate modern poetry; to get us away from the traditional and greeting card poetry; to improve my diction and establish a consistent voice; to learn the skills of writing, reviewing, and appreciating contemporary poetry; obey Rex's commands.

(*continued on page 238*)

(continued from page 237)

QUESTION	*SAMPLING OF RESPONSES*
3. Have you ever taken a poetry or poetry technique course before? If so, please briefly describe.	14—no 5—some sort of poetry work in public school
4. What other types of writing are you doing this semester?	Fiction Technique—4 Article/Essay—4 Other classes—8 Non-specific fiction—2 Non-specific personal writing—1
5. How is this class different from other writing classes you have taken?	it's heavy on poetry, you just don't dabble in it; besides poetry being the main subject, not very—same laid back atmosphere; most of my other classes have focused on critical essay writing; too early to tell; this class seems somewhat less structured from my just completed Article & Essay class; more creative and no so concrete as to what has to be written—I can use my imagination a lot more; it allows me to be, say, create whatever I want. There are no guidelines, there are no limits; group activities are helpful; more structured; more focused and definitely on a higher level; more variety in assignments; completely focused on poetry, rather than a melting pot of various fiction; more group oriented
6. What's a poet and are you one?	8—strong yes: yes, I think I am 4—hedging: I guess I am, I hope I am, I would like to be one 4—by association: everybody is a poet 2—not yet 1—who is to judge?

Based on my first meeting, I begin to refine my project as shown in the following extract from my working project description:

September 18. From Mini-Ethnography: Project Description
I wonder if students are somehow more focused or committed to their writing in this type of class as opposed to a class they must take to meet university requirements. My initial questions, the questions I think I really might be able to "get to" are: what does the teacher want to do

with this class; and why did the students register for a poetic technique class? What do they want? What do they think they are getting?

I have, at this point, decided to "let the class speak to me" and hope that it will speak loudly enough for me to hear, make connections, see patterns of behavior. I return to the classroom.

September 19. Second Meeting: *Bang-bang-bang, my head hurts/I'm tired and freezing. Students sit and read newspapers, the Flambeau and FSU-View.* Over on the other side of the room, two girls chit-chat—rather loudly—a few guys join in the discussion when one of the girls starts talking about someone (a friend) who just got a rat tattoo and got her belly-button pierced. The conversation moves on to tongue piercing; the pros and cons. *I listen and watch, a nonentity in this class; a nonentity in much of my school life it seems.* Everyone else in the classroom, and it's filling-up fast, is pretty quiet. *I read a newspaper, too—cover? or cower?* Rex arrives and has everyone come up to the front desk to pick up a handout. He writes next week's assignment on the board and explains the requirements. *WOW, this is fast paced. Hope these guys write fast.* Rex then dives right into looking at class poems, written sometime before I arrived. Rex says they will be looking at consistent voice and concrete detail and says, "If you can master these two, you're on your way to being famous" in a light tone. He then asks if anyone feels particularly vocal—"I need some volunteers here." A student comes in late, 10 minutes. A student finally volunteers to read and they begin reading the first poem aloud. A student comes in late, 11 minutes. When the reader is done, Rex asks, "What's going on here?"

At a pause in the discussion, which is light, Rex asks, "If this was a literature class, what would we say about this—what's the subject of the poem?" Light discussion follows and works to a standstill but then Rex asks, "Could it be sexual? Could the poem be about sex?" Rex then humorously comments that it's ok to talk about that possibility in this class—you can say sex or something like that. A slightly more lively discussion ensues and then Rex steers the conversation to a close and wraps-up this discussion.

Rex then asks for comments on problems in the draft and says, "and all drafts have problems." *One young man always wants to answer Rex's questions. There are many students who say nothing.* He introduces the term *abstraction,* and then asks the class for some examples of BIG abstractions—these he writes on the board (love, pain, piety, truth, hate, death) and then points the students to a few abstractions in the current poem and asks the students to point out any others. The next poem reading is much like the first except now the students automatically point to abstractions and possible "fixes" which leads to discussion about good concrete details.

Rex then has the class get paper out for in-class writing. He asks them to briefly list five of their most difficult choices. As they are writing, he writes several prompts on the board and has them freewrite from them. He then keeps adding another line until there about 19 prompts on the board. The students continue to write and there are occasional groans when Rex adds another prompt.

Rex then hands out a sheet that has the same starting prompts but defines what type of thing must be written. For example, the first line is: If I had only—[name something you have always been afraid to do]. They are to work on this poem for next Tuesday.

> "There are many students who say nothing."
> —field notes, 18 September

> I think some others are more inclined to write poetry than myself (Noah).
>
> I feel that I'm more party/sports/fun minded than the majority of the class. I don't really fit in with the rest of the class (Brian).
>
> I'm quiet in a group setting, so I see myself as something of an observer (David).
> —from 2nd Questionnaire

September 24. Third meeting: The class is chit-chatty before Rex comes in though I don't note anything in particular. *I am distracted, carrying questions/concerns from the last class into this one.* Rex arrives and writes the assignment for the next class on the board; major groans concerning number of copies required (6). Rex say they are going to talk about the Surreal Poetry from the prompt handed out on Thursday and asks everyone to get into their writing groups which have already been assigned. There's lots of talking, scraping of chairs, desks, etc. Three groups of five people each work inside the room and 2 groups go outside in the hallway. I ask Rex how they got into groups. He says he brings in an ugly hat and they put slips of paper in it with a name on each and then draw five names to form a group. They stay in these groups throughout the semester.

Rex tells the groups to choose one poem as a representative of their group. It will be read out loud to the rest of class. Rex then visits each of the groups for a brief time. *In an aside to me, Rex confides that he is not feeling well and is particularly cranky today. I don't think it shows at all.* The groups in the hallway come back into the room and examples are read from 3 groups. Rex asks, "What were you doing different between the autobiographical poem (handed in last week) and the surreal poem— what were you thinking as you wrote?"

Rex talks about giving poems back on Thursday. Rusty, in the back row, softly says, "Liar." Rex doesn't hear or chooses to ignore it.

Rex then asks, "What do you gain using autobiographical material?" And students respond slowly with authenticity, "Easier to tell a story than make one up." Then someone mentions that you might be too close to the material, so Rex asks about the negatives. He gets from one student the idea that the significance can be lost on the reader, "They don't know what's important like you do." This leads to a brief back and forth about audience.

Rex then asks what is gained by writing the poem in the surreal mode. Striking images and that you can see the writer's imagination better are offered, which leads to talk about images and dreams. Rex asks the class what, as a writer, did you find yourself doing when writing the surreal poem? Rex then shares via overhead projector a poem written by a prior student, asking what are the autobiographical elements and what are the surreal elements. [*It's quite a good poem.*]

Rex asks them to get back into their writing groups—3 groups in, 2 outside in the hall. The ones going to the hall file out like obedient children. Each group is given a different poem to read and discuss (one person is to read it aloud to their group). Again, Rex visits each group, easily moving in and out, prompting, questioning, encouraging. Rex then gets everyone back together again, reviews an assignment which is due on October 8th. The students are released from the class.

> "I don't know what's going on in this class at all. I just don't
> see anything."
>
> —Status Note, 25 September

> *If you had to describe this class as a living being, what would it be?*
>
> I guess I would say this class is like a spider making its web. It's very
> slow and everything has to be precise, only to be ripped apart
> minutes later (Noah).
>
> It would be an ex-living being if anything. Most of the class doesn't
> work with one another. I don't know. I don't see this class as
> anything but a class (Scott).
>
> —from 2nd Questionnaire

September 26. Fourth Meeting: Rex is ill and has cancelled class. However, Genevieve West is there to give back the graded poems as promised and to give guidelines for the next meeting. I notice that a lot of students are missing. Before she gets into all of that, she does let me address the class and hand out my 2nd questionnaire. I know this is a bad idea—this giving out the questionnaire and hoping they will bring it back—but since they already know that they will be leaving early, I don't think I will get very "good" responses if I hold them here. Anyway, I hand it out, explaining what it is and that I would like it back on Tuesday.

They get their graded poems and most leave immediately. Some students hang around the class, reading Rex's comments (I assume). I overhear one young lady remark, "I think he's mad at me."

Before I leave, one student gives me back a completed questionnaire.

> "I think he's mad at me."
>
> —field notes, 26 September

> I am not a poet. Rex hates my writings and I just get frustrated (Brian).
>
> Yes, I'm having trouble because I like to write with abstractions (Rusty).
>
> This is a 3000 level class and I am only a freshman. Some of the things I'm expected to know I haven't learned yet (Scott).
>
> —from 2nd Questionnaire

October 1. Fifth meeting: Seems to be more chit-chatting before class today. What I can overhear has nothing to do with class or poetry. Rex comes in and begins to pass out a revised calendar. He highlights what has changed and goes over the important dates. Rex invites the students to "come in to visit me" and says, "If you haven't been in to see me at least twice during the semester, you aren't getting your money's worth."

Rex reminds the class about the criteria for a good poem in this class: concrete, consistent voice, and connected to something outside the poem (broader view). He emphasizes that these criteria are for this class but that they apply pretty well to poetry in general.

The class then breaks into writing groups. Each person reads their own draft aloud and then they discuss it. I watch and listen to one group nearby. Rex joins the group early and prompts/questions, tries to engage other students. He asks about the concrete details and asks which ones work. They work on this awhile and then go on to deconstruct the abstractions in the poem. I hear one young woman say, "I need criticism . . . last time 'It was so good'." Rex leaves to join another group and this one continues with feedback. I hear the term "hallmark card" bandied about as an example of what they don't want in their writing. (I have heard Rex use this term in class discussion as well). This group talks about moving between fiction technique class and this poetry technique class, and how taking both classes in the same semester has caused some "problems" such as writing prosy poems and fragmentary stories. *I'm impressed that this group continues very much on task after Rex leaves. Their only digression is actually about writing and the writing program. I find out from Rex later that several of the members of this group have come in to talk to him about their poem drafts.* The group moves off task briefly and talks about other writing classes. I overhear one student say, "I hate all those literature classes—so much structure."

As the class comes to a close, I ask if anyone has a survey to give me and only get one.

October 3. Sixth meeting: *The natives don't seem terribly friendly today when I ask if anyone has remembered the questionnaire.* Poems (Poem 2) are to be turned in for a grade today. Rex writes the next meeting's assignment on the board and then asks everyone to get a blank piece of paper out and write a self-evaluation. Much silence ensues. *Thankfully, the classroom is not so freezing today. In the words of the great Berra, it's deja vu all over again. Boy, is it quiet in here. I can hear the cold air coming through the ac vents.* Students (2–3) arrive quite late, maybe 9–10 minutes. They are repeat offenders.

Everyone is asked to gather their documents and turn them in to Rex. Rex then hands out a slip with the "job" assignments for the class book and asks the groups to gather together to write their job description. There's lots of talk and lots of introductions. *I stay back here with the artists group. These people don't know one another and have to introduce themselves. I guess they only know their own writing group members.* This goes on for about 30 minutes and then the class forms a large circle to report back on what each small group requires or will require of the large group. *Hmm—this is a good idea, particularly to teach planning, organizing, communication, collaboration.* Once the reports are complete, everyone gets back into the typical class formation (see layout in Figure 5). The class now wrenches back to normal class activities. Rex passes out a poem, his

Figure 5

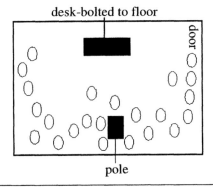

own poem, "Charles Burgin," and talks about writing from a photo (their third poem is to be written in relation to a photo or painting).

The class ends.

October 8. Seventh meeting: Once again I ask for my questionnaires. I offer another copy in case anyone has lost the original. I get blank stares and a sort of group "UH" floats in the air. I do get one back from a male student. Rex arrives and asks if I need a minute. I tell him no, I've already asked.

Rex writes the assignment on the board and then hands out a sheet about the photo poem. He says, as he is handing the sheets out to the class, "What I'll start doing for the rest of the semester is giving you some revision suggestions and the theory behind what I'm looking for." He goes over the sheet and emphasizes that his suggestions are suggestions not mandates, and encourages the students to try some, saying "Enjoy the ride." Rex then talks briefly about revision practices and that students may be feeling "finished" too early. He then passes out some of the drafts (with names removed) that were collected earlier. Each poem is read aloud by a student and then looked at for what's working: details, the connection to the outside world, etc. Also, students offer what else could be done with the poem. *As I look around this room the words dull, dull, dull come to mind—dead or dying off—wilting from lack of rain, from lack of nurture? But that's not it really; the nurture is there but these students are like robots: they will perform but only if their switch is hit. Rex most often has to call on someone to read and for input; they don't offer without prompt.*

One poem in particular sparks some resistance on the part of one student concerning abstractions, she saying that abstractions are ok sometimes and that poems shouldn't be labeled. *Oh, my—now here's a problem. The poem in question really does reek and Rex is being extremely kind to it and this young woman doesn't see it, doesn't want to listen because, I think, this undercuts her position, her view of herself (?).* Rex attempts to engage her with specifics but she is talking generalities. After a back and forth, back and forth, they move on to the next poem. No other students come forward to buttress the young lady's position.

> "These students are like robots: they will perform but only if their switch is hit."
>
> —field notes, 8 October

October 10. Eighth meeting: Rex introduces the villanelle as a possible form the students might want to consider and hands out a sheet of two examples. Both poems are read aloud. Amy, the girl who disagreed about abstractions on Tuesday, now states that she doesn't think much went into the writing of these villanelles. *Is this because Rex seems to value the difficulty of writing this form?* The class gets into their writing groups and goes outside. I opt to stay and talk with Rex. *Rex seems edgy about letting all the students out of his sight. He seems itching to go check on them.* One of the things we discuss is the lack of volunteering in group discussions.

> "Rex seems edgy about letting all the students out of his sight. He seems itching to go check on them."
> —field notes, 10 October

> *If you had to describe Rex as an animal, what animal would he be and why?*
> I guess an owl. He's pretty wise for such a young guy (Noah).
> I'd rather not answer that question (Brian).
> I'd describe him as a bee because he's always buzzing around (David).
> —from 2nd Questionnaire

October 15. Ninth meeting: *A different class today—much more chit-chat.* Poems will be turned in today for a grade. Before Rex arrives, Rusty says across the room to Amy, "Shoot for that B –." Rex arrives and a student asks, "Am I still held to the 30 lines?" Rex responds with, "Oh, no. I'd be glad to negotiate." (This exchange is from a student who wrote a 4-page poem last time.)

But they don't turn in the poems today but rather get into writing groups and work on lists of colors. Some of these colors are to be worked into to their current poems. As the students are working on their color lists, Yvonne hands out an "Assignment from the Editors" slip.

The class then gets into class book groups. I have the Editor group in front of me and right now the talk is about Yvonne getting a job at Barnes and Noble and how it works—i.e., availability and time off. Then, at the suggestion of the publishing group, the editors decide to include a group ode to Rex in the class book (they won't tell him about it).

Students dribble out of class as their respective groups finish.

October 17. Tenth meeting: Before class, one person (Sara) is showing her poetry journal to another student; two males are talking about music and then move on to talk of writing villanelles; other people are carrying on conversations; one or two isolated students are sitting apart and are quiet. Before the official start of class but after Rex arrives, I ask for help scheduling individual interviews. Poems are turned in by the established routine. The room is quiet.

Drafts of poems are read out loud. Rex then hands out a challenge word poem assignment sheet, explains the exercise, and asks everyone to get into writing groups. Students do so and begin to work on the words. *I am surprised at how difficult it seems for these groups to come up with words. I'm thinking poets—sensory description—attention to details—I don't know, just seems that poetry folks should revel in this.*

After class, Sara and Stacy volunteer for interviews. They are the only ones to do so.

October 22. Eleventh meeting: Rex hands out some advice on writing the review paper. He then quickly goes over some thoughts on punctuation using a fish tank analogy. *I'm stealin' this fish tank thing!* The class then leaves to go outside to form into writing groups and discuss their review drafts. I am to interview Sara after class.

SARA: Sara has just recently changed her major to English. She is a sophomore. She tells me several times that she has been writing for quite some time (13 years old) and that she has published some poems. Upon questioning, I learn that this is Sara's first poetry writing class though she did have some poetry writing/reading in high school. She describes her high school teacher as "pretty lame." I begin the interview by sharing my impression of the class and the lack of voluntary discussion. I hope by me introducing the subject, Sara will feel comfortable talking about "negatives" and I hope to keep the interview focused. Sara says:

> well, some have never written poetry before—me, I'm just shy. That's just like a class. . . . Rex is pretty good actually, he actually . . . whenever people don't talk that much he actually says what do you think of it and I like that because he makes people think . . . they all just sit there. . . . I like that about him.

Sara then tells me that she goes in to talk to Rex frequently. She is concerned with getting her poem "right." She tells me that she first had a lot of sentimental language in her poems but it's getting better. While she agrees with Rex about his emphasis on concrete images, she doesn't agree with all of Rex's views.

> all the stuff that he says is bad, I don't agree with him. . . . Partly he doesn't want us to resort back to 18th century poetry—I can see where that's what he's trying to do but I don't think that he should make such a big deal of it if people decide to do it that way. . . . I disagree with writing about certain topics. . . . I think that if you're at this level you can think of something to write about without being told to write about—like sleep. . . . I

like Rex. I just have a couple of problems with him.
I think he's a good teacher—it's just that his teach-
ing style. . . .

In the end, I find that my interview with Sara doesn't really point to anything in particular about the class as a group but I do get an idea of how Sara sees herself. I do not feel as if I have found a window into the class' culture, if there is one. Fortunately, I still am to have an interview with Stacy and later, one with Noah. Hopefully, one of them will help me *see* this class.

October 23. From mini-ethnography, take 1

This is a tale of an ethnography gone wrong, horribly wrong. It tells the saga of a lowly but earnest graduate student hoping for what can only be called a minor miracle: completing a class assignment while simultaneously achieving an intellectual epiphany—an aha! of the mind. . . . This is a disturbing tale for it speaks of confusion, uncertainty, temerity, silence, and surrender.

October 24. I interview Stacy this morning. I also arrange with Noah for a new interview time (next week, Tuesday 29th). I can't attend today's class meeting because of prior commitments.

STACY: Stacy proves to be a very interesting interview. She is thoughtful, deliberate, and articulate. Stacy is a philosophy major and has or will have an English minor. She plans on going to law school after she gets her undergraduate degree. Stacy is a junior, having transferred here from Ft. Walton–Okaloosa Community College. She tells me she started at FSU as a Freshman but had to go back home when she became quite ill (she doesn't elaborate). I begin the interview by telling Stacy a little bit about my perceptions of the class saying I get no sense of community.

as a class? I don't think there can be since we're
divided into groups and we tend to stick to those
small groups and we don't ever intermingle except
when we're all in the classroom and then it's still
like-these are my people. . . . I see people coming
in and they'll discuss things with people from their
group-it's sort of segregated like that.

About writing groups, Stacy says that's where most of the participation comes in:

I've gotten some good feedback from Jim and Bobbie
but I think people in these writing groups—at least
mine—they tend to be too polite or they want to be

and that's not very effective, beneficial but occa-
sionally I'll get some good [laughs] I hate this
line—you know. . . . Yeah, well it's too positive most
of the time and it takes up, it wastes a lot of time.

I then ask her if she noticed any change in the class after the first grades.

I know for a fact that most of the class was extremely
displeased with his . . . well . . . he had a right to
give what he did. . . . I just remember what I'd read
that first writing group—the poetry wasn't very good—
the grades were deserved but the whole class didn't
react well to it . . . why's he being such a hard
ass . . . I think he's a jerk . . . things like that.

As we continue to talk, Stacy begins to give me some insight into this class. I present the following statements somewhat out of sequence for the purpose of crystallizing what becomes a major theme in Stacy's interview and a viewpoint I take with me to Noah's interview.

I'm doing what he wants . . . concrete detail is the
only thing he seems to be stressing or consistently
stressing . . . he's driving us toward a goal
end. . . . I've progressed in this class towards
manufacturing poems that mean nothing to me which is
actually good practice—I guess that's what you have
to do in a class like this and he wants depersonal-
ization . . . it's like a vocational . . . sort of
practicing the method to write. . . . We've all just
fallen into this "I'm just manufacturing a poem, this
is a manufactured poem"—it's very technical, it's
gotten very technical and I think that's what he
wants and it, it's probably good that he does that
because the less attachment you have toward some-
thing the more willing you are to change it and ma-
nipulate it the way he wants it to be. . . . I think
people who come out of this alive, not weeping or
bruised will have benefited from it as far as the
technical part of writing poetry goes—they can bring
that with them—if nothing else the fact that you have
to write something, that you have to revise it, you
always have to be writing.

Stacy says she would recommend the class if someone's goal was to become a published poet but if someone was writing strictly for self, then she says they might get "burned." She says she has become used to the class.

October 29. Twelfth meeting: *Boy, the class is noisy/laughing/exuberant.—Has an alien mothership replaced all of the students with programmed-happy clones?* Poem 4 is being turned in, complete with self-evaluation. Amy has come in late and sits next to me. *Oh, she appears to have forgotten her poem—she goes through her back pack and all her folders at least twice then sits there looking around; she seems frumped-out, confused, frustrated and mad. I am thinking about my discussion this morning with Wendy, about resistance and investment. I wonder if students are shunning me (not participating) as a way of resisting Rex. Perhaps I am aligned with him in their minds. I wonder, too, about investment in classes, investment in poetry. I wonder if an investment in a poem or poetry in general does not necessarily equal investment in a poetry class AND if investment in poetry in general does not necessarily equal an investment in a particular poem written for this class.*

After the self-evaluations are written and everything turned in, Rex says that as a result of his survey last week concerning the usefulness of the course text, they will be trying something new. He asks the students to individually propose an assignment for the next poem complete with invention and revision suggestions. *My own suggestion, mentally given, is a theme of surrender.* When most of the class begins to exhibit signs of confusion/discomfort with the idea, Rex asks if they would like to do it in their writing groups. He gets a firm "no" from most everyone. So they work on suggestions for about ten minutes and then Rex has them swap with someone. He asks them to refine, add, pose possible revision strategies and not worry about whether they agree that it would be a great assignment or not. He says, "Just go ahead and go with the flow here." After everyone is done, Rex tells them that he will pick out 3–5, bring them back next class, and the class will decide which will be their next assignment. He then asks them to get into their class book groups. Amy leaves the classroom, *maybe going to her car to retrieve her paper?* The artists tell the group that they will be taking their class photo in the graveyard and everyone needs to wear black or something dark. *Seems like these groups are more familiar with one another now.* Amy asks me if I have some gum but I don't. I offer Tic-Tacs and she gladly accepts them. She says she gets psyched easily and she forgot her poem—she'd just finished printing it out at home and must have left it there. She is trying to reach someone and have them bring it to her. By the end of class, she does get her poem in.

Noah's interview immediately follows this 29 October class meeting—the last one I attend.

> "investment in poetry in general does not necessarily equal an investment in a particular poem written for this class"
> —field notes, 29 October

NOAH: I am very happy that Noah has volunteered for this interview. He didn't right at first but one day he came into class early and said he would talk with me. I particularly wanted to interview Noah because he had indicated on the first questionnaire that this was the second class he had taken with Rex. I find out that Noah took Rex's Article and Essay class this past summer. Noah is a bit older than some of the other students and, like Stacy, has transferred here from a community college. Noah started his college career at Rollins College—club Rollins, he calls it. He almost totally failed; he did fail his first English class at Rollins. He then went to Valencia Community College where he did much better in English and discovered he liked it. Noah is an English major and says he "couldn't imagine a better major." Noah describes this class as containing lots of quiet people saying, "I find it kinda frustrating . . . it's like, wake up . . . come on everybody." He says many are still young (Noah is 23) and are into the party scene (he says, "It's not what it's about for me anymore"). I ask him about his poetry writing.

> *[I] don't like it—well, not that I don't like it, it's just that I haven't been introduced to it before this class and apparently I'm not good at it according to Rex—he liked my essays more . . . too much structure to it. . . . I obviously have too much too say to edit that.*

I then ask him about the class and my perception of a change in attitude around the first grade.

> *I think everybody came into class thinking—we're going to write poetry la-de-dah and then they realized how he grades, hard—he's hard—he's real hard—he takes something you've worked really hard on and instead of giving you something for the effort, he's like this [sound] too wordy, this is too flowery, this is whatever—B— and you're like, but I tried really hard and so there's really nothing as far as effort goes—it's what he thinks works and that's what he grades you on—it's very subjective and it really pisses you off—but there's very little he's gonna change so you just have to deal with it. [LATER] He says this is something I couldn't write and yet he criticizes it and it gets frustrating 'cause you're not sure how you're supposed to please the guy—you really don't know what to do to please if you try your hardest to do everything he tells you to do and then he looks at it and says I could never do this but it still sucks—it's really frustrating. [GRADES?] B—, B—, B—the second I thought I nailed—that's when my morale dropped.*

I ask Noah if he thinks Rex knows of what he speaks.

> *Oh, absolutely, absolutely. I think he's very knowledgeable about the subject but at the same time really not open to suggestions other than what he knows. I feel bad about saying that because I like Rex—he's a hell of teacher, a great teacher. I mean I've learned a lot from him already, at the same time he knows what he wants and he expects to get that and if you don't give him that he's not*

real lenient on it—I think the rest of the class would probably agree with me on that.

Finally, I ask Noah if there is anything I should know that I haven't asked about and from this simple question I receive some great insight.

> *You're in here as much as I am—except for the poems. . . . I'm forced into the middle of it. As much as you sit here and stare at everybody and listen to what everybody said, I did the same and—I haven't figured anything out more than you have, I'm sure. . . . It's really the same in any class—kids sign up for the class, half of them don't want to be there, a few of them are excited to be there, then the class runs thru, lives its life and I don't think anybody here is gung-ho to write poetry except Rex and that one tall guy.*

I ask Noah if he would take another class with Rex and he responds positively. We talk about next semester's courses and I ask if he has registered. He says no and I urge him to talk to someone about what classes to take. I ask if Rex would be someone he would talk to and again, he responds positively. Despite the frustration Noah expresses about Rex's evaluations, Noah seems to genuinely like and respect Rex.

As a concluding act, I ask Rex (via e-mail) about grades at this point in the semester. I want to somehow assure myself that most of the students are doing "fine," so their discomfort about the class shouldn't be linked to overall failing grades. Rex reports that the grades are: 6 = A; 13 = B; 4 = C; 2 = F (dropped). This falls in line with my view that they are doing just fine; over half are above average.

I also ask Rex to write a brief "statement" of his impression of the class; the dynamics of the class and his role in the class. The following is his response:

```
I'm still trying to decide what actually took place
this semester, but somehow, early on, a good many of
the students made two unfortunate decisions which
both impeded their learning and made the course as a
whole disappointing for all involved (maybe they had
made these decisions long ago). First, they decided
poetry was such a subjective, indefinable entity, and
no teacher could possibly justify giving any student
a grade lower than an "A" in; thus in the first few
weeks, grades—not art, or expression, or creativity—
became their primary concern. Second, many students
decided early on that they already knew all there was
to know about poetry, and there was no more to learn;
thus, for them, the notions of doing multiple drafts,
of experimenting with voice, of using concrete de-
tail, of reading and learning about what contemporary
writers do, well, these were all inconvenient. Note
```

that I decided to abandon the *Best American Poetry
1996* text at midterm because students kept complaining that "all the poems are boring." Of course, these
students are the ones who keep insisting on defining
contemporary poetry using 19th century aesthetic
criteria (lofty in diction, abstract, melodramatic,
clichéd from the perspective of 1996). In short,
these students simply want approval for whatever they
dash off in a hurried last moment before class, which
some arrogantly confessed to doing; they are not interested in growing as writers. Bearing all this in
mind, it isn't surprising to me that students were
never (and still aren't, now in the 12th week) willing to give honest, critical feedback during peer response sessions. And it's interesting to me that very
few students took it upon themselves to see me in the
office, to ask for help, to discuss the important
ideas the course asked them to think about, or even
to protest. In general, students were defensive during class discussions, unwilling to listen to me or
each other. The lack of interest they have taken in
the class book, a project which puts them in control,
is further proof that this course simply asks them to
do more than show up, turn in a poem, and await their
well deserved *As*, which is, somehow, what they envi-
sioned a poetry class to be like.

Thus endeth my field work.

A Vampire in the Mirror *or* Reflections of Nothing

Surely it must be obvious that my observations center on Rex. Almost
every paragraph of my field notes begins with *Rex said this* or that, or
Rex did x. While I have edited my field notes for this document, the orig-
inals echo this same teacher focus. Some of the blame for this one-sided
reporting can be traced to my lack of participation in student writing
groups and, I think, my interest in the material being presented by Rex.
However, part of my own developing discomfort with this project was
based on a lack of student interaction/active participation in the class
itself. I felt as if I had little else to observe in the class but Rex. To be fair
to the students, the class is very much a teacher-fronted one and Rex
is—what did Wendy call it?—a charismatic teacher. In this class, he
runs the show even while he tries to generate participation.

After some six weeks attending this class, I was at a loss at to what
to say, what picture to paint. My questionnaires gave me the barest of
insights and the three interviews only provided partial glimpses. As I

struggled to name what it was that I had experienced, my own past presented me with an analogy—an analogy that seemed to bring all, or at least most of, the disparate pieces together. Certainly there are other possible interpretations—different eyes will see different things—but the following is what emerged for me. And its emergence has caused much questioning on my part—about Rex West's class and about the larger academic setting in which this class took place.

I spent ten years in the military, specifically the Air Force, and, at the risk of offending several sensibilities, I believe parallels exist between the military as an organization and academia. The military, as I knew it, is an extremely large, layered organization replete with rituals, rules, customs, and tiered authority. Similarly, the academy, as embodied in a university, has its customary rituals such as commencement exercises and dissertation/thesis defenses; has rules covering such things as course loads, research/teaching ratios, tenure; and operates under national standards for degree granting authority, grants degrees at several varying expert levels, and employs individuals for several classes of jobs. Careers in both the military, particularly for officers, and in teaching are often considered to be more of a calling than a career, likened to other ill-paying but satisfying life-long commitments such as the ministry.

Entry into the officer corps requires a basic college degree with advancement only possible through additional education and training. This is not unlike the situation in academia. If an individual is content with either an Associates or Bachelors degree and the careers made available with those degrees, no further education will be required. However, if there's a desire for an advanced teaching job or a desire to join the scholarly discourse about a particular subject, it's very likely that more education, more letters of the alphabet behind the name, will be required. New military officers are often not fully committed to the military organization's wider culture but, if these new officers continue their service, a certain allegiance to the organization develops. As the organization invests in the individual through training and economics, the individual invests in the organization, identifying more and more with its culture. The military life is not an easy one and so, I believe, it requires this aligning of self-constructed identity with organizational beliefs. I believe parallels can be found in academia.

As already mentioned, the military, like a university, has many layers of authority. Most Americans are somewhat familiar with the faces of Generals Schwartzkopf and Powell. While these two men had enormous authority and power, it is not at their level that the military's day-to-day multifaceted culture is most evident. In fact, it is at the squadron level that we find the strongest evidence of military culture. It is at this lower organizational level that several cultures meet, often clash, and sometimes meld into one.

The squadron is the basic element of a working unit in the Air Force. Whether it be concerned with supplies, transportation, or, to a lesser degree, flying missions, the squadron is where the work gets done. It is also at the squadron level that we can find the greatest variety of organizational values. Here there are officers committed to maintaining the organizational culture; new officer initiates who are just learning their specialty's culture as well as the larger military culture; enlisted personnel who vary as greatly in commitment to the organization as the officers but who also have their own culture that is "forbidden" to the officer corps; and finally, but not always present, is a civilian work force whose position and culture is better left unexplored. Within this setting, individuals are assigned roles to play. These roles are largely determined by officer/enlisted distinctions and rank within the two groups. Someone is the leader and everyone else becomes followers. Or so it would seem.

Like group dynamics everywhere, designated leaders are often constrained by their followers' willingness to follow. Sometimes the leader shares decision making, sometimes the larger organization is made the scapegoat for unpleasant requirements, sometimes leaders simply don't care what the followers want/think, and sometimes leaders abandon all previous commitment to the organization's culture and attempt to surrender their positions of authority completely. During my brief time in the military, I think I saw all of these positionings. I also witnessed followers' reactions and one that I think is particularly pertinent to this ethnography is one that I would call the *well, this is stupid but we'll do it for you anyway* reaction.

In the military, there's a lot of practice. There's practice weapons firing. There's practice chemical weapons training. There's practice loading and unloading aircraft. There's practice digging foxholes and living in tents. There are practice wars, conducted on paper and simulated by computers. Over and over again, year after year practice goes on. The idea, of course, is that if everyone practices enough, when the time comes to do these things for real no one will have to wait to learn how to do something, that what has been practiced will now be a natural action. Needless to say, all this practice doesn't endear itself to too many people. It's repetitive, dull, and is most often done under guidelines that limit the spontaneity and creativity often needed to get jobs completed in a real-world environment. As unwelcome as these practices are, if (and it is a hugely important if) a leader is well respected/well liked by the group, all goes well. Lots of bitching ensues, things are done in a very perfunctory manner; there's little personal investment given to the task at hand but the job gets done. Sometimes the leader tries to explain why things are as they are; more often, people are just told that tasks must be done because they must be done. Again, if the mini-culture of the working unit is such that the leader is held in some esteem, things get done. If not, and I have witnessed this as well, followers are willing to risk failing at a task or, at the least, to perform at the bare minimum for the sole purpose of shaming the leader in the presence of the larger culture. At the extreme poles of this leader–follower relationship we might place blind obedience or "taking that hill against all odds," and absolute resistance or "fragging the Lieutenant." Experience, at least my experience, shows that in everyday practice the military actually operates between these poles.

What does all this have to do with Rex West's Poetic Technique class? I believe his students respect him as a poet and many like him as an individual. I believe that most of these students agree, on a mental level, with what Rex is teaching them about concrete detail, consistent voice, and connecting with a larger world. However, I also believe many students have disengaged from their work for this class. They are not participating in the class on an emotional level because they have lost their emotional investment in the poetry they are producing for the class. While they may, indeed, revere poetry they do not revere the poems they write for this class. They seem to me to be less in a resisting mode than in a position of acceptance and surrender. They are in the *well, this is stupid but we'll do it for you anyway* mode.

I want to make clear that Rex does not in any way conduct his class in a military fashion, stereotyped in society's mind as barked orders, rigid structure, and unmediated authority. Rex has established rules for his class; goals and expectations for the course; requirements and criterion—but nothing that can't be found in just about any class syllabus. He also provides opportunity for student input, student participation, and peer interaction. During my observation period, I heard Rex repeatedly invite students to come and talk to him about their poetry. Why then did the military analogy come to mind?

Like military officers immediately upon commissioning, Rex owns power by virtue of his position and role. He owns the red pen, if you will. And as long as he, or any other teacher, owns the power of the grade book, the superior/subordinate relationship will exist. Further, Rex is not only a member of an academic organization to which many students desire entrance, he is also a published poet. He has, therefore, already attained two levels of distinction that many of his students are struggling to gain. I don't believe Rex, nor for that matter any instructor, can totally escape the mantle of authority—and perhaps this is a good thing. In this class, it appears that students not only acknowledge Rex's authority as an instructor but they also recognize Rex's authority of the subject material. Rex's institutional power is occasionally challenged but students respect him as a poet. Lucky for Rex and lucky for these students, too: Rex didn't have to deal with active aggression in his class and his students probably learned something from the 14 weeks of study. But watching this class has also caused me to wonder about how acceptance and surrender is a part of the university process. It has caused me to wonder about the academic institution and how, despite its own sense of itself as a learning space, students are still compelled to take classes as designated by a variety of programs (liberal studies hours, major fields). And finally, it makes me wonder about members of the academic institution—how professors become professors, how they become gatekeepers of institutional norms/values, and how they pass institutional creeds and ways of being onto their students.

Bibliography

American Psychological Association. 1983. *Publication Manual of the American Psychological Association.* 3rd ed. Washington, D.C.: American Psychological Association.

Anderson, P. V. 1996. "Ethics, Institutional Review Boards, and the Involvement of Human Participants in Composition Research." In *Ethics and Representation in Qualitative Studies of Literacy,* eds. P. Mortensen & G. E. Kirsch, 260–76. Urbana, IL: National Council of Teachers of English.

Anderson, W., C. Best, A. Black, J. Hurst, B. Miller & S. Miller. 1990. "Cross-Curricular Underlife: A Collaborative Report on Ways with Academic Words." *College Composition and Communication* 41: 11–36.

Anson, C. M. 1987. "The Classroom and the 'Real World' as Contexts: Re-Examining the Goals of Writing Instruction." *Journal of the Midwest Modern Language Association* 20: 1–16.

Applebee, A. N. 1986. "Problems in Process Approaches: Toward a Reconceptualization of Process Instruction." In *The Teaching of Writing.* Eighty-fifth Yearbook of the National Society for the Study of Education, eds. A. Petrosky & D. Bartholomae, 95–103. Chicago: University of Chicago Press.

Atkinson, P. 1990. *The Ethnographic Imagination: Textual Constructions of Reality.* London: Routledge.

———. 1992. *Understanding Ethnographic Texts. Qualitative Research Methods 25.* Thousand Oaks, CA: Sage.

Barbee, A. 1997. "Listening to the Voices of College 'Basic' Writers." Thesis. Florida State University.

Becker, H. S. & B. Geer. 1969. "Participant Observation and Interviewing: A Comparison." In *Issues in Participant Observation: A Text and Reader,* eds. G. J. McCall & J. L. Simmons, 322–31. Reading, MA: Addison Wesley.

Berkenkotter, C. 1989. "The Legacy of Positivism in Empirical Composition Research." *Journal of Advanced Composition* 9: 69–82.

———. 1991. "Paradigm Debates, Turf Wars, and the Conduct of Socio-Cognitive Inquiry in Com University Press Position." *College Composition and Communication* 42 (2): 151–69.

Berkenkotter, C., T. Huckin & J. Ackerman. 1988. "Conventions, Conversations, and the Writer: Case Study of a Student in a Rhetoric Ph.D. Program." *Research in the Teaching of English* 22: 9–44.

Berlin, J. 1984. *Writing Instruction in Nineteenth-Century American Colleges.* Carbondale: Southern Illinois University Press.

———. 1987. *Rhetoric and Reality: Writing Instruction in American Colleges, 1900–1985.* Carbondale: Southern Illinois University Press.

———. 1990. "Writing Instruction in School and College English, 1890–1985." In *A Short History of Writing Instruction: From Ancient Greece to Twentieth Century America,* ed. J. Murphy, 183–220. Davis, CA: Hermagoras Press.

Bishop, W. 1989. *A Microethnography with Case Studies of Teacher Development Through a Graduate Training Course in Teaching Writing.* Dissertation Abstracts International, 49, 11A. (University Microfilms No. 89–05, 333).

———. 1990a. *Something Old, Something New: College Writing Teachers and Classroom Change. Studies in Writing and Rhetoric.* Carbondale: Southern Illinois University Press.

———. 1990b. "Writing Students as Livestock, Walls, Weasels, Little Kids, and Other Transformations." *Oklahoma English Journal* 5 (1): 6–14.

———. 1991. "Teachers as Learners: Negotiated Roles in Writing Teachers' Learning Logs." *Journal of Teaching Writing* 10 (2): 217–40.

———. 1992. "I-Witnessing in Composition: Turning Ethnographic Data into Narratives." *Rhetoric Review* 11 (1): 147–58.

———. 1993. *The Subject Is Writing: Essays by Teachers and Students.* Portsmouth, NH: Boynton/Cook.

———. 1997. *Teaching Lives: Essays and Stories.* Logan: Utah State University Press.

Bissex, G. 1980. *GNYS at WRK: A Child Learns to Write and Read.* Cambridge, MA: Harvard University Press.

———. 1987. "Why Case Studies?" In *Seeing for Ourselves: Case-Study Research by Teachers of Writing,* eds. G. Bissex & R. H. Bullock, 7–20. Portsmouth, NH: Heinemann.

———. 1990. "Small is Beautiful: Case Study as Appropriate Methodology for Teacher Research." In *The Writing Teacher as Researcher: Essays in the Theory and Practice of Class-Based Research,* eds. D. A. Daiker & M. Morenberg, 70–75. Portsmouth, NH: Boynton/Cook.

Bissex, G. L. & R. H. Bullock, eds. 1987. *Seeing for Ourselves: Case-Study Research by Teachers of Writing.* Portsmouth, NH: Heinemann.

Bizzell, P. 1986. "Composing Processes: An Overview." In *The Teaching of Writing.* Eighty-fifth Yearbook of the National Society for the Study of Education, eds. A. Petrosky & D. Bartholomae, 49–70. Chicago: University of Chicago Press.

———. 1988. "Arguing about Literacy." *College English* 50: 141–53.

Bizzell, P. & B. Herzberg. 1996. *The Bedford Bibliography for Teachers of Writing.* 4th ed. NY: Bedford, St. Martins.

Bleich, D. 1993. "Ethnography and the Study of Literacy: Prospects for Socially Generous Research." In *Into the Field: Sites of Composition Studies,* ed. A. R. Gere, 176–92. New York: Modern Language Association.

Brand, A. G. 1980. *Therapy in Writing: A Psycho-Educational Enterprise.* Lexington, MA: Heath.

——. 1985. "Hot Cognition: Emotions and Writing Behavior." *Journal of Advanced Composition* 6: 5–15.

——. 1987. "The Why of Cognition: Emotion and the Writing Process." *College Composition and Communication* 38: 436–43.

——. 1989. *The Psychology of Writing: The Affective Experience.* Westport, CT: Greenwood.

Brandt, D. 1998. "Sponsors of Literacy." *College Composition and Communication* 49 (2): 165–85.

Bridwell, L. S. 1980. "Revising Strategies in Twelfth Grade Students' Transactional Writing." *Research in the Teaching of English* 14: 197–222.

Britton, J., et al. 1975. *The Development of Writing Abilities, 11–18.* London: Macmillan.

Brodkey, L. 1987a. "Writing Critical Ethnographic Narratives." *Anthropology & Education Quarterly* 18: 67–76.

——. 1987b. "Writing Ethnographic Narratives." *Written Communication* 9: 25–50.

Brooke, R. 1987. "Underlife and Writing Instruction." *College Composition and Communication* 38: 141–53.

——. 1991. *Writing and Sense of Self: Identity Negotiation in Writing Workshops.* Urbana, IL: National Council of Teachers of English.

——. 1997. "Ethnographic Practices as a Means of Invention: Seeking a Rhetorical Paradigm for Ethnographic Writing." *Voices and Visions: Refiguring Ethnography in a Postmodern Era,* eds. K. Kirklighter, C. Vincent & J. Moxley, 11–23. Portsmouth, NH: Boynton/Cook.

——. 1998. "Modeling a Writer's Identity: Reading and Imitation in the Writing Classroom." *College Composition and Communication* 39: 23–41.

Brooke, R. & J. Hendricks. 1989. *Audience Expectations and Teacher Demands. Studies in Writing and Rhetoric.* Carbondale: Southern Illinois University Press.

Brooke, R., T. O'Connor & R. Mirtz. 1989. "Leadership Negotiation in College Writing Groups." *Writing on the Edge* 1: 67–85.

Brueggemann, B. J. 1996. "Still-Life: Representations and Silences in the Participant–Observer Role." In *Ethics and Representation in Qualitative Studies of Literacy,* eds. P. Mortensen & G. E. Kirsch, 17–39. Urbana, IL: National Council of Teachers of English.

Bruffee, K. 1983. "Writing and Reading as Collaborative or Social Acts." In *The Writer's Mind: Writing as a Mode of Thinking,* eds. J. L. Hays et al., 159–69. Urbana, IL: National Council of Teachers of English.

——. 1984. "Collaborative Learning and the Conversation of Mankind." *College English* 46: 635–52.

Calkins, L. M. 1983. *Lessons from a Child.* Portsmouth, NH: Heinemann.

———. 1985. "Forming Research Communities among Naturalistic Researchers." In *Perspectives on Research and Scholarship in Composition*, eds. B. McClelland & T. R. Donovan, 125–44. New York: Modern Language Association.

Casey, M., K. Garretson, C. P. Haviland & N. Lerner. 1997. "Ethnographic Dissertations: Understanding and Negotiating the Traps." In *Voices and Visions: Refiguring Ethnography in a Postmodern Era*, eds. K. Kirklighter, C. Vincent & J. Moxley, 116–27. Portsmouth, NH: Boynton/Cook.

Cashulette-Flagg, A. 1994. "Preparing for Peer Response: Student and Teacher Perceptions in the First-Year Writing Classroom." Thesis. Florida State University.

Chase, G. 1988. "Accommodation, Resistance and the Politics of Student Writing." *College Composition and Communication* 39: 13–22.

Chiseri-Strater, E. 1991. *Academic Literacies: The Public and Private Discourse of University Students*. Portsmouth, NH: Boynton/Cook.

———. 1996. "Turning in Upon Ourselves: Positionality, Subjectivity, and Reflexivity in Case Study and Ethnographic Research." In *Ethics and Representation in Qualitative Studies of Literacy*, eds. P. Mortensen & G. E. Kirsch, 115–33. Urbana, IL: National Council of Teachers of English.

Clandinin, D. J. & F. M. Connelly. 1994. "Personal Experience Method." In *Handbook of Qualitative Research*, eds. N. K. Denzin & Y. S. Lincoln, 413–27. Thousand Oaks, CA: Sage.

Clifford, J. 1988. *The Predicament of Culture: Twentieth-Century Ethnography, Literature*. Cambridge, MA: Harvard University Press.

Clifford, J. & G. E. Marcus. 1986. *Writing Culture: The Poetics and Politics of Ethnography*. Berkeley: University of California Press.

Collins, J. 1984. "The Development of Writing Abilities During the School Years." In *The Development of Oral and Written Language in Social Contexts*, eds. A. D. Pellegrini & T. D. Yawkey, 201–11. Norwood, NJ: Ablex.

Collins, J. & M. Williamson. 1981. "Spoken Language and Semantic Abbreviation in Writing." *Research in the Teaching of English* 15.1: 23–35.

Cook, D. 1996. "Literacies at Work: The Writing Lives of Working Students." Dissertation. Florida State University.

Cooper, M. 1986. "The Ecology of Writing." *College English* 31: 134–42.

Corbett, E. P. J. 1965/1990. *Classical Rhetoric for the Modern Student*, 3rd ed. New York: Oxford University Press.

Cushman, E. 1996. "The Rhetorician as an Agent of Social Change." *College Composition and Communication* 47 (1): 7–28.

Daiker, D. A. & M. Morenberg, eds. 1990. *The Writing Teacher as Researcher: Essays in the Theory and Practice of Class-Based Research*. Portsmouth, NH: Boynton/Cook.

Daly, J. A. 1985. "Writing Apprehension." In *When a Writer Can't Write*, ed. M. Rose, 134–65. New York: Guilford Press.

Daly, J. A. & M. D. Miller. 1975. "The Empirical Development of an Instrument to Measure Writing Apprehension." *Research in the Teaching of English* 9: 242–48.

Daniell, B. & A. Young. 1993. "Resisting Writing/Resisting Writing Teachers." In *The Subject Is Writing: Essays by Teachers and Students on Writing,* ed. W. Bishop, 223–34. Portsmouth, NH: Boynton/Cook.

Daumer, E. & S. Runzo. 1987. "Transforming the Composition Classroom." In *Teaching Writing: Pedagogy, Gender, and Equity,* eds. C. Caywood & G. Overing, 45–63. Albany: SUNY Press.

Dean, J. P., R. Eichhorn & L. R. Dean. 1969. "Limitations and Advantages of Unstructured Methods." In *Issues in Participant Observation: A Text and Reader,* eds. G. J. McCall & L. Simmons, 19–24. Reading, MA: Addison Wesley.

Denzin, N. K. 1989. *Interpretive Biography. Qualitative Research Methods Series 17.* Thousand Oaks, CA: Sage.

———. 1994. "The Art of Politics of Interpretation." In *Handbook of Qualitative Research,* eds. N. K. Denzin & Y. S. Lincoln, 500–15. Thousand Oaks, CA: Sage.

Denzin, N. K. & Y. S. Lincoln, eds. 1994. *Handbook of Qualitative Research.* Thousand Oaks, CA: Sage.

Diesing, P. 1983. "Ethnography." *The English Record* Fourth Quarter: 2–5.

DiPardo, A. 1993. *A Kind of Passport: A Basic Writing Adjunct Program and the Challenge of Student Diversity.* Urbana, IL: National Council of Teachers of English.

Durst, R. K. & S. C. Stanforth. 1994. "'Everything's Negotiable': Collaboration and Conflict in Composition Research, 61–62." In *Ethics and Representation in Qualitative Studies of Literacy,* eds. P. Mortensen & G. E. Kirsch, 58–76. Urbana, IL: National Council of Teachers of English.

Eichhorn, J. et al. 1992. "A Symposium on Feminist Experiences in the Composition Classroom." *College Composition and Communication* 43: 297–322.

Elbow, P. 1986. *Embracing Contraries.* New York: Oxford University Press.

———. 1990. *What Is English?* New York: Modern Language Association.

Emig, J. 1977. "Writing as a Mode of Learning." *College Composition and Communication* 28: 122–28.

Fagan, W., J. Jensen & C. R. Cooper. 1985. *Measures for Research and Evaluation in the English Language Arts.* Vol. 2. Urbana, IL: National Council of Teachers of English.

Faigley, L. 1986. "Competing Theories of Process." *College English* 48: 527–42.

Fetterman, D. M. 1989. *Ethnography Step by Step. Applied Social Research Methods Series.* Thousand Oaks, CA: Sage.

Fine, M. 1994. "Working the Hyphens: Reinventing Self and Other in Qualitative Research." In *Handbook of Qualitative Research,* eds. N. K. Denzin & Y. S. Lincoln, 70–82. Thousand Oaks, CA: Sage.

Finkel, L. 1993. "Knowledge as Bait: Feminism, Voice, and the Pedagogical Unconscious." *College English* 55: 7–27.

Firestone, W. A. 1987. "Meaning in Method: The Rhetoric of Quantitative and Qualitative Research." *Educational Researcher* 16 (7): 16–21.

Florio, S. & C. M. Clark. 1982. "The Functions of Writing in an Elementary Classroom." *Research in the Teaching of English* 16: 115–30.

Flower, L. 1979. "Cognition, Context, and Theory Building." *College Composition and Communication* 40: 282–311.

Flower, L. & J. R. Hayes. 1981. "A Cognitive Process Theory of Writing." *College Composition and Communication* 32: 365–87.

Flynn, E. 1988. "Composing as a Woman." *College Composition and Communication* 39: 423–35.

Fontana, A. & J. H. Frey. 1994. "Interviewing: The Art of Science." In *Handbook of Qualitative Research,* eds. N. K. Denzin & Y. S. Lincoln, 361–76. Thousand Oaks, CA: Sage.

Fulwiler, T. 1982. "The Personal Connection: Journal Writing Across the Curriculum." In *Language Connections: Writing and Reading Across the Curriculum,* eds. T. Fulwiler & A. Young, 15–31. Urbana, IL: National Council of Teachers of English.

Geertz, C. 1988. *Works and Lives: The Anthropologist as Author.* Stanford, CA: Stanford University Press.

———. 1993. "Deep Play: Notes on the Balinese Cockfight." In *Ways of Reading: An Anthology for Writers,* 3rd ed., eds. D. Bartholomae & A. Petrosky. Boston: Bedford Books of St. Martin's Press.

Gere, A. R., ed. 1985. *Roots in the Sawdust: Writing to Learn Across the Disciplines.* Urbana, IL: National Council of Teachers of English.

Goetz, J. P. & M. D. LeCompte. 1984. *Ethnography and Qualitative Design in Educational Research.* Orlando, FL: Academic Press.

Goswami, D. & P. Stillman, eds. 1987. *Reclaiming the Classroom: Teacher Research as an Agency for Change.* Portsmouth, NH: Boynton/Cook.

Grant-Davie, K. 1992. "Coding Data: Issues of Validity, Reliability, and Interpretation." In *Methods and Methodology in Composition Research,* eds. G. Kirsch & P. A. Sullivan, 270–86. Carbondale: Southern Illinois University Press.

Gros, A. G. 1991. "Does Rhetoric of Science Matter? The Case of the Floppy-Eared Rabbits." *College English* 53 (8): 933–43.

Gubrium, J. 1988. *Analyzing Field Reality. Qualitative Research Methods Series 8.* Thousand Oaks, CA: Sage.

Haimes-Korn, K. 1996. "The Subject of Experience: How Students Negotiated Learning in a Composition Classroom." Dissertation. Florida State University.

Harste, J. C., V. A. Woodward & C. L. Burke. 1984. *Language Stories and Literacy Lessons.* Portsmouth, NH: Heinemann.

Hartwell, P. 1981. "Writers as Readers." Paper presented at the Conference on College Composition and Communication, March.

————. 1987. "Creating a Literate Environment in Freshman English: How and Why." *Rhetoric Review* 6: 4–21.

Haswell, J. & R. H. Haswell. 1995. "Gendership and the Miswriting of Students." *College Composition and Communication* 46 (2): 223–54.

Hayes, J. R. et al. 1992. *Reading Empirical Research Studies: The Rhetoric of Research.* Hillsdale, NJ: Lawrence Erlbaum.

Heath, S. B. 1983. *Ways with Words: Language, Life, and Work in Communities and Classrooms.* New York: Cambridge University Press.

Herndl, C. G. 1991. "Writing Ethnography: Representation, Rhetoric, and Institutional Practices." *College English* 53 (3): 320–32.

Herrington, A. 1981. "Writing to Learn: Writing Across the Curriculum." *College English* 43: 379–87.

Hillocks, G. 1986. *Research on Written Composition: New Directions for Teaching.* Urbana, IL: ERIC and National Council of Teachers of English.

Huberman, M. A. & M. B. Miles. 1994. "Data Management and Analysis Methods." In *Handbook of Qualitative Research,* eds. N. K. Denzin & Y. S. Lincoln, 428–44. Thousand Oaks, CA: Sage.

Huckin, T. N. 1992. "Context-Sensitive Text Analysis." In *Methods and Methodology in Composition Research,* eds. G. Kirsch & P. A. Sullivan, 84–104. Carbondale: Southern Illinois University Press.

Hunt, J. C. 1989. *Psychoanalytic Aspects of Fieldwork. Qualitative Research Methods, Series 18.* Thousand Oaks, CA: Sage.

Irmscher, W. F. 1987. "Finding a Comfortable Identity." *College Composition and Communication* 38: 81–87.

Janesick, V. J. 1994. "The Dance of Qualitative Research Design: Metaphor, Methodolatry, and Meaning." In *Handbook of Qualitative Research,* eds. N. K. Denzin & Y. S. Lincoln, 209–18. Thousand Oaks, CA: Sage.

Kamil, M., J. A. Langer & T. Shanahan. 1985. *Understanding Reading and Writing Research.* Boston: Allyn & Bacon.

Kantor, K., D. R. Kirby & J. Goetz. 1981. "Research in Context: Ethnographic Studies in English Education." *Research in the Teaching of English* 15: 293–310.

Kincheloe, J. 1997. "Fiction Formulas: Critical Constructivism and the Representation of Reality." In *Representation and the Text: Reframing the Narrative Voice,* eds. W. G. Tierney & Y. S. Lincoln, 57–80. Albany: SUNY Press.

Kincheloe, J. L. & P. L. McLaren. 1994. "Rethinking Critical Theory and Qualitative Research." In *Handbook of Qualitative Research,* eds. N. K. Denzin & Y. S. Lincoln, 138–57. Thousand Oaks, CA: Sage.

Kirk, J. & M. L. Miller. 1986. *Reliability and Validity in Qualitative Research. Qualitative Research Methods Series 1.* Thousand Oaks, CA: Sage.

Kirklighter, C., C. Vincent & J. Moxley. 1997. "Introduction." In *Voices and Visions: Refiguring Ethnography in a Postmodern Era*, eds. K. Kirklighter, C. Vincent & J. Moxley, v–xii. Portsmouth, NH: Boynton/Cook.

Kirsch, G. E. 1993. *Women Writing the Academy: Audience, Authority, and Transformation. Studies in Writing and Rhetoric.* Carbondale: Southern Illinois University Press.

Kirsch, G. & P. Mortensen. 1996. "Introduction: Reflections on Methodology in Literacy Studies." In *Ethics and Representation in Qualitative Studies of Literacy,* eds. P. Mortensen & G. E. Kirsch, xix–xxxiv. Urbana, IL: National Council of Teachers of English.

Kirsch, G. & P. A. Sullivan, eds. 1992. *Methods and Methodology in Composition Research.* Carbondale: Southern Illinois University Press.

Kleine, M. 1990. "Beyond Triangulation: Ethnography, Writing, and Rhetoric." *Journal of Advanced Composition* 10 (1): 117–25.

Knoblauch, C. H. & L. Brannon. 1983. "Writing as Learning Through the Curriculum." *College English* 45: 465–74.

———. 1984. *Rhetorical Traditions and the Teaching of Writing.* Portsmouth, NH: Boynton/Cook.

Knoeller, C. 1998. *Voicing Ourselves: Whose Words We Use When We Talk About Books.* Albany: SUNY Press.

Lauer, J. M. & J. W. Asher. 1988. *Composition Research: Empirical Designs.* New York: Oxford University Press.

Lofty, J. & R. Blot. 1997. "Covering One's Tracks: Respecting and Preserving Informant Anonymity." In *Voices and Visions: Refiguring Ethnography in a Postmodern Era,* eds. K. Kirklighter, C. Vincent & J. Moxley, 45–56. Portsmouth, NH: Boynton/Cook.

Maimon, E. P. 1987. "Maps and Genres: Exploring Connections in the Arts and Sciences." In *Composition and Literature: Bridging Gap,* ed. W. Horner, 110–25. Chicago: University of Chicago Press.

Marcus, G. "What Comes (Just) After 'Post'? The Case of Ethnography." 1994. In *Handbook of Qualitative Research,* eds. N. K. Denzin & Y. S. Lincoln, 563–74. Thousand Oaks, CA: Sage.

Martin, N. 1987. "On the Move." In *Reclaiming the Classroom: Teacher Research as an Agency for Change,* eds. D. Goswami & P. R. Stillman, 20–28. Portsmouth, NH: Boynton/Cook.

McCarthy, L. P. 1987. "A Stranger in Strange Lands: A College Student Writing Across the Curriculum." *Research in the Teaching of English* 21: 233–65.

McCarthy, L. P. & S. M. Fishman. 1996. "A Text for Many Voices: Representing Diversity in Reports of Naturalistic Research." In *Ethics and Representation in Qualitative Studies of Literacy,* eds. P. Mortensen & G. E. Kirsch, 155–76. Urbana, IL: National Council of Teachers of English.

Meloy, J. M. 1994. *Writing the Qualitative Dissertation: Understanding by Doing.* Hillsdale, NJ: Lawrence Erlbaum.

Miles, M. & A. M. Huberman. 1984. *Qualitative Data Analysis.* Thousand Oaks, CA: Sage.

Miller, S. 1992. "Writing Theory: Theory Writing." In *Methods and Methodology in Composition Research,* eds. G. Kirsch & P. A. Sullivan, 62–83. Carbondale: Southern Illinois University Press.

Minh-ha, T. T. 1988. *Woman, Native, Other.* Bloomington: Indiana University Press.

Mohr, M. 1985. "Appendix A: What Happened in Their Teaching." In *The Teacher-Researcher: How to Study Writing in the Classroom,* ed. M. Myers, 127–29. Urbana, IL: National Council of Teachers of English.

Mountford, R. D. 1996. "Engendering Ethnography: Insights from the Feminist Critique of Postmodern Anthropology." In *Ethics and Representation in Qualitative Studies of Literacy,* eds. P. Mortensen & G. E. Kirsch, 205–27. Urbana, IL: National Council of Teachers of English.

Morse, J. 1994. "Designing Funded Qualitative Research." In *Handbook of Qualitative Research,* eds. N. K. Denzin & Y. S. Lincoln, 220–35. Thousand Oaks, CA: Sage.

Mortensen, P. & G. E. Kirsch, eds. 1996. *Ethics and Representation in Qualitative Studies of Literacy.* Urbana, IL: National Council of Teachers of English.

Moss, B. J. 1992. "Ethnography and Composition: Studying Language at Home." In *Methods and Methodology in Composition Research,* eds. G. Kirsch & P. A. Sullivan, 153–71. Carbondale: Southern Illinois University Press.

Murphy, R. 1990. "Anorexia: The Cheating Disorder." *College English* 52: 898–903.

Myers, M. 1985. *The Teacher-Researcher: How to Study Writing in the Classroom.* Urbana, IL: National Council of Teachers of English.

Nelson, J. 1990. "This Was an Easy Assignment: Examining How Students Interpret Academic Writing Tasks." *Research in the Teaching of English* 34: 362–93.

Newkirk, T. 1991. "The Politics of Composition Research: The Conspiracy Against Experience." In *The Politics of Writing Instruction: Post-Secondary,* eds. R. Bullock & J. Trimber, 119–35. Portsmouth, NH: Boynton/Cook.

———. 1992. "The Narrative Roots of the Case Study." In *Methods and Methodology in Composition Research,* eds. G. Kirsch & P. A. Sullivan, 130–52. Carbondale: Southern Illinois University Press.

———. 1996. "Seduction and Betrayal in Qualitative Research." In *Ethics and Representation in Qualitative Studies of Literacy,* eds. P. Mortensen & G. E. Kirsch, 3–16. Urbana, IL: National Council of Teachers of English.

North, S. 1987. *The Making of Knowledge in Composition: Portrait of an Emerging Field.* Portsmouth, NH: Boynton/Cook.

O'Connor, T. & R. Mirtz. 1989. "Leadership Negotiation in College Writing Groups. *Writing on the Edge* 1: 67–85.

Odell, L., D. Goswami & D. Quick. 1983. "Writing Outside the English Composition Class: Implications for Teaching and for Learning." In *Literacy for Life: The Demand for Reading and Writing,* eds. R. W. Bailey & R. M. Fosheim, 175–99. New York: Modern Language Association.

Olesen, V. 1994. "Feminisms and Model of Qualitative Reseat." In *Handbook of Qualitative Research,* eds. N. K. Denzin & Y. S. Lincoln, 158–75. Thousand Oaks, CA: Sage.

Olson, G. 1991. "The Social Scientist as Author: Clifford Geertz on Ethnography and Social Construction." In *(Inter)views: Cross-Disciplinary Perspectives on Rhetoric and Literacy,* eds. G. A. Olson & I. Gale, 187–210. Carbondale: Southern Illinois University Press.

Perl, S. 1979. "The Composing Processes of Unskilled College Writers." *Research in the Teaching of English* 13: 217–38.

———. 1983. "Reflections on Ethnography and Writing." *The English Record* 10–11.

Perl, S. & N. Wilson. 1986, 1998. *Through Teachers' Eyes: Portraits of Writing Teachers at Work,* 2nd ed. Portland, ME: Calendar Islands Press.

Pianko, S. 1979. "A Description of the Composing Processes of College Freshman Writers." *Research in the Teaching of English* 13: 5–22.

Polkinghorne, D. E. 1997. "Reporting Qualitative Research as Practice." In *Representation and the Text: Reframing the Narrative Voice,* eds. W. G. Tierney & Y. S. Lincoln, 3–22. Albany: SUNY Press.

Potter, W. J. 1996. *An Analysis of Thinking and Research About Qualitative Methods.* Hillsdale, NJ: Lawrence Erlbaum.

Powers-Stubbs, K. 1992. "Watching Ourselves: Feminist Teachers and Authority." *College Composition and Communication* 43: 311–15.

Pratt, M. L. 1986. "Fieldwork in Common Places." In *Writing Culture: The Poetics and Politics of Ethnography,* eds. J. Clifford & G. E. Marcus, 27–50. Berkeley: University of California Press.

———. 1991. "Arts of the Contact Zone." *Profession* 91: 33–40.

Rankin, E. 1994. *Seeing Yourself as a Teacher: Conversations with Five New Teachers in a University Writing Program.* Urbana, IL: National Council of Teachers of English.

Ray, R. 1992. "Composition from the Teacher–Researcher Point of View." In *Methods and Methodology in Composition Research,* eds. G. Kirsch & P. A. Sullivan, 172–89. Carbondale: Southern Illinois University Press.

———. 1993. *The Practice of Theory: Teacher Research in Composition.* Urbana, IL: National Council of Teachers of English.

Reason, P. 1994. "Three Approaches to Participative Inquiry." In *Handbook of Qualitative Research,* eds. N. K. Denzin & Y. S. Lincoln, 324–39. Thousand Oaks, CA: Sage.

Rhodes, K. 1997. "Ethnography or Psychography? The Evolution and Ethics of a New Genre in Composition." In *Voices and Visions: Refiguring Ethnography in a Postmodern Era*, eds. K. Kirklighter, C. Vincent, & J. Moxley, 24–36. Portsmouth, NH: Boynton/Cook.

Rhoman, D. G. & A. O. Wlecke. 1964. *Pre-writing: The Construction and Application of Models for Concept Formation in Writing*. East Lansing, MI: Michigan State UP.

Richardson, L. 1990. *Writing Strategies: Reaching Diverse Audiences. Qualitative Research Methods, Series 21.* Thousand Oaks, CA: Sage.

Ronald, K. & J. Volkmer. 1989. "Another Competing Theory of Process: The Student's." *Journal of Advanced Composition* 9: 81–96.

Rose, M., ed. 1985. *When a Writer Can't Write: Studies in Writer's Block and Other Composing Process Problems.* New York: Guilford.

Rose, M. 1980. "Rigid Rules, Inflexible Plans, and the Stifling of Language: A Cognitivist Analysis of Writer's Block." *College Composition and Communication* 31: 389–401.

———. 1985. "The Language of Exclusion: Writing Instruction at the University." *College English* 47: 341–59.

———. 1990. *Lives on the Boundary.* New York: Penguin.

Rosenblatt, L. M. 1978. *The Reader, The Text, The Poem: The Transactional Theory of the Literary Work.* Carbondale: Southern Illinois University Press.

Schaafsma, D. 1993. *Eating on the Street: Teaching Literacy in a Multicultural Society.* Pittsburgh: University of Pittsburgh Press.

Schriver, K. A. 1992. "Connecting Cognition and Context in Composition." In *Methods and Methodology in Composition Research*, eds. G. Kirsch & P. A. Sullivan, 190–216. Carbondale: Southern Illinois University Press.

Schwandt, T. 1994. "Constructivist, Interpretivist Approaches to Human Inquiry." In *Handbook of Qualitative Research*, eds. N. K. Denzin & Y. S. Lincoln, 118–37. Thousand Oaks, CA: Sage.

Sewell, D. N. 1995. "Encountering Writing: The Literacies and Lives of First-Year Students." Dissertation. Florida State University.

Shaughnessy, M. P. 1977. *Errors and Expectations: A Guide for the Teacher of Basic Writing.* New York: Oxford University Press.

Smith, F. 1994. *Understanding Reading: A Psycholinguistic Analysis of Reading and Learning to Read*, 5th ed. Hillsdale, NJ: Lawrence Erlbaum.

Sommers, N. 1980. "Revision Strategies of Student Writers and Experienced Adult Writers." *College Composition and Communication* 31: 378–88.

Spindler, G. & L. Spindler. 1987. "Teaching and Learning How to Do the Ethnography of Education." In *Interpretive Ethnography of Education: At Home and Abroad*, eds. G. Spindler & L. Spindler, 17–33. Hillsdale, NJ: Lawrence Erlbaum.

Stake, R. E. 1994. "Case Studies." In *Handbook of Qualitative Research*, eds. N. K. Denzin & Y. S. Lincoln, 236–47. Thousand Oaks, CA: Sage.

Sternglass, M. 1997. *Time to Know Them: A Longitudinal Study of Writing and Learning at the College Level.* Hillsdale, NJ: Lawrence Erlbaum.

Sullivan, P. A. 1992. "Feminism and Methodology in Composition Studies." In *Methods and Methodology in Composition Research*, eds. G. Kirsch & P. A. Sullivan, 37–61. Carbondale: Southern Illinois University Press.

———. 1996. "Ethnography and the Problem of the 'Other'." In *Ethics and Representation in Qualitative Studies of Literacy*, eds. P. Mortensen & G. E. Kirsch, 97–114. Urbana, IL: National Council of Teachers of English.

Sunstein, B. S. 1994. *Composing a Culture: Inside a Summer Writing Program with High School Teachers*. Portsmouth, NH: Boynton/Cook.

———. 1996. "Culture on the Page: Experience, Rhetoric, and Aesthetics in Ethnographic Writing." In *Ethics and Representation in Qualitative Studies of Literacy*, eds. P. Mortensen & G. E. Kirsch, 177–202. Urbana, IL: National Council of Teachers of English.

Tanaka, G. 1997. "Pico College." In *Representation and the Text: Reframing the Narrative Voice*, eds. W. G. Tierney & Y. S. Lincoln, 259–304. Albany: SUNY Press.

Thompson, B. M. 1979. *A Theory of Teacher Change Developed from Teachers of Writing*. Urbana, IL: ERC/RCS. ERIC ED 188 197.

Tinberg, H. B. 1998. *Border Talk: Writing and Knowing in the Two-Year College*. Urbana, IL: National Council of Teachers of English.

Tobin, L. 1989. "Bridging Gaps: Analyzing Our Students' Metaphors for Composing." *College Composition and Communication* 40: 444–58.

———. 1993. *Writing Relationships: What Really Happens in the Composition Class*. Portsmouth, NH: Boynton/Cook.

Tyler, S. A. 1986. "Post-Modern Ethnography: From Document of the Occult to Occult Document." In *Writing Culture: The Poetics and Politics of Ethnography*, eds. J. Clifford & G. E. Marcus, 122–40. Berkeley: University of California Press.

Van Maanen, J. 1988. *Tales of the Field: On Writing Ethnography*. Chicago: University of Chicago Press.

Walvoord, B. E. & L. P. McCarthy. 1990. *Thinking and Writing in College: A Naturalistic Study of Students in Four Disciplines*. Urbana, IL: National Council of Teachers of English.

Welch, N. 1993. "Resisting the Faith: Conversion, Resistance, and the Training of Teachers." *College English* 55 (4): 387–401.

———. 1997. *Getting Restless: Rethinking Revision in Writing Instruction*. Portsmouth, NH: Boynton/Cook.

Williams, C. L. 1996. "Dealing with the Data: Ethical Issues in Case Study Research." In *Ethics and Representation in Qualitative Studies of Literacy*, eds. P. Mortensen & G. E. Kirsch, 40–57. Urbana, IL: National Council of Teachers of English.

Wolcott, H. F. 1987. "On Ethnographic Intent." In *Interpretive Ethnography of Education: At Home and Abroad*, eds. G. Spindler & L. Spindler. Hillsdale, NJ: Lawrence Erlbaum.

————. 1990. *Writing Up Qualitative Research. Qualitative Research Methods.* Vol. 20. Thousand Oaks, CA: Sage.

Wu, R. 1997. "Writing Bio (Life) into Ethnography. In *Voices and Visions: Refiguring Ethnography in a Postmodern Era,* eds. K. Kirklighter, C. Vincent & J. Moxley, 77–85. Portsmouth, NH: Boynton/Cook.

Wyche-Smith, S. 1993. "Writing Rituals or Time, Tools, and Talismans." In *The Subject Is Writing: Essays by Teachers and Students on Writing,* ed. W. Bishop, 111–23. Portsmouth, NH: Boynton/Cook.

Yager, K. 1997. "Composition's Appropriation of Ethnographic Authority." In *Voices and Visions: Refiguring Ethnography in a Postmodern Era,* eds. K. Kirklighter, C. Vincent & J. Moxley, 37–44. Portsmouth, NH: Boynton/Cook.

Index